Blag, Steal & Borrow

BY

GARY RAYMOND

PERCY
PUBLISHING

This book is a factual account of real events.

Enquiries should be addressed to
Percy Publishing
Woodford Green,
Essex. IG8 0TF
England.

www.percy-publishing.com

1st Published June 2016
1st Edition
1st Print

ISBN: 978-0-9932916-6-1

Cover Design Copyright © 2016 Percy Publishing
Photo Copyright © 2016 Jill Taylor
Percy Publishing is a Clifford Marker Associates Ltd Company

Print: Svet Print, d.o.o., Ljubljana

Dedication

To Louise, you mean the whole wide world to me.

To my lovely daughters Hayley, Kerry, Amy and Holly.

To Mum and Dad for all their support and inspiration.

To my little sisters, Susan, Mandy &
Jill for putting up with me.

To all the family that are no longer with us – you will
never be forgotten.

"Why join the navy if you can be a pirate?"

Steve Jobs

Gary Raymond

Gary Raymond is a writer, tweeter and maverick music manger. His artists have had numerous top 40 singles and albums. He now lives in a quiet village in Essex leaving well behind him those days in the music industry of alcohol excess, drugs and massive egos.

www.mrgaryraymond.com
Facebook: mrgaryraymond1960
Twitter: @Mr GaryRaymond

Foreword

It is my distinct honour to have been asked to write this foreword. However, I had no clue how to do it, I'm a songwriter not an author, but I wanted to do it, so here is what I have to say about our ex-manager and good friend Gary Raymond.

We first met Gary outside a venue in Birmingham. His band 'Twenty Twenty' were performing that night and we were outside busy handing out flyers to the crowd promoting our own band 'Room 94'.

As he approached I thought he was going to have a go about us poaching his crowd, but instead he politely said hello, and we had a short chat and then we found ourselves on his personal guest-list for his show.

A few minutes later guys from another band walked up to him and asked if they could also get on his guest list. He stared at them and then said "You can get lost – I saw your comments slagging 'Twenty Twenty' off on Facebook," and there and then I knew he was the person I wanted to manage 'Room 94'.

Working with Gaz (we always call him Gaz – even though he hates being called it by anyone else) was always a great time with never a dull moment. We would always come up with cheeky ideas and schemes to try get us to where we wanted to be - some of them worked, some of them didn't and some of them were just plain fucking crazy – like shooting a music video underwater!

"Don't worry, what's the worst that can happen?" he said, "One of you drowns and album sales go up!"

We had a great working relationship and developed an even better friendship which made for some very interesting moments on tour.

We once flew out to Poland to play a sold-out DVD launch show and as a tradition on those very early in the morning flights we started with a pint, then another...then another.

We had some radio and TV spots to do throughout the day before the big launch the following day so we drove about slightly pissed (and by that we mean that we had a driver who drove the van around while we drank) and got what we needed to do done and then as soon as we had finished we left the venue, where the final TV spot was being filmed and made our way to the nearest pub.

We ended up visiting a lot of pubs that day where eventually we were spotted by a group of fans who joined us for a few drinks, and later on we found ourselves in the VIP lounge of a fancy club in Warsaw drinking free booze by the bucket load.

It was here that a very busty blonde barmaid took a shine to Gaz, well that was until we got kicked

out when Gaz and Sean our lead guitarist decided to jump up and play the bongos that were on the club's stage.

The night ended with a group of us walking through a McDonald's drive through and Gaz ordering about twenty cheeseburgers for everyone – that's twenty cheeseburgers shared between us all, not each!

The next day we played to a packed venue and had a great DVD release show and like the true professional he is, Gaz made sure that everything was sorted for us and all we had to do was concentrate on the performance.

Gaz has always been great at sorting things out and making things appear from nowhere, we were a small band with no name for ourselves but he managed to sort us a mammoth UK HMV signings tour, 2 a day for a week where we visited fourteen different cities in 7 days. He also managed to blag us a wad of Nando's gift vouchers and a few crates of 'Innocent' smoothies for the week to help keep us sustained.

5 grown men in a car travelling up and down the country, farting and burping was an experience that was full of banter and inappropriate jokes, we had a real laugh, no in fact we pissed ourselves laughing most of the time as he told us of his tales of growing up in the seventies and those fucking amazing exploits with the 'Koopa' boys and at the same time we all worked our bloody asses off.

I think the only bone of contention we ever had was the music choices, as he would prefer glam rock to our choice of Justin Bieber.

One of the funniest things that happened that week was when we went into a pub to watch The Champions League match between PSG and Chelsea and decided to have some food. Gaz wanted to order some nachos but the barman said "I can do them but we don't have any sour cream, salsa or guacamole."

"That's just fucking crisps," Gaz replied in amazement and we all fell about the floor laughing.

That's something else about him, he's sharp as a razor unless his pissed then he just falls asleep.

At the end of the week we managed to secure a top

30 album as an unsigned act with no press team, no money, just the music, our amazing fans and of course a great manager.

With the album in the charts Gaz noticed we had received a lot of tweets from fans in Glasgow who had not managed to meet the band on the signings tour - as we could not fit the final one in. He spoke to them via Twitter and having realised how upset some of them where, he set up a signing in Glasgow and in his little Renault Clio he picked us up and drove us all the way to Glasgow from Hertfordshire. The journey was horrendous and due to traffic problems it ended up taking about 10 hours– but get there we did and the Glaswegians turned out in force and made it a special night for the all.

After the signing we decided to go to the casino and get very drunk and while there we noticed Charlie from 'Busted' – and while we all sat there staring at him debating whether or not to go and say hello as he looked like he was chilling Gaz walked past him and he turned around and said "Hell Gary, how you doing?"

That's the other great thing about Gaz, people know who he is and he has their respect.

He is the type of bloke you want in your corner and on your team and with him it was always about doing what you can at that moment in time and making the most out of every situation and opportunity that arose and, unlike almost everyone else in the music industry there was never any bullshit from him.

As a manger he understood our needs and even if we wanted to stand out in the cold after a show having photos taken with fans then no matter how long it took he was there, standing like he does with his arms folded – just keeping an eye out – what a legend.

I was allowed to read this book prior to it being published and all I can say enjoy it, it's a fucking riot!

Kieran Lemon,
Lead singer, Room 94
www.room94.co.uk
Twitter @Room94

Now Let's Get to It

They Told Me I Needed an Intro. So Here's Mine.

'I wish I knew then what I know now.'

Have you ever said that? I have on many occasions.

The contents of this book is a story of what I know now and definitely not what I knew back then. If I had known back then, this book would tell a very different story.

There would've been no all-night van rides slogging up and down the country, far fewer pints of lager, most definitely no drugs, possibly no fighting, and, it has to be said, a lot less fuck-ups and who knows maybe never would've ended up managing a little-known pop punk trio from rural Essex called 'Koopa'.

Not heard of them? Well, they were the first unsigned band in history to land a top 40 single and became a part of a landmark moment in the internet revolution that was sweeping the music industry in 2007.

A most notable feat in anyone's book, except 'Koopa' went on to do it a further two times.

Still not ringing any bells? Well there's a pretty good reason for that!

Before I started writing my story and delve in to the who's, why's, where's and what's, I had a big question that only I could answer - and that question was why?

Why would anyone in the world want to read a book about someone they have never bloody heard of?

Who would be interested in my story of EastEnders,

the seaside, dolphins, wild animals, sex toys, sticky tape and almost bringing the music industry to its knees?

Well we are all aware that for every worthwhile person making a contribution to society there are thousands filling their time doing jack-shit – I just thought it was my time to stop doing jack-shit and try to do something worthwhile.

I had grown tired of spending most of my days on Twitter reading peoples tweets who rant on about why 'Batman' is better than 'Superman' or looking at the latest Facebook post from someone informing the world of their highest score on that mind-numbing game Candy Crush.

So, I would just like to make things very clear from the start. I'm not some footballing superstar who wants to spill the beans on his former teammates and manager. Nor I am some former football hooligan who wants to share all those terrace tear-ups against rival gangs held on cold Saturday afternoons to repent all his sins – although I do have quite a few sins from which I need redemption.

Finally, I am definitely not some movie star who needs to regale you with tales of attending plush Hollywood parties with beautiful woman on tap and how I bedded some Oscar winning movie stars, male and female!

This is just a simple story about a normal guy who, after an unusual and colourful upbringing, went to sleep for 25 years, metaphorically speaking, before deciding to break free from the stranglehold of a potentially mundane life and manage a pop punk band. It is as simple as that - Well actually nothing in life is that simple.

So where and, more importantly, how did this all begin? How did I end up managing a band?

I had no experience whatsoever in the music industry and in fact I didn't even really listen to music that much.

When I was younger I lived and breathed music. I loved collecting vinyl and going to gigs but by the time I met 'Koopa', music was just a passing hobby.

I was living a normal existence. I was married to my second wife and we had two beautiful daughters. I mowed the lawn at weekends, I painted the garage doors and I saved vouchers out of the newspaper for a bargain caravan weekend away with my family – I was just normal. Normal! Don't make me laugh.

I lived how people expected me to live. I was just like everyone else. I had nothing to say. I had no identity. I was simply going through the motions – I was a pretend husband and father.

Then out of the blue, three strange looking individuals who had created a pop-punk band and who were in dire need of a manager and a Svengali came into my life.

Maybe if I had known what I was doing, things would have turned out differently for all four of us. Perhaps if we had played by the music industry rules and not our own, things would have taken a very different path – who knows!

Suddenly I found myself in the dark, shark infested, waters of the music industry and slam dunk on the firing line is a risky place to be. I was an armchair manager running the project from the comfort of my living room with limited knowledge of how the industry conducted its business.

I was blagging my way through every day blissfully unaware that, if you exposed any of the music industries flaws or took advantage of any of its loopholes that it would simply close its ranks on you, slam its doors shut in your face and kick you right in the bollocks as hard as it could as you fell flat on your face.

Right from the start the great thing about us all was that we were a totally unknown entity to the music industry and we would not let any fucker pull the wool over our eyes. I know I'm not the first to point out that these days the music industry is dead but having experienced the greed and arrogance of almost everyone in it, from the labels, agents, PR and even the bloody teaboy I can understand why – they have forgotten the one thing that made us all fall in love with music in the first place – the fucking music!

These days it's all about the bottom line profit and how many fake sodding followers you have on social media.!

"We got this far with no money and this is what real music sounds like," was the boast as the bands satirical lyrics sent a shiver through the industry for a brief moment in time and what I do know for sure is that 'Koopa' should have gone on to become anti-establishment rock and roll legends and that I could have been there very own Malcom McLaren.

This book is written as I experienced those times. Through my own eyes, which occasionally might have been obstructed by my ill-chosen addictions.

There may also be occasions where events have been seen through very rose tinted glasses, but this is the story of my life and the way I choose to remember it. I needed to get things off my chest and it's written straight from the horse's mouth - so please forgive me for all the foul fucking language!

Writing my story has been a cathartic experience, releasing feelings I'd locked away deep at the back of my mind as well as provoking memories of the pain and distress I caused family and friends. But it was

not all doom and gloom, there were also lots of fun times sometimes far too many fun times, and I must confess that on many occasion I have had to stop

writing because I've been pissing myself laughing - I hope you will laugh along, but we'll wait and see – won't we.

That said, I'm not proud of everything I've done and neither should I be; but I felt everything needed to be included. And, I don't blame anyone other than myself as I leapt at the opportunity to manage the band and, dived head first into the lifestyle with no safety harness or thought for anyone else..

The whole experience was like being in a mash up of television shows like 'The Prisoner', 'Lost' and ''Twin Peaks - you just never knew what the fucking hell was going to happen next.

So sit back and enjoy 'Blag, Steal & Borrow' the story of how I ended up just like my old man and how I orchestrated the cunning plan that saw an unknown three-piece band from Essex become the most famous band in the world – for just one day and how the bands very mischievous manager, yes, yours truly, carried off what was the rock and roll blag of the century that put them in the 'Guinness Book of World Records'.

We know what steal and borrow mean but what's a blag?

Definition of blag - to 'manage to obtain (something) by using guile or, con or scam.

See where this is going?

"So can I start reading the fucking book now?" you ask....

Yes of course you fucking can!

Chapter 1

Drop Your Trousers and Cough

There's two sides to this story, so before boarding the rollercoaster ride to self-destruction that was 'Koopa' I feel you need to better understand how I became the person I am today and why everyone in the family looks at me these days and says; 'You're turning into your dad.'

Is that a bad thing to become just like your dad?

Of course it depends on the type of man your father was. If he was a good man, yes of course it's great, but if your dad turned out to be a mass murderer or a total fucking moron, then maybe that's not such a good thing.

Well, luckily for me he was a good man, no wait, he was and still is a great man and I have most definitely inherited many of my current traits from him, including; my sarcasm, my lack of patience, my grumpiness and my sudden realisation that all music is far too loud these days.

To better understand me, you first need to understand where I come from and the roots of the family that helped shaped my life. In particular, you need to know a bit about my dad, and why without much success in my teenage years, he tried to get me into his way of thinking and how I did eventually realise that he was trying to pass down the flame-of-life, which I needed to grab hold of and run with.

I heard my dad say 'make every move count' on numerous occasions during my childhood and at the time I had very little appreciation of the power of those four little words, but as I entered the murky depths of the music industry I came to realise that he had taught me very well. He was also an advocate of the phrase 'stand your ground', which although these days seem to be more associated with football hooliganism, was something I was taught as a youngster to help me stand up to bullies in the playground and, in later years the many bullies and complete wankers that I would encounter in the music industry. Although it turned out that sometimes this phrase was not always best followed.

Making my 'every move count' I guided Koopa's career to the pinnacle point where they would go on and create music industry history — that would shake the record labels to their very core and ensure that the band for a brief moment in time and, against all the odds, would be the most famous band in the world; even if it was for just one single day.

My Dad, Brian Victor Raymond, was born into this world on the 19th March 1939 to parents Alfred and Caroline Raymond and the youngest of seven children; three brothers, Alfred, Arthur and Ronald and three sisters Irene, Louise and Doris. There was quite a large age gap between Dad and the rest of his sibling's, so as you can imagine everyone made quite a fuss of the new arrival and he became completely mollycoddled by his sisters.

But the very fact that I was even born in the first place is somewhat of a miracle given the extraordinary experiences of my father and his family when he was a baby.

On September 1st that same year, the then Prime Minister Neville Chamberlain, solemnly announced to the nation "I have to tell you now that no such undertaking has been received and consequently this country is at war with Germany." This announcement would have a huge impact on our family and their beloved East End.

Just after the war broke out, it was discovered that the local vicar who had christened my Dad, was actually a German spy and had been secretly sending the Nazi's information on the most populated areas in East London; allowing the Luftwaffe to concentrate their bombing raids on those particular locations in order to cause mayhem amongst the residents, along with as many casualties as possible. He had apparently also been harbouring German agents in the parish rectory, but eventually got caught when a sixty-year old parishioner overheard him speaking in a foreign language and following excessive snooping by the locals; the vicar was caught bang to rights.

I'm not sure what happened to him, but my dad seems to recall his father telling him in later years, that the vicar was executed for treason, but he also remembers his sister saying that the local residents got together, snatched him one night and gave him a bit of a beating before covering him in sackcloth's, tying him up and weighing him down with some bricks before lobbing him into the Thames.

Dad's eldest sister Irene, was given the choice of munitions or forces and chose to join the women's branch of the British Army - the Auxiliary Territorial Service better known by its acronym ATS.

After passing her basic training, Irene was deployed to the Royal Artillery and returned to London, where she spent the rest of the war on the anti-aircraft guns and, by all accounts, contributed to the shooting down of at least two enemy aircraft, as well as avoiding enemy gunfire and bombs that were falling on London's East End.

Dad's two eldest brothers, Alfred and Arthur joined the Royal Navy with Arthur becoming a Petty Officer serving in British coastal waters, and Alfred being one of the heroes of the D-Day Normandy landings on 6th June 1944; during which he bravely transported ground troops on a landing craft to the beaches while under intense German gunfire. I Can only imagine what that must have felt like.

Dad still has a letter that he cherishes that Alfred wrote to Arthur during the war asking if he could borrow £5 to take a girl on a date. That just about sums up the Raymond brothers, as they were all good-looking and always on the pull; no matter what was going on in the world around them - even during a war.

Luckiest of all though was my Dad, he was just a babe in arms when in the safety of the bomb shelter during the first blitz on London, September 1940, the family home was obliterated by a German bomb. The council moved the family to 135 Earlham Grove, Forest Gate,

E7 which shortly after, during another air-raid was also totally destroyed by German bombers, but luckily enough once again the whole family were in the safety of the underground shelters. It was now 1942 and they had been moved into 115 Earlham Grove — yes the very same street. In those days there was no way that families would submit to German oppression and it was a time when, as a nation, we would stand our ground even if it meant living in the same street where you had been bombed-out before.

One bitterly cold winter afternoon Dad's grandmother popped round to the house complaining of a really painful toothache asking if they would accompany her to the dentist surgery, which of course my nan agreed to do.

Nan wrapped little Brian up all nice and snug and they left the house heading towards the surgery, which was situated not far from the local swimming baths. At the end of Earlham Grove, they turned right into Sprowston Road where Dad picked up a stick and started running along with it while dragging it along some fencing, making a kind of percussion sound – he was obviously destined to be the professional drummer he became in later years.

At that very same time he heard a strange sound, like a lorry engine going extremely fast high in the sky, looking up, he saw a long object with fire blasting from the back — it was really quite close.

Nan instantly recognised this horrific sound as a dreaded Doodlebug. These were basically bombs with wings that kept flying until their fuel ran out. They were a marvel of German technology, but nan knew that as long as you heard the engine you were safe; once it cut out though, its descent was rapid. There and then the engine stopped – there was silence, it was time to start worrying and run for cover as fast as you could.

Nan and Grandma grabbed little Brian, who was still playing with his stick and rushed to take cover in the nearest sheltered place, which happened to be the doorway of Dad's favourite sweet shop. They heard the whistling sound as the Doodlebug descended and then the huge explosion that followed.

My Nan once described the sound to me as being a loud 'Whomph,' thankfully they were all unharmed, but left tearful and very shaken.

They heard screams coming from around the corner and they rushed back only to see the complete carnage and the total devastation of what once was 115 Earlham Grove. I can't begin to imagine what it must have looked like, but I've been to places like Margate, Doncaster and Skegness with bands, and they do look like bombs have been dropped on them.

Amidst the sound of the ear piercing screams, Nan could see that their house was gone; along with the houses either side. Those bastard Germans had once again blown up the family home and everything they owned. It was starting to seem as if Hitler actually had some kind of personal vendetta against the Raymond family and, in particular, my Dad! The bombing left the families of Earlham Grove with only one possession - courage. The Germans weren't going to take that!

Years later I would be told that a childhood friend of my dad's was killed in that explosion and that Dad had been traumatised for a while, having seen the poor boy's body parts, along with those of the boy's mother strewn across the ground where the house had once stood. Suffice to say they sent little Brian to spend what was the remaining of the war to the safety of the countryside and, surprisingly, no more bombs ever landed near the family home.

Although during this time he did get dive-bombed by a swarm of bees, which left him with some nasty stings. Apparently the doctor had to calm him down and ensure him that they were not German and sent by Hitler.

Nan would forever refer to the Germans as 'Those dirty German fuckers' until her dying day.

When the war was eventually over, people went about rebuilding their lives after all the tragedy and the hardship they had endured — they just got on with it. You have to stand back and admire that good old-fashioned determination.

My Grandparents eventually became landlord and landlady of The Five Bells Public House located at 535, Old Ford Road, Bromley-By-Bow, London E3.

They were the salt-of-the-earth East End publicans, born and bred in the East End tradition and above all were the most wonderful people you could ever meet. The Five Bell was decked with dark wooden furnishings and the walls and the bar were adorned with horse-brasses. The pub had a dark wooden floor, which would receive a covering of fresh sawdust every morning ready for the day's trading.

The pub was the hub of the local community, full of humour and comradeship, a place where people met to drink, drink some more and gossip about her-at-number-seven or Jim-the-scrounger. It was also the place where people came to do the odd trade, sometimes legal and all above board and sometimes not so legal and all above board. There were some real characters about and all with one thing in common; they all loved the East End, they were born and raised there and would never dream of leaving.

I would only get to spend the first three years of my life there while my Grandad Alfred was alive, so never really got to know him that well, but I'm told he was a tough, no-nonsense man who didn't suffer fools gladly. He would never be seen unshaven or unkempt and always wore a shirt and tie.

Once my Grandad quite literally picked up a burly, drunken, loud-mouthed South London dockworker by his collar and pinned him to the dartboard with two darts, one in each ear, after my Nan had been threatened by him because she had refused to serve him another pint of bitter.

Luckily for the chap involved my Nan grabbed hold of the third dart before Grandad managed to use it; so we'll never know what body part he had in mind for its final destination.

My Dad was one of those lucky, or some would say unlucky, young men who would be conscripted to do National Service. Conscription ran for two decades after the war and finished around the birth of The Beatles in 1963. Around 6,000 young men were called up every fortnight and now it was Dad's turn.

Can you imagine that happening these days given the attitude of some of today's youth? – it would be total mayhem.

Like every ex-conscript, the medical is etched into his memory, performed in a somewhat comic book style and ending with the dreaded moment the lady doctor would ask you to drop your trousers and cough.

After having his head shaved, not by some lovely modern style, hairdresser, but someone with the attitude of a Sioux Indian collecting scalps, and being kitted out with his uniform all within a few hours of arrival on day one, he looked just like all the other rookie national servicemen. Next it was time for the parade ground where the breaking-in process by the abusive drill sergeants would begin in earnest, and after which 'young men' would just be called 'men' and the strong separated from the weak. One thing is for sure they were taught to look after themselves.

After finishing basic training, he was sent to Paderborn in Germany, where he learnt to drive a Chieftain tank. Even now in his late seventies, he drives his little car as if he's still driving a Chieftain tank.

While he was off doing his National Service in Germany his mum was introduced to sixteen-year old Doreen Wotton. She was a beautiful and very intelligent young lady born and raised in the East End by Emily and John Wotton. This was the woman who would become my Mother.

Her real name was Doreen Sheila Wotton, but there were lots of girls called Doreen amongst family and friends so everyone called her by her middle name, Sheila which has stuck to this very day. She worked as a chemist's assistant just off the main market and history has it that a lot of the young chirpy Cockney bar-row-boys were chasing after her affections, so she was never short of admirers, flowers and chocolates.

Nan was very impressed with her and set about organising some serious matchmaking, persuading young Doreen to write to her son while he was away. Dad was very pleased by this and eventually they ended up writing nearly every day and their initial pen friendship gradually turned to romance as their letters became evermore amorous.

When he finished his National Service, Dad was naturally keen to get back to England as soon as possible to meet the new love of his life — whom he had still not met in person. The family laid on a small homecoming party and his mother informed him that he was to have his first meeting with Doreen at her aunt's house the following evening and she gave him the time and address.

The following night he had a bath, put on his best whistle and flute, splashed some cologne on his boat, combed his hair and headed off remembering to pick up some flowers on the way.

When he arrived, he approached the door and reached for the doorbell. He was nervous, more nervous than he had ever felt before and he could feel himself shaking. The door was answered by Rosa, who was acting as chaperone for the evening, even though she was only the same age as my soon-to-be Mum.

In fact, Rosa was my Mum's sister's daughter so technically my Mum was her aunt. Mum and Rosa had grown up together and were actually more like sisters.

The one thing about Rosa that stood out a country mile was just how tall she was standing over six-feet two inches and that was barefooted, so imagine how tall she looked standing there in front of my Dad as his jaw fell to the floor in her six-inch heels?

She quickly introduced herself and he, just as quickly, breathed a huge sigh of relief as he entered the house. It's not that Rosa was not pretty, in fact the complete opposite, she was stunning; it was just that he was only five-feet ten inches tall so at that moment he thought that it was never going to work. So imagine his delight when he found out this was not Doreen.

Rosa showed him into the kitchen and apparently that's when he first set eyes upon my Mum, who sat there all nervous and shy. He was already in love with her and she with him, but this was the very moment that confirmed that love.

They went to the cinema on their first date that same evening. Dad says it was to see 'Horrors of the Black Museum', which was infamous for its gruesome murders including the spikes out of the binoculars scene. But my Mum seems to recall that they went to see 'Carry On Teacher'. Throughout the movie Rosa sat behind them to keep a close watchful eye.

After they had been dating for a while my mum fell pregnant with yours truly early in 1960 and with both of them not wanting to cause any family fall-out or scandal and, owing to the fact they were very much in love, they decided to marry as soon as possible and became Mr. and Mrs. Raymond on the 7th May of that year, and then on 6th October 1960 at Queen Mary's Hospital in West Ham Lane, E15, I arrived kicking and screaming.

Mum often likes to remind me of that day; when apparently the doctor took his first look at me, smacked me on the arse until I cried and then turned to my parents and said, "Congratulations – you have a beautiful baby girl."

Chapter 2

Great Big Porky Pies

I'm not a true Cockney, as I wasn't born within the sound of The Bow Bells, but that doesn't mean that I wasn't raised as one and West Ham tends to come under the 'Cockney banner' anyway. I do like to use the odd piece of slang though, so the odd Orchestra Stalls, Tom Tit, or Hampton Wick may be heard on occasion.

The first thing about being born in the East End of London is that you were expected to be an Iron (not an iron hoof of course) or Hammer and support West Ham United.

Obviously the nickname the 'Irons' came from the team's original name, Thames Ironworks and the nickname the 'Hammers' came from the club badge that proudly displays two crossed rivet hammers.

All the family were West Ham United supporters and they would fully expect, in fact fucking insist, that it was your duty to become part of the forever-blowing bubbles crowd at Upton Park on a Saturday afternoon, but I was having none of that bollocks and much to everyone's bitter disappointed — I became a Spurs fan.

That's Tottenham Hotspur if you've no idea who I'm talking about.

I think it was watching the 1967 F.A Cup Final between Spurs and Chelsea that sealed the deal, as this was the first time I ever saw Jimmy Greaves on a football pitch. He was majestic, masterful and magnificent and he tore Chelsea apart with his silky skills and it made quite an impression on me aged six and a half years old. And that's when it happened; I became Yid Army for life.

At the start of managing Koopa I discovered that they, and all their mates, were Arsenal fans, which lead me to suffer their abuse for the entire time we worked together — they were Gooners and I was the yid.

There were so many warning signs surrounding Koopa that I'm surprised I never spotted a single one.

***

Mum and Dad were living above their parent's pub while they were saving for a place of their own, which was proving even tougher at the time as I had just arrived on the scene. Mum recalls bathing me in the kitchen sink, as there was no spare money to invest in luxuries like a baby bath.

When I was a nipper my Grandad Alfred would sit me on the pub bar and put a pint in one of my hands and an unlit cigarette in my mouth to amuse all the pub regulars. My parents also used to slip some beer into my bottle at night or when I was teething as apparently throughout our family history this had helped the children sleep, something that still helps me sleep these days — six pints of lager and I sleep like a baby, although I snore like a rhino.

Sadly, in 1963 my Grandad Alfred passed away, and

shortly after the council decided to reclaim the land in the local area to build a new bypass, so my Nan moved to another pub in East London called The Palmerston. Also around this time Dad started playing the drums, after his mum had purchased him his very first drum kit for his birthday.

Dad soon formed his own band, The Palmerston Trio, which was a strange name for the band as they actually had four members, including Dennis the blind pianist. Dennis called himself the Ray Charles of Hackney, but I'm not sure everyone shared his opinion. For a laugh the band would quite often place the piano on the stage so that Dennis performed the set with his back to the audience.

The guitar player was called Johnny, he was always very suave and when not strumming, could be found at the bar necking back Buchanan's Black & White

Old Scotch Whiskey on the rocks while chatting to the numerous ladies who seemed to be attracted to him. And then there was Derek the lead singer, who had beautiful long flowing blonde locks and was a real hell-raiser; he lived the swinging sixties lifestyle to the max.

Growing up in East London was a real life adventure for me and I remember that Mum would take me to Victoria Park to have a run-around when I was about 5 years old. Victoria Park is the East End's very own version of Regents Park although, of course, much less busy and obviously has no zoo, but even to this day it's very green, beautiful and full of life. It's bounded on two sides by canals, which helped make it an adventure playground for youngsters such as myself and although I was never allowed to play alongside the canals, it was truly the place your imagination would run wild; I would be Tarzan swinging through the trees in the jungle while rescuing Jane from the fierce lions and stampeding rhinoceros while avoiding the canals full of hungry crocodiles.

Nan eventually moved to another pub that was situated on Albion Drive near London Fields, E8 called very appropriately The Albion. The pub was always alive with the sound of music, albeit Nan on stage belting out 'Maybe It's Because I'm A Londoner' or Eight-Fingered-Bert tickling the ivories on the piano. Bert was on the front-line during the war and had two fingers shot off by a German sniper, which did limit his repertoire a little, but he never let it get him down.

Once a very old lady got on the stage to sing 'Puppet On a String' which had become her favourite, ever since she watched Sandie Shaw perform it at The Eurovision Song Contest and to cut a long story short — half way through the song, she dropped to the floor stone-cold dead leaving one local to remark "Someone has cut her bloody string!"

***

Mum and Dad had now saved enough money to put a small deposit down on a tiny flat just up the road from The Albion and Mum set about making it our family palace. I had started school and was attending St. Paul's in Welshpool Street; I loved it and it was there I first encountered sand.

I was allowed to walk to the shop at the top of the

street on my own and go outside and play with friends, as long as I didn't stray too far away. I'm not saying they were safer times and I don't remember it was ever like the old adage, that every back door was open and you could just pop in for a cup of tea, however, I do remember it as being a time that families and communities stuck together and everyone knew everyone. It just felt safer than it does today, which obviously it wasn't… it just felt like it.

Back in those days we had milkmen who would deliver your milk direct to your doorstep, they still exist today, but you just don't see that many around. The sound of the milk cart's electric motor whining around early in the morning and the sound of clinking bottles as the milkman delivered his goods is something I will never forget. I also remember telling Mum that she should be more like the woman living next door as she had a special relationship with the milkman as I'd seen him taking her milk inside her flat for her, rather than just leaving it on the doorstep.

"You should ask him to do that for you Mum," I told her.

She just clipped me round the ear and told me not to tell anyone else.

I don't think the next door neighbour was the only cat in the street getting the cream, as a few days later I saw the milkman looking a bit flustered leaving Mr. Jones house a few doors down.

Now, let it be known that I was a little on the naughty side when I was around seven years old and one day my Mum gave me some money to get a pint of milk from the shop on the corner. On the way back I bumped into one of my school friends and whilst running around having a kick-about with his new orange plastic football, I dropped the bottle smashing it into pieces.

I watched totally distraught as the milk flowed into the gutter and I knew I was in big trouble, so quick as a flash I concocted a plan.

I ran home and Mum looked at my flustered red face and asked, "Are you OK?"

"A man grabbed me and made me drop the milk, Mum!"

'Are you sure you're ok?'

"Yes, I kicked him as hard as I could and ran away!' I replied.

At this point, mainly through embarrassment, I burst into tears. Mum called Dad and relayed the story. I watched Dad make a phone call and the next thing I knew, two very tall policemen walked into the house. I thought they had come to lock me away for telling great big porky-pies and I could feel the tears start to run down my cheeks.

What they actually wanted to do was ask me some questions about the man who grabbed me. I'm not sure what I told them, but I do know that for the next few weeks everyone was on the lookout for a man with a funny moustache who was wearing a red and purple hat and long purple coat.

You may have just guessed that I have described none other than 'Dick Dastardly', the fictional character and antagonist who appeared in various Hanna-Barbera animated series, including 'Wacky Races' and

'Dastardly & Muttley'; I was watching a lot of cartoons and reading a lot of comics at the time.

As you can imagine they never found him and to my parents I would like to take this opportunity to apologise — as I've never confessed to this previously.

I did seem to develop a fine skill for telling porkies and this would come in handy when I started working in the music industry, as being the biggest bull-shitter you can is essential, especially when trying to get a band a gig.

"Do you think they can sell 50 tickets?" the promoter would ask.

"Of course!" I would reply. Obviously we couldn't, but we needed the gig as it was key to our plans.

One of the things I loved most about growing up was going to see my other Nan who lived in the tower block in Jamaica Street, the location for the film 'Sparrows Can't Sing' starring Barbara Windsor. This was always exciting as she lived in the clouds high in the sky above London.

I looked upon it, as her living in a concrete beanstalk and I would be Jack climbing the beanstalk (especially when the lift was broken which, as you will read happens often) to find the gold or in this case the sixpence that Nan would give me on every visit.

One Saturday, as we reached the lobby of Nan's block I rushed off into the lift quickly pressing as many buttons as I could and to my Mums dismay the doors started to close before she could reach me. She was carrying a bunch of freshly cut flowers she had just bought from the market, which got stuck in the door as it closed, ripping the heads off all the stalks.

Things then took a turn for the worse as the lift, instead of going up just shuddered to a grinding halt.

"Mum!" I yelled, "Help me!" before bursting into flood or tears and screaming.

I was stuck in the lift. It would appear that pushing all the buttons at once was not the brightest of ideas and I would end up stuck in that lift for two hours until an engineer came and rescued me. The experience was made worse by the terrible stench of urine.

Let's be honest and say that if you get stuck in a lift as a child, you generally hope for the following:

The lift is not haunted.

You don't have to poop.

It doesn't last too long.

Well, at least it was not haunted.

Every time we visited Nan after the lift incident mum would make us walk up the stairs, I guess it was once bitten, twice shy.

The other good reason for visiting my Nan, was that on the way home we would stop and have 'pie and mash' for tea, or in Dad's case sometime eels and mash. 'Pie and mash' is an East End tradition. It was the food of the working class Cockney and I bloody loved it and on the Roman Road there was the king of pie and mash shops... Kelly's Pie & Mash.

There it stood with its white tiled walls adorned with large mirrors and black marble floors, tables and worktops. When I was a child pie, mash and liquor was and still remains the best thing I had ever tasted. If you have never tried it, push your Cockney prejudices to one side and give it a go.

I read recently that none other than David Beckham

loves pie and mash so much, that he had some delivered to his private jet to enjoy while on a flight from the UK to America.

There was just one thing about the 'pie and mash' shop that disturbed me, and I have vivid and scary memories of the man outside the shop chopping the heads off the live eels as people walked by. Bet you can't do that these days – it's health and safety all gone PC. I also remember that if I got food on my face that my Mum would spit on a hanky and wipe it off; she never carried antibacterial wipes with her, in fact they may not have been invented back then. Come to think of it everyone would just spit in their hankie and wipe your face without a second thought – disgusting.

After the lift incident I was very upset and spent most of the time at my Nans either crying or doing that thing where you have stopped crying, but continue to do those stuttering gasps; while breathing in and out as you try to calm down. Anyway, Mum was obviously cross with me and we ended up leaving.

The most annoying thing about that was I never got to watch the wrestling with Nan and listen to her shout abuse at the television at the top of her voice; she absolutely adored the wrestling.

Nan's favourite wrestler was the blonde bombshell with the ponytail Jackie 'Mr. TV' Pallo who had a fierce rivalry with Mick McManus. Nan had a special way with words and told me when I was around eight-years old that Mick McManus "Was a fucking dirty old bastard."

"What's a fucking dirty old bastard?" I asked Mum.

"Where did you learn those words?" she replied as her hand clipped my ear.

"Nan," I said — as I grassed her up.

"Oh dear," Mum sighed.

Chapter 3

The Cockney Costa Del Sol

In the late sixties Dad was offered the opportunity, via one of his Mum's contacts at the brewery, to become the landlord of his very own pub and he happily accepted as he had always wanted to follow in his father's footsteps and become a pub landlord.

The pub was called The Pegasus and, unbeknown to him it was a real hellhole and full of bad people from both sides of the law planning bad things. The police frequented the pub to keep their eyes on the local East End villains and those very same villains would drink in the pub just to keep an eye on the police.

Undercover policemen (who informed everyone that they were undercover – thus blowing their cover) would spend all day in the pub knocking back drinks like they were going out of fashion and then jump in their motors to drive home. This was a different time — it was London in the sixties and I'm not even sure that drink-driving laws were enforced (especially by the police force on their own people), all I know is that everyone thought nothing of drinking and driving. It wasn't ever frowned upon and seemed socially acceptable; it was regarded a little more seriously than we regard littering these days and you were unlikely to ever be stopped and forced to take a breathalyser test – probably because the coppers themselves were pissed.

There were always fights breaking out and I witnessed quite a few. Once this monster of a man, casually walked up to some chap sitting quietly having a drink at the bar and with one punch, hit him so hard that he flew across it as if he had been hit by a freight train. Dad looked down at me and said "When a man that big casually walks up next to you, something bad is about to happen."

Some of the men that drank in the pub were proper hard-as-nails villains and those were just the policemen.

I remember there was real tension in the household once that caused my sister Susan and I not being allowed to go to school or even leave the pub on our own for about a month, after someone who had started a fight in the pub and had subsequently been barred, threatened to kidnap me, Susan and our new born sister Mandy. The police deemed it to be a very viable and a serious threat, so Mum and Dad were instructed to take every precaution to protect themselves and the three of us.

Of course, I was more than happy not to go to school and I spent hours playing with my toy soldiers and cars that my uncle, who worked at the Matchbox factory in Hackney would bring home by the boxful every time he visited. He always told Mum that they were rejects — but he told me that they were brand new. How I wish I had kept that toy van with the Weetabix logo on the side; they fetch up to £3000 at auction these days.

I even had time to play with the chemistry set I had received at Christmas and finally unbox that 'Cutta Matic Dr. Who & The Daleks' set, which basically involved cutting out Dalek shapes from sheets of polystyrene with a heated wire. The chemistry set and 'Cutta Matic' were among a range of children's toys on sale that had the potential to poison, maim and seriously injure children in the sixties.

With the threat to the family ongoing Dad decided to go out and purchase a double barrel shotgun. I'm not sure where he got it from or if it was legally purchased, but I don't think he had a receipt. I remember seeing it and thinking 'I could use that to have a great game of war with my sister.' Thankfully I never saw it again as it was kept hidden away behind the bar; in the hope that it would never have to be used.

On a particularly dark and stormy night during another power cut (which we had a lot of) my cousin Richie, who worked as our bar manager and also lived with us above the pub, was very late home after a long drinking and poker session at a local club. Having forgotten his keys and not wanting to wake everyone up, he decided in his infinite wisdom to shimmy up the drainpipe onto the ledge and climb in through the skylight. Dad upon hearing the commotion grabbed the shotgun and crept up the stairs to deal with the intruder and seeing the shadowy figure climbing in — fired two barrels that luckily just missed.

The noise was deafening and, after the unpleasant ringing in his ears finally stopped, Dad looked up at Richie and shouted,

"Stupid bastard, I nearly killed you!"

"Well, you missed, you shit shot! Next time make sure you're wearing your glasses you blind fucker!"

The next morning Dad, disturbed by the fact that he had almost killed his brother's son, explained to Richie what had happened, as he had no memory of the previous night at all, and then realising just how close he had come to death, he apparently threw up in the kitchen sink. He then threw up again after Dad in a stern and villainous voice said, "After you called me a blind-fucker I considered reloading and shooting you for real!"

Soon after that shotgun incident, at the tender age of nine-years old Mum and Dad decided enough was enough and with another child on the way, it would be best to get themselves and us away from living in such an unruly and borderline nasty establishment like The Pegasus.

It might also have had something to do with the fact that Dad had discovered who the would-be kidnapper was and had dealt with him personally – I have heard rumours and gossip from family members as to what exact vengeance was delivered, but I've never been brave enough to ask him outright what exactly did happen.

We had extended family living in Southend in Essex, so they set about looking for a new home in that area and, after a short search found the perfect property on the seafront. So they served their notice at the pub, sorted new schools and put publican life on hold for the time being, while Dad concentrated on further pursuing his career as a drummer. And so in the summer of 69 (no bursting out into the Bryan Adams song, please) we upped sticks and moved lock, stock and barrel to The Cockney Costa Del Sol — that is Southend-On-Sea.

Southend is like Gibraltar, it's built on rock – but in this case; sticks of rock. When I was young the place was alive with the sound of day-trippers in kiss-me-quick hats who flocked to the seaside to enjoy the sand and sea between their toes, while tucking into ice creams and candy floss — people really did like to be beside the seaside.

Southend was all about the wind whistling from the sea, bringing with it the smell of the seaside: salt in the air mixed with sweet candy floss, hot dogs, fresh doughnuts sizzling and fish and chips frying, as well as all those screaming kids wanting more money, more ice cream and more rides on the merry-go-round.

Southend is home to the world's longest pleasure pier. The Pier is a major and historical landmark, which extends 1.34 miles into the Thames Estuary and is so famous that Sir John Betjemen once said, "The Pier is Southend and Southend is the Pier." It was certainly a stunning and standout feature of our new hometown and this was long before it was burnt down, not once, but twice and also had a ship crash into it.

The summers were fantastic and we had heatwaves that went on for weeks and weeks. The sun burning down reflecting off the pier, the grey and freezing cold sea as it lapped against the edges of the cigarette-butt laden beaches and the sound of the penny arcades clunking and chinging with every coin dropped into them.

The bank holiday carnival parades with all those

highly decorated floats, the beautiful Carnival Queens, marching bands all bold as brass and all those people in fancy dress running around from side to side of each float with their carnival buckets, collecting coins for charity – such happy days indeed.

Then there was the night time; the sun setting over the sea, giving way to those amazing sparkling illuminations that lit up the Golden Mile, filling the darkness with vivid colour that flashed all around you overloading your senses and turning the whole of the seafront into Southend's very own version of Las Vegas.

Viva Las Vegas! Viva Las Southend!

And finally, let's not forget the Dolphinarium, well, I say Dolphinarium, actually it was little more than a corrugated tin-shack erected on the seafront with rack seating inside, but everyone loves dolphins don't they!

I worked there for a while when I was the boyfriend of the owner's daughter. They were called Sally and Sinbad – no, not my girlfriend and the owner… the bloody dolphins! They were both grey in colour and had cone-shaped teeth and pronounced beaks – let's not go there you know I'm talking about the dolphins.

If he was in a very good mood, which usually meant the sun was shining and the place had been sold out all week, the owner would let us swim with the dolphins in the tank. They were so intelligent and adorable – yes, I do mean Sinbad and Sally the dolphins, as my girlfriend was thick as a plank (she was very good looking though).

That one summer at the Dolphinarium was great fun and although my duties were mainly sweeping up after each show and cleaning the piss off the floor in the men's toilets, on one very special occasion I was asked to step in and assist the trainer during the show, after her usual assistant had been taken ill with a stomach bug.

So imagine my surprise when they asked me to climb to the top of the ladder and hold out a fish in order for Sinbad to jump up and take straight from my hand.

I was shitting myself, mainly as I hated heights, but also at the thought of having my hand bitten off, as I had recently read the Peter Benchley novel 'Jaws' about a great white shark. I used to think that sharks only swam in the oceans, but after my experiences in the music industry I now know that they walk among us.

I climbed the ladder, which to be honest, was only about ten feet high and on command Sinbad sprung from the water below gracefully and grabbed at the fish in my shaking hand. However, totally forgetting the instruction to let go of the fish as the dolphin grabbed it, I panicked and held onto it even tighter, which meant as Sinbad grabbed the fish and descended back to the tank, I followed.

The crowd gasped in horror as I too hit the water, the trainer immediately dived in and helped me out. Dripping wet from head to toe and highly embarrassed I stood there while the crowd first laughed and then applauded, so I bowed and accepted the applause before walking off to dry out.

I do have a vague recollection that as I was being pulled out of the tank both Sinbad and Sally swam past laughing, in fact Sinbad gave me a wink as if to say "I did that on porpoise" – that's such a bad joke, I do apologise. I did however receive a special treat from my girlfriend that night, who was impressed with my heroics.

A few days later I became quite ill and Mum blamed it on the fact that I had probably swallowed some dolphin shit that had polluted the water. All I remember is being sick for a few days and Mum making me a bed up on the sofa so I could watch television.

A cure for most ailments in those days was a bottle of Lucozade from the local chemist, it came in a glass bottle complete with a yellow cellophane wrap.

Funny, but back then the chemist was the only place you could buy Lucozade as it was deemed a medicine, but these days it's on very cold-shelf in every shop you walk in. I accidentally knocked the bottle over and it spilt on Mums brand new faux fur white rug and no amount of scrubbing or cleaning with her brand new Bissell carpet-cleaning machine could remove the stain.

The Dolphinarium was locked up and abandoned soon after my escapades and the dolphins along with the owners just vanished into thin air; but they did leave piles of rotting fish and rubbish stacked up inside that wafted along the seafront for a few weeks, before the council cleaned it up.

We lived in a large three-bedroom house on the seafront, and shortly after we had moved in my little sister Jill was born. I loved this house and my bedroom had a view of the sea opposite. In the living room Dad had built a bar, which he decorated in a Hawaiian style, all yellow and blue with parrots and hula girls painted on it. It was very exotic and it was always fully stocked with wonderfully coloured bottles. I particularly liked the red soda syphon which sat on the side, ready for action at any time; it was also great for spraying at my sisters with when they annoyed me.

Best of all was my bedroom with its football wallpaper and my beloved poster of Raquel Welch — you know that one with her dressed in the skimpy furs, which I spent a lot of time concentrating on and my favourite poster of all which showed all the flags of all the countries in the world – nerd alert!

The house had steps leading to the front door where, as kids we would sit watching the ships go by.

I had just acquired a pair of slingshots from a kid at school called Oily-Ian, named because of his very greasy hair, which I had exchanged for a pair of Clackers.

Clackers, also known as Knockers and Click Clacks and consisted of two large acrylic balls, which hung on either end of a heavy string. The two balls would swing apart and back together, making the loud clacking noise that gave the toy its name and I use the term toy very loosely – it was more of a weapon.

You could clack away for maybe 30 seconds at a time, but eventually you would lose your rhythm and they would lose their trajectory and those fucking hard acrylic orbs would rebound off each other and wrap around your hand and slam you on your wrist bone, causing you to scream out, followed inevitably by the words "I'm never ever doing that again!" Sometimes the balls shattered sending dangerous flying shards every which way, notably toward nearby pairs of eyes.

The biggest problem with them was that you couldn't resist trying again.

You would try it again — and of course you would bruise your wrist again and again and again...

Eventually my Clackers had caused me too much pain (let's not get childish) that when Oily-Ian presented an opportunity of a swap —it was most welcome. He came into school a few days later with a plaster cast on his wrist having suffered a fracture due to an accident involving those balls of death.

One particular sunny day I asked my Sister Susan if she fancied joining me in a slingshot session. We crossed the road to the beach and collected some pebbles mixed with stones before returning to our front steps to begin having some fun. We started firing them back across the road at the seagulls on the beach that were becoming more and more agitated after every shot.

In fact, we may have invented an early version of the now popular game 'Angry Birds' that afternoon. This was all great fun until I accidentally let fire just as a car passed and my inaccurate shot went straight through its back window causing it to shatter.

The car shuddered to a halt and a very angry looking man got out screaming at us both.

Without a second thought I looked at my Sister and yelled "Look what you have done," causing her to burst into tears. My lying techniques were coming on a treat by the time I was in senior school.

Hearing all the commotion Mum rushed out of the house and started talking to the man.

I don't know what she said to him, but he quickly calmed down.

She grabbed us and shouted "You two, get in the house!"

Mum most certainly was an 'Angry Bird' I watched as she picked up her purse and went back outside. Peeping through the orange patterned curtains (everything in our house apart from the Hawaiian themed bar was orange or brown – it was the fucking seventies) I saw her hand over some money to the man and then turn back towards the house.

We both tried to run off to our respective rooms, but were stopped in our tracks.

"Come here, both of you!" she shouted as we cowered in terror.

The inquest began and the truth was told — well, not really. I went on to explain exactly what Susan had done and best of all she was under the impression that she had actually fired the window smashing shot.

Mum did what all parents would in that situation, clipped us both round the top of the head with her palm and sent us to our rooms while shouting "Your father is going to hear about this when he gets home!"

I felt bad, so I crept out of my room to say I was sorry to Susan and confess that it was me that fired that fatal shot at which point she screamed at the top of her voice "MUUUUUMMMMM!"

"Gary said he did it Mum!" grassing me right up.

"She's lying," I replied as I did my best 'stand there and look innocent' move.

"Get to your rooms!" Mum shouted.

"I'm in my room," Susan replied. Mum clipped Susan round the ear again and shouted,

"Don't be cheeky to your Mother."

Susan cried most of the day, I was still denying everything and when Dad came home I stuck to my story that Susan fired the shot that hit the car, but I still ended up sharing the punishment — no pocket money for six weeks.

"Where did you get the slingshots?" Dad asked.

"I got them from Oily-Ian at school."

"Who the bloody hell is Oily-Ian?"

"He's…" I started to answer before being interrupted.

"Oh, never mind. Where are the sodding slingshots?"

"Mum's got them."

Dad marched off, collected the slingshots from Mum snapped them in half and then threw them in the bin. I felt like saying that's a bit harsh, but decided it would be best to keep quiet given the circumstances.

I also heard him tell Mum "Those fucking kids are a bloody nightmare, I don't know how you cope with them."

I always meant to own up to this, but never got around to it until now.

Sorry Susan. Sorry Mum. Sorry Dad. Sorry man in the car. Sorry seagulls.

Chapter 4

There are Ninjas in the Playground

Our house (at the bottom of our street) was always filled with music, whether it was Dad filling the air with classics on his brand new eight-track tape deck like Dave Brubeck, Mum listening to Englebert Humperdinck's 'Release Me' (Please don't read anything into that — she loved my Dad, but did have a soft spot for Englebert) or Susan singing and dancing to her favourite's, The Osmonds in the living room.

The only problem with the eight-track was that every time a new song came on, you heard a loud click.

Doing my best impression of an idiot's guide-to; the eight-track tape was basically an up-market cassette tape.

What's a cassette? Please just fuck off and Google it if you don't know.

I had a second-hand record player in my bedroom which wore out many a needle listening to my collection of 45rpm vinyl singles (that's 7-inch singles to anyone under 25). It was my pride and joy and was a Fidelity HF33 portable record player, built into a striking red case (now considered kitsch) and had an integrated speaker – mono, of course!

It had an arm which held a needle that you had to manually place on the record in order to play a song, but you had to be extra careful carrying out this manoeuvre because the slightest pressure could scratch the record.

Now, if you were really adept at using your record playing, you could find the specific groove for the beginning of any song – something they call 'shuffle' these days.

I would spend hours in my room listening to my singles collection that mainly consisted of Slade, Sweet, David Essex, Mud and Barry Blue records. Strange that in the years to come Barry Blue's son would be the person that signed up one of my bands called Twenty Twenty.

Albums were a bit sparse in my collection, but I did have a few including Rod Stewart's 'Every Picture Tells a Story', Bowie's 'Hunky Dory' and a comedy album called 'Interesting Facts' by Kenneth Williams, which had been a present from my Dad who always laughed out loud when he heard me playing it.

Once to my horror, I came home from school and could hear music be played from my room and upon immediate inspection, I discovered my sister Mandy was using my record player to listen to some 'Pinky & Perky' records Mum had given her and, worst of all, she was just picking up the arm and dropping the needle on the record causing it to bounce around. I ran towards her, but tripped over a pile of magazines and stubbed my toe on her 'Look-in' annual which annoyed me even more.

"Oh my God! Don't drop the needle like that!" I

shouted, causing her to burst into tears and she run off crying as usual to Mum. 'Oh well, that's me in more trouble,' I thought. My Mum subsequently told me off and told me that they had actually got me from the circus and threatened to give me back if I shouted at my little sister ever again.

Mum would say crazy stuff like that. Once, when she caught my sister Susan picking her nose and told her that bogies and snot were actually her brain cells so she was slowly destroying her own brain – she was absolutely terrified, but never picked her nose again.

It was time to get a new stylus or, or what the un-initiated would call, a needle for my record player and decided I would pick one up on our next trip to the record shop. When I was growing up I would hop on the bus on a Saturday morning, or if the weather was nice, take a slow stroll into town with my mates whilst having a chat about the football or in most instances, girls. Arriving at the record shop ready to explore and discover all the hidden gems that deserved to be in your music collection.

The experience of buying a single or album is lost on the new generation of music lovers. This doesn't mean they love music any less, but the modern music lover seems to want everything right-now. They have come to be a generation with no patience and worse still, a generation who mostly despise paying for the music they listen to.

There is no anticipation, no excitement. Now it's just a click on a laptop or phone and you have it. I'm not knocking the modern way of purchasing and down-loading singles or albums, as I'm a big fan myself. But there's just something magical missing and I'm sure a hell of a lot of people would agree with me.

These days you are, quite simply, missing the adventure of owning music. Downloads play a major part in this story and, in fact, without them I would've never put pen to paper or fingers to keyboard in the first place.

The pleasure of holding an artist's latest album is lost on the new generation. The delight of seeing the artwork, reading the sleeve notes and hearing it for the first time are moments you come to cherish forever. If you were really lucky your new album purchase would include all the lyrics on a separate sheet in order for you to sing along in the privacy of your own room — thankfully vinyl is making a comeback!

Today bands and singers are far too accessible and that's why the likes of David Bowie, Elton John, The Beatles and many more artists became massive stars – they had a mystery about them and weren't to be seen every minute of every day. Now a fan can simply keep refreshing a band's site and see updates of them talking shit, eating pizza and feeding their fucking cat. And let's not get me started on the fact you can tell what a band is going to sound like these days by their fucking haircuts and the clothes they wear.

My best mates from school were Ali-the-Turk (yes, he was Turkish), Ginger-Keith (obviously named), Denis-The-Menace (obviously he was a bit of a lad), Trout, who was actually called Graham Fish and Terry-All-Gold — we called him this because he once bought a girl a box of Terry's All Gold chocolates and made the big mistake of telling us.

There was also Fumble who was actually called Freddie, but he told us he once touched a girl's breast under her top in the cinema and thus became Freddie-Fumble, then just Fumble. Fair play to Freddie though, as he was the first of our gang to officially finger a girl.

Then there was the smallest member of the gang William known to us all as Little-Willy and named after The Sweet hit single "Little Willy" which we would randomly start singing every time he was being a knob-end. Let's all sing together, "Little Willy, Willy Won't Go Home…." Let's just say we sang it to him a lot.

There was also a girl called Janette Barnes, who used to hang around with us as she was a bit of a tomboy. She played football with us in the park, hung about on the seafront and generally acted like a boy. I know Ginger-Keith tried to kiss her once so she kicked him in the balls and called him a ginger wanker. Ouch!

Oh, and of course finally there was me. I was obviously called Gazza making me the one true Gazza. Paul Gascoigne may have something to say about this, but to be fair, even he called me Gazza when I met him at White Hart Lane when he was playing for Spurs – so there!

We would always start our music buying at Woolworths, mainly because Tracy Moore worked there on Saturdays; she had an enormous pair of breasts, which she always found hard to keep in place in her tight company-branded blouse she was forced to wear. Then we would move on to the little record store located downstairs in a music shop in the High Street the name of which escapes me.

I was into glam rock to start, so was always excited to be picking up the latest single on my radar. So it could be 'Tiger Feet' by Mud on Rak Records, which usually came without 'middles' meaning you had to use your spindle to play it, or another week it could well be 'The Bump' by Kenny; whose lead singer, the teenage heart-throb Rick Driscoll would strangely play a part in my venture into the music industry years later.

After hanging around outside the record shop chatting for a while, our gang would gather our belongings and head for that 'holiest of holies', the holy grail of fast food restaurants... The Wimpy.

What's The Wimpy? Please! No! You've Never heard of The Wimpy?

Well, you have not lived until you have eaten there.

Let me educate you in the best burger ever created. Let me introduce you to 'The Original Quarter-Pounder with Cheese'. There will never be another like it. Why? Because of that oh-so-delicious secret-sauce that oozed from the burger bun and covered that sumptuous flame-grilled burger.

The Wimpy Burger Bar also had a secret weapon in its desert locker. A desert that would take your taste buds into outer space. A dessert, if purchased on a date with your girlfriend, would almost guarantee you being able to put at least one hand under her jumper for a cop-a-feel moment, a dessert that now purports to an almost mythical status as if it actually never existed at all —the doughnut and ice cream combo with chocolate sauce finished off with chopped nuts on top that was 'The Brown Derby'. My mate Freddie-Fumble always maintained that this was a euphemism, but I never understood his train of thought.

I enjoyed hanging around with my mates at the weekend, but as Monday morning arrived you knew it was time to go back to the school with the most fearsome reputation in Southend — Southchurch Hall High School for Boys.

There wasn't a single girl in sight unless of course you included Dirty-Doris and Big-Betty the dinner ladies; all the girls from junior school had gone to Dowsett High School for Girls.

Dirty-Doris had earned her nickname after a boy had seen her picking her nose while stirring some custard and Big-Betty, well you guessed it, she was a slobbering twenty-stone monster who was once accused of having an affair with the school janitor; who just happened to look like Catweazel.

The chasing and chatting up of girls would have to be something saved as an after school activity. Apart from our school playing fields being next to the girls' school, we never got any opportunity to use our cheeky chat up patter that we had been perfecting, like – "I'm not a photographer, but I can picture you and me together."

They didn't always work as Little-Willy once found out, after he said to a girl he saw in W.H. Smith "Are you retarded? Because you sure are special," and she punched him in the face.

The school had earned its reputation for having the toughest pupils in the area and I have to admit it was actually pretty rough there. The teachers were all as hard-as-nails ex-military and wouldn't give a second thought to giving you a clump round the head for any reason they deemed fit; and astonishingly and they all swore like troopers. I once got whacked round the head just for being wet when it was raining as we walked to school that morning.

"You're dripping on the floor, Raymond!" Was the shout I got as I walked into the classroom, just before his hand clumped me round the head, and when you did get whacked by a teacher you wouldn't tell your parents for fear of getting another punishment.

Some teachers were always angry, just being at the school made them angry, seeing our ugly faces made them angry and it appeared that just being alive made them angry. Anyway, they were to be avoided in the corridor and you dare not look at them in class or speak out of turn.

School wasn't about the classroom, it was all about fitting-in during the breaks and being able to get-in with the cool kids in the playground. If you didn't, then you were pretty much fucked for your entire school life.

Everyone had nicknames; if you were unfortunate, then you might not be given a complimentary one. There was one lad called Patrick, whose mum was Egyptian – he was called 'CleoPatrick' and another lad was called 'Tea-Pot' because he was short and stout.

There were some that were far worse including one thirteen-year old boy simply known as cunt!

Bullying was also rife; luckily though I could look after myself a little bit and bullying is something practiced by the insecure and the cowardly and was something I never encountered or ever indulged in.

I remember uniform codes being really rather strict, especially in the footwear department – teachers were obsessed with what you were wearing on your feet. Then there were those little pricks known as Prefect's sitting in wait at the school gates, ready to pounce if you dared to arrive just a few seconds later than the assembly bell.

I walked into school one day with my tie loose and out, pounced Simon Carter; he was a shitty little Prefect-grass and he loved his job – he probably went on to be a traffic warden.

"That's a late violation, oh and a tie violation!" he announced in his piffy little voice.

"Fuck off grass!" I whispered as I walked past.

"That's the use of foul language as well!"

"So you are actually going to report me for swearing are you?"

"Yes, you're on report," he declared with pride, "I have everything written down in my report book."

"Well. in that case, why don't you go fuck yourself wanker!" I replied.

The problem was that he did bloody write everything down because the deputy headmaster called me into his office later that day and showed me the report book and, after a severe telling off regarding my use of the English language, I got given detention for a week and worst of all had to help out at the Film Club after school.

I really didn't care to have to sit through 'Lord of the Fucking Flies' – that's not its actual title!

A teacher once shouted "If you talk at all during this lesson, you will be given detention. Do you understand?" I didn't reply and got detention for ignoring him – that sums up teachers in the seventies.

Our school was very old and so were most of its teachers. Mr. Bull the history teacher quite often just nodded off during his own lessons while Mr. White the elderly geography teacher was going a bit senile and once forgot where France was on the map of Europe.

"It's here, sir, in between Germany and Spain," a pupil pointed out.

The teachers were nothing short of thugs; if you dared admit to not understanding something most teachers would just explain it the exact same way, but just louder and in a more exasperated voice. And if you spoke out of turn during a lesson, well, you were likely to be struck on the head by a chalk-duster, which was the teacher's favourite weapon of choice or, even worse pulled out to the front to receive the punishment of the slipper. You have to question the morals of teachers that kept an old slipper in their desk ready for action.

There was a maths teacher The-Ten-Foot Misery, his real name Mr. Critchley and he was a real bastard. He was very tall and picked on the inoffensive and mild mannered; he would hurl chalk at pupils if they failed to pay attention. He had a bad back for a while and had to wear some kind of support that made him look even taller and scarier – he went absolutely berserk in class once and gave us all a week's detention when he found someone had chalked 'Chas the Spaz' on his blackboard. I once made the mistake of putting my hand up to say I didn't understand the question and he screamed in front of the whole class "You don't understand the question because you're a stupid fucker!" – WTF!

The French teacher Mr. Brown hated me with a passion, not because I was rubbish at learning French, but because every Wednesday, as captain of the school football team, I would have to leave his class before the lesson ended and he objected every single time. This would mean that the Head of P.E. Mr. Grant, who was a rough-tough ex-soldier and extremely proud Scotsman, would have to storm into the class and insist I was allowed to leave – he may have even threatened Mr. Brown with physical violence once.

Mr. Brown then made it his job to make my life hell at every given opportunity; like making me lie on the floor for the rest of the lesson once, after I fell backwards off my chair.

He was a right, as the French would say 'Branlcr.'

Mr. Grant, Head of Physical Education to give him his full title, was little more than a sadist who loved inflicting pain on anyone and, at our school there always seemed to be a someone. If you stepped out of line in his presence, he had his own unique form of discipline, he would grab a small piece of hair on your temple and lift you up onto your tiptoes – it was most effective.

During P.E. he would make us play 'murder-ball', yes, it was actually called 'murder-ball' and it was as brutal as its name; a game invented to inflict pain upon the pupils. It seemed to have no rules and no teams and involved Mr. Grant and his assistant Mr. English spending half an hour chasing you around the gym in an attempt to hit you with tennis balls — thrown with as much force as they could muster.

If they happened to hit you in the face you would hear them cry out "Yes!"

If you got hit you sat to the side and the winner, or idiot, was the last boy standing. I was down to the last two once and to win the other boy grabbed me and used me as a human shield leading me to receive a thumping ball to the head and another straight to my bollocks. Ouch!

One daring kid called Eddie Hewitt once picked up a ball and threw it back at Mr. Grant making it bounce off his forehead; everyone stopped running and there was total silence Mr. Grant threw an evil glare at poor Eddie, who stood white faced, before picking up a medicine ball walking over to him and telling him to lie on the floor. Once lying flat on his back Mr. Grant aimed the medicine ball at his stomach and let it fall. Eddie winced, puffed his cheeks out and tried to hide his pain. Mr. Grant turned, picked up a tennis ball, blew his whistle and the game was back on. I don't remember anyone else ever throwing a ball at Mr. Grant again.

I had a really strange relationship with Mr. Grant, as I was the captain of the school football team, he always treated me differently to the others and we would discuss the future and the chances of me making it as a footballer. He was a great teacher and he had a passion for sport with endless knowledge to pass on. His greatest gift was giving me encouragement and making me mentality tougher – something that came in very useful once I was managing the bands.

However, we always fell out over one thing; cross-country running, he was mystified at just how bad I was at it. Truth is, I hated long distance running and always just dawdled along at a nice easy pace. On occasion, given the opportunity, I would nip in for a fizzy drink and a bag of crisps at my auntie's house that backed onto the cross-country field. Luckily Mr. Grant never found out otherwise he would have killed me.

The school playground was huge and sloped naturally to one side. One winter we decided to create an ice-slide, which over a few days became one solid sheet that went down the slope straight into a high wall. We must have been fucking mental to do it, but one night as the leaving-bell sounded, we sneaked out and poured a few buckets of water down the slope in the hope that it would freeze perfectly overnight. Alas, we never actually got to use it, as early the following morning the headmaster on his daily site inspection stepped onto it and ended up sliding down into said wall — causing him to require medical attention for concussion.

I recall there were some very unpleasant playground games around at the time including; The Dead Arm Game. which involved taking turns punching each other in the arm as hard as you could until someone caved in and pleaded for mercy, and Slap which. unlike the usual format of slapping hands was adapted to slapping faces.

There were also far more brutal games like Knee Conkers and Head the Brick, but I tried to avoid those, especially Head the Bric' as only the slightly strange kids — that you tried to avoid from the special classes — seemed to want to play.

My bruises came to my mum's attention on one occasion causing her to ask what had I been up to. "Just playing games in the playground Mum – nothing to worry about."

I swear for a moment that she thought I was getting bullied or even worse being physically abused by some teacher, but she never mentioned it again.

I suppose the ultimate punishment of all was being dragged to the headmaster's office for the cane; now that bloody stung!

I only received the caned once and that was for making those Ninja style Kung Fu stars in metalwork and then flinging them around the playground. How someone never got killed or seriously injured is beyond me; the playground could be a most dangerous place.

On the very odd occasion that I did find myself in a fight, I always tried to stand my ground as my Dad had taught me. The boys would form a circle and two would enter the inner sanctum, but only one would leave triumphant.

The first time I got into a fight at school, I think we just tapped one another a few times before a teacher broke it up, but the second time I knew I was in big trouble. After football training I had accidentally trodden on the bare foot of the school-bully Billy Whitehead with my boots on, he already resented the fact that I was captain of the school team, so I guess he decided now was the time to put me in my place. He was the teams centre half and was bloody huge. I knew I had a painful beating coming.

I did consider taking the cowardly way out of which I had three options; doing a runner after school, faking illness and going home early or running home at lunchtime and asking Dad to send me to another school for the rest of my education, but in the end after much debate and being called a fucking coward by some of the other lads, I decided to just get it over and done with.

The home-time bell rang and from my history classroom window, I could see everyone gathering for the spectacle of me getting my head kicked-in. I walked out and into the circle to face Billy looking about ten-feet tall and very menacing.

I took off my blazer and tie remembering the golden rule; if in a fight — take off your tie. I once witnessed a boy almost strangled to death because he had forgotten this rule and I wasn't going to get caught out by that old trick.

I puffed out my cheeks and walked to the middle of the circle ready to be battered.

Billy walked up to me and looked me up and down.

"Didn't think you would be here!" he snarled.

"Well, let's just say I'm not scared of you Billy," I replied defiantly. In actual fact I was fucking terrified.

He pulled back his very large arms, clenched a fist and I watched in slow motion as it headed towards my face with a – Wallop! The blow hit me hard on the cheekbone and it hurt like hell.

He stepped back and I moved forward to throw my first punch, I swung and he stepped away causing me to miss. He then stopped and looked at me. Everyone around was baying for him to finish me off, well, except for my mates who were looking at me as if to say — it was nice knowing you Gazza!

I waited for the next punch, but it never came, Billy stopped and paused.

"I didn't think you would have the guts to take me on!" he said.

"Best get it over and done with I thought mate."

Billy moved closer and just when I thought he was going to reach out and offer me a handshake... Bang! He had me again!

He hit me straight in the face and I fell straight to the ground out for the count. When I came to I saw Mr. Grant, the P.E. teacher shouting at him.

"What's wrong with you? We have a cup match against Eastwood tomorrow and I need everyone fit!"

I eventually pulled myself up and looked around to see there was only myself, Billy and Mr. Grant left in the playground, everyone else had scarpered.

"Sorry sir, it was my fault – I started it," I said.

"I doubt that very much." Mr. Grant replied.

We were marched into the gym given the slipper and then let go. He told us that he was annoyed with us because we had made him leave school late and that he did not have time to do his weekly food shop.

"That's a bit of a gay thing to say," I whispered to Billy on the way out.

"Yeah."

"So is that it?"

Billy looked at me and said, "See you tomorrow we need to beat that Eastwood scum."

After that incident, we were kind-of mates and that was great and yes, we did indeed beat the Eastwood scum that following afternoon, both scoring goals helping to put a smile on the usually grumpy Mr. Grant's face.

I have very good memories of school, but perhaps that's because I choose to and that I was also one of the lucky ones. Yes, I suffered some verbal abuse from teachers, especially Mr. Brown during French lessons and on occasion I might overstep the mark and get a detention, but there were the weaker minded boys who suffered terrible mental abuse from teachers and quite often pupils.

Some boys would shake with fear and even piss themselves as a teacher unleashed their verbal wrath upon them. It was horrifying to have to sit and watch as the teacher got so close to them that both his hot breath and his venomous spit hit the pupil in the face.

I thought long and hard about the abuse that went on at school before deciding whether to write about it or not, but it would be wrong not to include some of the things that I witnessed and encountered that to be honest just felt normal when we were teenagers.

There were those times when you would get the odd slap on your bare arse from the sports teacher as you walked naked to the showers, which sometimes was so hard it left a red mark on your cheeks.

There were times when teachers would tease you as you stood showering; telling you to make sure you didn't miss any bits and going on about your growing or not growing pubic hair. In certain classes there was a lot of knee touching by certain teachers as they leaned over you to look at your work or explain to something. Back in the early seventies, these types of things never felt that creepy, but in the light of how the seventies are perceived today it now makes my fucking skin crawl to the max.

Dishing out punishment was something that some teachers seemed to enjoy and in particular one teacher whose name escapes me, obviously enjoyed it more than most; he was a fucking monster who would stalk the corridors at lunchtime seeking his next victims and when he found them he would make damn sure that they suffered for their misdemeanours.

His favourite weapon of choice was the slipper, but playground gossip had it, that his slipper was stuffed with a few pennies to help inflict even more pain on the poor sod who stood bent over his desk.

He seemed to get some kind of thrill from handing out the punishment and he was very enthusiastic about it too, and quite often would get all sweaty and out of breath such was his exertion. I can hear his weasly little voice in my head right now and it makes me feel sick – he was a total bastard and he was hated by all.

Upon a recent visit to the school, which is now an adult learning centre, I was told that everything regarding the building when it was a school was destroyed years ago — I do find it strange that nothing remains of those times though, just one of those things I guess — but it does make you think.

The smells and sounds of your school days are forever emblazoned in one's mind and mine are definitely of the school playground; those 30-a-side football matches with a tennis ball at dinner time will remain with me forever, as well as memories of amazing friends and actually getting a great education in the end – despite all the pain inflicted. Southchurch was not a happy school, it was an aggressive school even violent at times, but it prepared the boys for real life.

We left Southchurch toughened-up and prepared for the trials and tribulations of our lives ahead.

Besides, I bet there's not one person at that school who will ever forget that day in the playground when in a fit of rage, a boy called Daniel shouted at the headmaster "Fuck off, you wanker!"

The look on the headmaster's face was priceless.

The look on Daniel's face as he realised what he had just said was priceless.

The fact that the headmaster punched him straight in the face, well, that's something you didn't see every day.

Chapter 5

I'll Tell Your Mum to Pack Your Bags

Dad was concentrating on his music and the Palmerston Trio was actually making a name for themselves on the jazz circuit, having eventually evolved into an actual trio consisting of Derek, who, as well as being lead singer played the keyboards, Johnny on guitar and of course my Dad on not just the drums, but percussion – that's a posh term for drums with the addition of a set of bongos.

They performed at prestigious London venues such as The 100 Club, The Marquee Club and the legendary Ronnie Scott's. Doing the circuit performing in various working men's clubs around the UK meant Dad would be away quite a lot of the time, something I would come to understand better when I myself started out in the music industry. I would spend hours and hours with Koopa trudging up and down motorways consuming fast food, alcohol, breathing in weed and pissing in cola cans.

The Palmerston Trio even had some radio play with their recording of the song "Quando, Quando, Quando," which translates as "When, When, When."

It was a cover version of an Italian song, which they performed in a Bossa Nova style. The song had a simple, but very catchy lyrics and was most famously covered in the sixties by Englebert Humperdinck.

It was at this time that I first encountered a music agent by the name of Albert Pringle affectionately named Albie by all. He was a flamboyant loud character with outlandish fashion sense, who once boast that he turned down managing Tom Jones and just missed out on signing The Who before Lambert and Stamp stepped in to snap them up. He was a chain smoker, a heavy drinker and he had an interesting list of clients that included, singers, bands, comedians and strippers — compared to the modern day agent he was a knight in shining armour

Dad had become an amazing drummer and had now turned fully professional, his talent had not gone unnoticed and so he was very much in demand most weeks for session work, which proved very lucrative. He did recording sessions with amongst others; Shirley Bassey, Cleo Laine and Acker Bilk, which led him to appear on many hit albums of the time. He was a bloody handsome bloke my dad — he had a real swagger about him.

I've seen many drummers throughout my years, but I can state categorically that I have never seen one better than him and growing up with a Dad who was in a band was a very cool thing. Take a bow Brian Victor Raymond.

My Dad was aware I loved music and tried for years to get me to learn to play the drums. I once told him I was thinking of learning to play the guitar.

"A guitar player, are you kidding? – I'll tell your mum to pack your bags!"

Being a drummer was never going to be an option for me. I grew up aspiring to be a famous footballer and for a short time in my teens and I almost made the grade. Football was one of the things that I was passionate about when I was growing up – here's the top 5:

Football.

Girls.

Music.

Bruce Lee.

Raquel Welch.

Did I mention that I've no ability whatsoever of making my hands and feet do different things at the same time? As Eric Morecombe proudly stated, "I'm playing all the right notes, but not necessarily in all the right order" and that pretty much sums up my musical talent.

What the hell is a Hi-hat anyway, surely that's something Edwardian gentlemen wore isn't it? As for the rest of the kit; snare, bass, pedals, crashes, sticks it was just all too much for me to remember, and anyway I wanted to be the next Jimmy Greaves, George Best or even that silky skilled, long haired footballer with the fantastic moustache that played for Crystal Palace, Don Rodgers. I wanted to be Jimmy, George or Don and most of all I wanted long hair and a fantastic moustache!

In the summer of '73 the Palmerston Trio was offered a residency on the Isle of Man. Mum decided it would be great if we all went along in tow, so Dad booked a chalet for the season and we all headed off to the island's capital and largest town, Douglas; best compared to towns like Blackpool or even the fantastic Southend-On-Sea.

Douglas is most famous for hosting the annual Isle of Man TT motorcycle road-racing event. Motorcycles zooming around the town is common place even off season, as is the sound of the following ambulance bells.

It was a summer to remember, the band had a slot in The Palace Lido Theatre and when they were not performing we would spend time on the beach doing all the fun stuff that families get up to on their holidays, although Mum did sometimes refer to it as a busman's holiday. It was during this holiday that my sisters became addicted to an ice-lolly called the 'Lolly Gobble Choc Bomb' made by Lyons, this was an ice-lolly made up of chocolate centred strawberry ice cream, dipped in chocolate and covered in 'hundreds & thousands', they were bloody addicted to them and I always roared with laughter when my sisters asked the man in the shop for a Gobble!

My life was changed that year because on the 8th July 1973, I went to see Slade. I was twelve-years old and this was to be a show I would remember for the rest of my life, but the fact that the gig even took place is simply staggering.

It was the climax to the most tempestuous week for Slade and after playing a gigantic show at Earls Court the previous weekend, tragedy struck when drummer Don Powell was involved in a car crash.

But instead of having to cancel the show the band was thrown a lifeline because Don's brother Frank, who was a plumber by trade stepped in – turns out that Frank had been taking drumming lessons from Don and knew the entire Slade set list.

On Friday Frank rehearsed with the group, on the Saturday his picture appeared in the papers and on the Sunday he was on stage in front of my sister and myself and I didn't even notice the difference.

The memories of that gig are etched in my mind and it seems like yesterday and definitely not over forty years ago. I remember Slade coming on stage in all their famous clobber. Noddy Holder with his red shirt, tartan trousers and yellow striped socks and Dave Hill dressed like a gypsy with a mirrored headscarf.

I can still remember them blasting out their huge hits and it was on that very night on the Isle of Man that I became a Slade fan for life; being able to skip the queue and go backstage and meet the band after the show just completely top it off.

That night Frank 'the now stand-in drummer' told my Dad he would be going back to being a plumber the following week and as it turns out my Dad the drummer would be going back to being a publican as he had received a phone call asking if he would be interested in becoming landlord of a busy pub on Southend seafront. It was an offer he couldn't refuse – the chance of a lifetime, so after an emergency band meeting to arrange a replacement drummer we all headed back to Essex.

Sadly, although it was an offer of a life time, it also signaled the end of an era for my Dad-the-drummer and he would never play full-time again — choosing to concentrate on being the perfect pub landlord instead.

The pub was called The Ship and it was instantly recognisable with its very distinctive bright green roof tiles. It was huge inside and had both public and saloon bars and it had a large car park to the rear, that created additional income from all the parked coaches full of day-trippers enjoying a sunny and booze filled day out at the seaside. Bar prices were so cheap in 1973 compared to today and you could get a pint of Harp lager for just 16p – yes, 16 fucking pence.

My parents loved the idea of running a public house so we were all moved the short distance along the seafront from our house into the pub. The living space above was massive and for once we all had our own bedrooms. I was particularly impressed with mine as it was right at the back and had a window that over looked the stage of The Foresters pub next door. If I looked down through their skylight I could see all the acts on their stage.

It turned out that my room was a blessing in disguise as The Foresters was most famous for having strippers on stage every night and, for a while I sold tickets to my mates. Every Friday night they would come round and we would cram into my room all after the best view of some old slapper taking her clothes off next door.

My entrepreneur skills funded the purchasing of my new World Cup Subbuteo set complete with fence surround, TV tower, floodlights and manager, trainer and press photographer figures.

The Ship was always busy and during the summer months was packed to the rafters and we seemed to have an interesting collection of people working for us including a large number of drag queens who made up the core of the bar staff, serving drinks, flirting with the customers, male and female, and randomly bursting into song and dance, mainly 'Cabaret' by Liza Minnelli.

It was a real entertainment, pub with lots always going on, if it wasn't a live band, then it would be a seventies-style DJ pumping out the hits of the time whilst drunken ladies and gentlemen danced around like idiots. On occasion things got a bit out of hand and a western-style bar room brawl would break out. I'm telling you that you haven't seen anything until you see a drag queen in full-dress and make-up knock out a fifteen-stone loud mouthed Cockney with a single punch.

The biggest memory I have of the pub was the awful cloud of thick smoke that hung over the entire bar area from all the smokers puffing away and, even after the last bell when everyone had left, all that remained was that foul smelling cloud. During the seventies people could smoke anywhere; buses, planes, cinemas, shopping centres and of course in pubs – it seemed that the whole of the seventies was shrouded in a haze of thick cigarette smoke. It wasn't just the fact that people smoked, it was the total lack of care for those that didn't, including us children. Everyone smoked everywhere, they didn't take it to a secluded smoking area, they did it right in front of your face without a second thought for you, your hair or your clothing... and of course your health.

***

So I'm guessing that losing your virginity is an important life event for any young man and I remember being fifteen and losing mine to one of the barmaids. Her name was Angie and just to be clear she was a woman. She was in her late twenties and was very pretty with soft blonde hair and dark eyes. She always wore bright red lipstick, short skirts and low cut blouses, which showed off her ample cleavage.

It was one afternoon when she was on her shift chatting to my mate Terry and I, when she asked me to do her a favour and help her move some furniture that evening.

"Yes, of course," I replied naively.

She wrote down the address, which was not far from school and said to arrive about 8.30pm.

As we left Terry gave me a funny look "You're in mate?" he said

"What do you mean?"

"Tonight you are going to bang one in the back of the net."

"What? No, I'm not — why would you say that?"

"Did you see the way she was looking at you?"

"Shut up wanker," I said as we headed to the amusement arcade next door to the pub.

All that afternoon I thought a lot about what Terry said, so decided to have a bath and put on some clean underwear just in case. There were rumours that if she got one sniff of 'Fabergé Brut' aftershave then her knickers were round her ankles in a flash, so I washed using my luxury 'Brut 33' soap that I was given for Christmas and splashed on some of Dad's Brut before I left.

It was dark when I arrived outside her flat and the

outdoor light above the door was not working, so I felt around until I found her buzzer — now stop that right now this was a major moment in my life!

She opened the door and I was surprised to see she was only wearing a short silky bathrobe through which I could see the contours of her body beneath. She appeared to be totally naked, I could feel my heart start to beat fast and my body was shaking like an unbalanced washing machine.

She ushered me in and asked if I would like a drink, I said yes so she poured us both a glass of wine. I hated the taste of wine so only sipped at it and placed it down on the table. She asked if I would like some of her 'Fry's Five Centres' — now before you start wondering what the hell is going on here, let me explain that 'Fry's Five Centres' was one of the best chocolate bars ever! Fruit fondant in dark chocolate with five different flavours! Strawberry, lime, orange, pineapple and raspberry, they were bloody delicious, so I got stuck in. From that point on, the rest is bit of a blur and like a ride on the roller coaster it was exciting, fast and over way too soon.

I do remember that no furniture was moved.

Although I wasn't a complete novice, this was however my first home-run and I will always remember those nights spent with Angie that followed over the next few weeks. She was not my girlfriend, but she will live long in my memory. Of course, even though she was adamant that we kept it to ourselves, I felt obliged to tell the lads at school of this momentous occasion and cries of 'you bloody lucky fucker!' rings a bell.

My favourite place of all growing up by the seaside was The Kursaal Ballroom, which in the seventies happened to be one of the country's pre-eminent and most vibrant music venues around, and my mates and I would spend an awful lot of time there during that time.

Luckily for us one of my Dads mates known to me as Uncle-Ted, ran this music venue, giving us free access to every show, every week and we certainly took full advantage and abused the privilege.

It also meant it was easy to impress the girls; taking them there to scream at their favourite pop stars all helped to get to the next level of your relationship at the end of the night. Although I hated that awful high-pitched girlie scream that pierced your ears as The Bay City Roller's or David Essex took to the stage and it would be a sound that I would come to hear a lot when I started managing bands.

We got to see huge rock acts like, Black Sabbath, Deep Purple, Mott the Hoople, and Queen. When we saw Hawkwind we also got to see the naked woman dancing that always accompanied them, she had the most enormous breasts I have ever seen and was very hairy down below and Ginger-Keith reckoned she looked like she was wearing a Sporran.

In October 1974 we went to see The Sensational Alex Harvey Band. This was the first time I'd ever encountered him and I swear that he was the blueprint for the Johnny Depp creation Captain Jack Sparrow as he waltzed around the stage in a creepy, yet mesmerizing manner, seducing you.

Then there was Zal Cleminson an absolutely brilliant and most underrated guitarist with his scary clown-painted face and stage moves that would make even The Scissor Sisters seem butch. This performance was like nothing I had ever seen from a rock and roll band before.

As the throbbing intro of 'Faith Healer' began, Alex strode menacingly to the centre of the stage and started singing unaware that a fight had just broken out at the front of the crowd. After a few minutes, Alex realised what was happening; lifted his left hand and gestured to the band to stop playing, which they did immediately.

He then asked the lighting engineer to turn up the house-lights which glared down at the men scrapping and he shouted, "No one fights at my fucking concerts! Do that again and I'll come down there and kick the shit out of you both!"

The now petrified men looked up at Alex who then nodded before he flicked his wrist up and the band roared back into 'Faith Healer.'

We just stood, our mouths agape. His songs just oozed with humour, human emotion, bitterness and sometimes-borderline flippancy. That night we all became fans of this phenomenal band and as the crowd started leaving, we stood in our usual spot singing a chorus of 'Gang Bang,' when Uncle-Ted came over to ask if we had enjoyed the show and then asked if we would we like to go backstage and meet them.

This would be my first taste of sex, drugs and rock and roll. We were escorted to the bands dressing room and introduced and, to be completely honest I couldn't understand a single word they were saying; they were all either completely off their heads on booze or their

Glaswegian accents was just so thick. But they were most welcoming and seem to have no concept of the fact that we were just teenagers.

They offered us lager, whiskey, vodka and rum. We drank and drank some more, then out came the drugs. I had absolutely no idea what I was doing, but I do remember popping some yellow pill and feeling quite chilled. There were loads of women around too, and some half naked; there were breasts all over the place, but we were not complaining. I looked towards the back of the room and saw the drummer having full on sex with some dark skinned woman who seemed to be enjoying the moment most enthusiastically.

We were having the time of our lives until their manager, who must have realised that we were maybe a little too young, asked someone to escort us out.

I saw so many bands during this time Including 10cc, Sweet and Slade and I'm not ashamed to say that I also went to see Gary Glitter. However, I may have had a lucky escape that night as I was invited backstage by staff, but I had other plans. This was probably for the best as I was a decent looking teenager. I admit though I'm still a fan of his music, but it's very hard to listen to 'Do You Want to Touch Me' these days without throwing up in your mouth a little bit. The same rule applies to The Lost Prophets; great band – but unlistenable these days. I still have both in my iTunes collection, as I just don't want to delete them — even though I should.

I did however delete 'Two Little Boys' by Rolf Harris.

Chapter 6

The Mystery of the Flower Pot Stand

In 1976, quite out of the blue my parents were offered the opportunity to run a village pub in the countryside and they decided it was a good time to move on.

The village was called Boreham. Where?

I asked exactly the same question, not having a bloody Scooby Doo where Boreham was.

Again, there was no way they could refuse such an exciting opportunity and the family moved once again to the quaint country village, which as it turned out was located just a few miles away from Chelmsford in Essex.

I was being forced to drop out of school in my final year, leave all my best friends to live in the bloody country. After only two weeks at my new school and facing a totally different curriculum, I decided that I fucking hated it. On top of this, my sister Susan had set fire to the school playing field, after a teacher had hit her. I had then chased him and punched a hole through the door that he had hid behind.

Southchurch Hall High School had taught me one thing in particular — take no shit from anybody and, as for my sister Susan, well, she had become a badass after the slingshot incident.

After a heart-to-heart Mum and Dad arranged for me to go back to Southend and stay with my aunt and uncle while I finished school and took my final exams. I was relieved to be back with my mates, although they were mystified that I had given up the opportunity to be at school with girls; so I duly accepted the chants of gay-boy on my first day back at Southchurch Hall School for Boys.

The new pub The Red Lion was in a prime location for making money as it was situated on the only road between London and seaside resort towns like Clacton, Dovercourt and the rather oddly named Walton-On-The-Naze. Or as spellchecker in Microsoft Word would prefer it to be spelt Walton-On-The-Nazi - try it and you'll see what I mean.

After a long week at school, I'd would get the bus home to see my parents. The bus journey was long and boring and you had no Apple iPhones or iPods to keep you company back then; they were still quite a few years away from being invented.

It was a very good decision to send me back to the boy's school as I left school with some decent results including 'O' Level Grades in English Language, English Literature, Math's, History, Geography and most surprising of all was passing my technical subject Woodwork as I hated all those craft and technical subjects; Woodwork, Metalwork and especially, the tedious and most boring of all, Technical Drawing.

So how did I pass my exam? What item of wooden beauty would get me through?

Well, it was a lovely flower pot-stand and the only part of it that was actually mine —was the beautiful varnish that coated the wood.

A few weeks before the exams another pupil, who was also making a flower pot stand, had to leave school because his parents had been posted to another county with the Police Force.

Seizing the opportunity, I swapped his carefully manufactured and very well designed stand for my shabbier effort. I did take the time to make sure it was varnished properly and a few weeks later handed it in as my own submission for the final exam. I passed — and Mum still has the flower pot stand in her garden so it's stood the test of time; the varnishing was obviously perfect!

I finally left school and reluctantly went to live with my parents in Boreham beginning a new chapter in my life. I felt that living in a country village was always going to be a big challenge for a young man with an East End attitude and his heart, as well as all his best friends, left back in Southend — but I had passed on the possible opportunity of going to University, as well as passing over the chances of joining The Fire Brigade and Royal Marines both for the best probably, as I would've definitely been the first shot dead as the troops landed somewhere in battle, and I would've made a terrible fireman; as I hate heights and the sight of blood, so going home was the only option open.

It was also around that time Ali-the-Turk and his family were leaving to set up a chain of kebab restaurants in the North of England and Little-Willy was moving to London, so perhaps it was the right time to move on after all.

I would keep in touch with Terry-All-Gold and the others long after moving away and we still had more crazy times ahead of us. I would sit on the stairs for hours on the phone talking to my mates and girlfriends back in Southend, our seventies version of keeping in touch and what today is called social media.

Boreham was a quiet little village not unlike those you see on television shows like 'The Vicar of Dibley' or 'Father Brown' but without the comedy or the murders. Life was slow paced and the village had the kind of people you would expect it to have; the local policeman who was called John-the-Copper who spent all day drinking in the pub and never seemed to get a callout, the vicar who spent most of the weekday drinking, the postman who really was called Pat who, after delivering the mail, spent the rest of the day drinking and so on and so on.

Village life in the seventies was slow.

The Red Lion was best described as having an old-world feel. The ceilings had exposed wooden beams and there was a welcoming stone-built fireplace at the end of the main bar, which added to the appeal of a very snug pub.

It was decorated with horse-brass, which always brought back memories of my nan – she loved them. Horse brass is a brass plaque originally used for the decoration of horse harness gear, especially for shire and parade horses, but they were also ideal wall decorations in pubs in the seventies. The Red Lion was warm and inviting and Mum and Dad made the perfect Landlord and Landlady.

Being situated on the main road between London and the seaside resorts, the pub was in an ideal location and dad devised a cunning plan to get even more people in the pub at the weekends. He paid the coach drivers taking day-trippers from London to the coast to stop at the pub for refreshments. It was a very successful plan and got huge amounts of people in the pub drinking and became a very lucrative investment.

They even started serving food, well, that's if your definition of food is a selection of fresh rolls in a glass display cabinet situated on the bar. This was a great addition to the pub, providing you liked your rolls filled with cheese, cheese & onion, cheese & tomato, ham, ham & tomato or ham and cheese!

Dad had the mind of an entrepreneur and was constantly having new ideas, some fantastic and some just plain crazy and I realised that this was something I inherited from him – Like Father, Like Son!

I was now working full-time in the pub, I would restock the shelves in the bar and I remember with a great fondness all those strange drinks that were always kept on the bottom shelf; Barley Wine, Cherry Brandy and of course that sparkling Perry drink that all the ladies loved called Babycham. There were so many types of beer around as well, Light Ale, Pale Ale, Worthington E and Double Diamond to name, but a few.

My job also entailed changing the beer barrels and generally helping around the place, all for a nice weekly wage of course. Eventually at the grand old age of eighteen, I became a barman. It was at this time that another Garry came into my life. Garry, yes spelt differently, came to live and work in The Red Lion the extraordinary thing about Garry was he was a dwarf. I'm not racist, homophobic or in this case dwarf-ist — but I just hated him.

Firstly, because I had to share my bedroom with him, secondly, that he was a real kiss-arse to my parents and thirdly he was just such a complete knob. Talking of knobs, I saw his once when he was undressing and it was massive; he could stand like a tripod!

I walked into my room once while he was having a quick 'tommy tank' rubbing his hand over my brand new Farrah Fawcett-Majors poster — you know that one with the erect nipples. That was my poster and only I was allowed to have erotic fantasies about Farrah and he had now violated her.

"You dirty little shit!" I shouted as he hurriedly retreated under his covers, "If I ever meet Lee Majors, I'm telling him you wanked on his wife!"

I took Farrah Fawcett-Majors down and put up another Bruce Lee poster and informed Garry that if I caught wanking over Bruce I really would punch his fucking lights out.

If you watch 'Game of Thrones' you will know exactly what I mean about him, he was just like the fictional character 'Tyrion Lannister'. He was calculated and cunning and would cause endless issues between myself and my parents; reporting me like a little school Prefect — if I was late for work or had upset my sisters — you know how much I hated bloody Prefects.

My cousin Ray, also came to work with us in the bar

which was great, and he was just as annoyed by Garry, so the pair of us used to take our revenge with the 'no-sale' button on the till, making it pop-out every time he walked past hitting him square in the head then after he ran off to squeal, we hung him up on the coat hook in the bar.

We both laughed until Dad sacked us both right on the spot before realising that he now had no staff for the weekend, so had to reinstate us just as fast.

Garry eventually left to go to Los Angeles shortly after that episode and I heard that he went on to become an 'Ewok' in 'Star Wars – Return of the Jedi.'

Working in the pub and being a barman meant my mates, new and old and I started drinking more heavily. In that era, it was the norm for kids to start drinking when they were 16 years old (the legal age was of course 18) and while this was illegal, it was very common and not really condoned much.

I was actually given the taste of alcohol at a very early age, mainly because at the age of eight I managed to consume the remaining drinks left on the tables at the end of a family party; apparently I threw up and then slept well.

We soon became regular drinkers, often getting drunk, but the alcohol did tend to make us act like idiots and we did put ourselves in some dangerous situations. One night we ended up pushing our mate Mark around in a shopping trolley before letting him go down a hill straight into the river almost drowning him.

Love and hugs were common place between me and my mates with us shouting 'I love you man!' at the end of every drinking session.

***

Just like myself when I started to manage Koopa, dad had a vision of doing something out-of-the-box and unorthodox, so he decided to bring live entertainment to The Red Lion and his vision; to turn the pub into Boreham's very own version of The London Palladium having live entertainment every weekend to attract some top cabaret artists.

The first task was the building of the stage. It was to be situated at the end of the main bar area. Dad thought this would be a good opportunity for me to show off my newly found woodworking skills since I had passed my exam. Oh Dear! I was in deep trouble.

I managed to scrape by this issue by pretending I had hurt my arm playing football and I suggested that it would be best if I just helped while he built it.

My Dad was brilliant he could do anything, so in no time at all there was a raised stage with a nice sound and lighting system complete with spotlight; all tailored to be a 'one-size fits all' set-up.

On the stage sat a drum kit and small keyboard ready to burst into action at any time and then there was the pièce de résistance - the metallic gold foil fringe curtain that hung at the back of the stage.

Dad set about booking acts and asked me to help in contacting the booking agents to see who we could afford. This would be a good introduction to the world of 'being a booking agent' for me and something that I would become for a brief while in the future.

Many acts were booked during my time and it all ended up a little bit like Peter Kay's creation 'Phoenix

Nights'. But we did actually manage to attract some of the nation's top talent of the time, including Bobby Crush, who won ITV talent show 'Opportunity Knock's' and one of Britain's leading ventriloquists Roger de Courcey whose 'Nookie Bear' was not at all like we had seen on TV, but instead was a proper foul-mouthed little fucker who, at one point during the show, rolled his eyes made strange sexual grunting noises towards a young lady in the audience and then suggested that they have sex later that evening.

I vaguely remember chart toppers Lieutenant Pigeon performing their one-hit 'Mouldy Old Dough' at the pub and rumours are rife that Keith Harris and 'Orville' once performed, but I must've been away or just not interested. A variety of other entertainers would perform over the time at The Red Lion including, cabaret singers, jazz bands, balancing acts, jugglers, organists, comedians and drag queens.

Dad still made time to perform. He loved music and entertaining and played part-time in a country and western band who often performed at the pub. I can't remember the name of the band, but the lead singer was a very polite gentleman called Tom Weston, which I always thought was very appropriate for a country and western singer, and I always thought that perhaps he should have adopted the use of his surname in the band's name.

Dad had also made a new best-friend in another chap called Derek. He was a very funny guy and was always telling jokes or singing songs. Dad and Derek would also do little comedy skits based on classics previously performed by Kenneth Williams, Tony Hancock and

Peter Sellers. Dads "Hands up, this is a stick-up" sketch — legendary!

One of the most bizarre bookings Dad ever made was a personal appearance by 'Red Rum', yes the famous racehorse! Three-time Grand National winner! Crowned king of Aintree. My little sister Jill even got the opportunity to ride Red Rum, which made her little eyes light up. The pub garden was crammed full of people who had travelled from miles around to catch a glimpse of their all-time favourite racehorse. It was as if a hurricane had hit the village, in the end there were people fighting one another to get closer to the superstar horse.

I did however, overhear one woman saying, "I haven't seen anything like this since I went to see The Beatles – and this is just a fucking horse."

Chapter 7

If You Build It They Will Come

With his very own version of The London Palladium up and running Dad set about adding new features to attract more business and next up was the purchase an old red Routemaster London Double Decker bus, which was to be turned into a children's adventure bus filled with stuff for the kids to play with, or seriously harm themselves in some cases — while their parents drank themselves stupid.

Our job was to paint it from its current faded red, to a lovely blue and white whilst inside Dad ripped out seats and added some extras —like a punch bag and a few sweet dispensers.

The bus was so successful that it was soon joined by an old fire engine, which, along with the addition of a giant trampoline, a slide and some swings, completed the children's playground and made the pub a very attractive proposition for customers with small children.

Health & Safety had been just three words back in the seventies and meant nothing; our local park was a complete death trap. The slide was far too high, there was no safety padded area or even grass – just rock, hard concrete or tarmac at the bottom and there was a pretty good chance that someone would be scalded by the hot metal as they slid down each summer. The climbing frame looked like The Chuckle Brothers had constructed it using scaffolding poles and some old rope – one false move and you could have killed yourself.

Meanwhile being hurled from a spinning merry-go-round, skidding across the gravel at full speed and cutting your elbows and knees to shreds was always high on the risk scale, as was the possibility of needing a tetanus shot.

In the seventies Health & Safety Laws meant that a public place would have to house a first aid kit on site, which must contain some bandages, plasters and the smallest pair of surgical scissors ever made. In the UK these days Health & Safety is a serious issue, but from my experiences of touring Europe with Koopa I'd say that the band's Health & Safety were not high on the agenda of most European promoters.

There was always one other thing that really bothered me about the seventies and it wasn't that everything was coloured orange and brown. It was all the adults who used to drive to the pub, leave their children in the car with a bottle of pop and a packet of crisps whilst they enjoyed themselves inside the pub for the next three or four hours and thought nothing of it. You just wouldn't do that these days, but they were different times with different attitudes to life. I guess it was great for our pubs profit margins.

The facilities at the pub were forever expanding, my parents got to work building a burger-bar in the main garden and the garage got transformed into a café, which sold coffee, tea, cake, ice cream and sandwiches.

One of the most popular soft drinks that were on sale in the café was 'Cresta' - "It's frothy man!" declared a talking polar bear in the ad. 'Cresta' was bloody disgusting it was thick and of course frothy, but children loved it and drank it by the bucket load, but if you drank too much, you ended up throwing up a strange coloured frothy vomit - you get the same result if you drink too many Redbulls.

Our next addition was the seafood stall, selling everything fresh straight from the sea. With the exception of prawns and crabsticks, which I loved, the rest all looked disgusting. Other delights on sale included cockles and mussels (all together now 'singing cockles and mussels, alive alive oh…' that's enough of that, thank you) as well as more revolting delights such as winkles, whelks and most disgusting of all, Jellied Eels.

For a while I had to work on the seafood stall and I hated it except for one particular occasion when I got a blow-job from a certain new barmaid. My cousin Tony who also worked at the pub had also fancied her and had been chatting her up for some, told me after that he thought something fishy had been going on that night!

Finally, well, not quite as something big was looming around the corner — Dad built an open-air stage in the garden for music and other events. The stage was enormous and with the summers being long and so sizzling hot, he could plan outdoor events for June, July and August.

You can't do that these days and I've lost count

of how many festivals I've attended in the summer months with bands when it's been pissing down with rain all day – far too many gigs, when everyone is wet and miserable.

Two of the best events took place on that outdoor stage. A huge country and western festival, which caused chaos due to the amount of people attending; the village was clogged up due to the sheer volume of traffic and the police had to be brought in for traffic control, as wave after wave of cowboys and girls descended on the pub.

The other event that springs to mind takes me back to professional wrestling. Dad booked Jackie Pallo, Mick McManus and Giant Haystacks for a charity event held on the outdoor stage.

When the wrestlers arrived, Dad suggested to one of their managers, that as it was a charity event could he get in and have a bout with Giant Haystacks. The manager agreed and thought it was a splendid idea.

It was to be a bit of fun only; no real contact. So it was arranged that Dad would land a forearm on the giant man and he would take a dive. However, someone forgot to inform Giant Haystacks of the arrangement.

The gardens were packed with people having a wonderful time and you could hear the ringing of the tills, clinking of glasses and the air filled with conversation, excitement and, of course, cigarette smoke.

The main event passed with the crowd favourite, Jackie Pallo, seeming to come back from the dead, as he always did, to defeat his arch nemesis, Mick McManus. Now it was time for the big charity match, Brian 'The Landlord' Raymond vs. Giant Haystacks —

surely a mismatch, but Dad knew he was safe and not in any danger.

Giant Haystacks stood six-foot-eleven inches and weighed around forty-three stones. His party piece was to throw an opponent onto the canvas before finishing them off with a hideous belly-flop. He was the one that everyone loved to hate and now he was about to take on the new crowd favourite, my Dad. The crowds were cheering and there was genuine excitement in the air.

The bell rang and Dad danced around a little, did a little bobbing and weaving and then started hurling insults at his opponent in a Muhammad Ali style "I'm gonna chop you down like a tree!" He shouted as Giant Haystacks just stood and stared back at him. Dad went in with the 'forearm', but it was like he had hit a brick wall. He started to look worried as Giant Haystacks stared at him and then with a huge grunt walked over, picked him up and held him with his arms straight up above his head. The crowd gasped in horror, Mum and my sisters all burst into tears and I feared for my dad's safety.

Giant Haystacks grunted again and with a quick flick of his wrists hurled Dad out of the ring onto the grass by the side of the stage. Ouch! The crowd went silent, I rushed over to see if he was alright, but he just started laughing, stood up, albeit a little gingerly, and bowed to his new fans. The crowd cheered and Giant Haystacks put his arm through the ropes to shake my Dad's hand.

That night my parents raised a fortune for charity and later was told by the wrestler's management that it was always better if it looked real; even if it could have killed him. The manager said Dad was lucky that Giant Haystacks hadn't belly-flopped on him, Dad laughed nervously, then got very drunk on his favourite tipple of gin and tonic to help ease the pain.

We had now christened The Red Lion Pub — *The Red Lion Resort*, and the only thing missing was a gift shop. Oh no wait! my parents *did* open a small gift shop inside the converted garage/café, selling all manner of souvenirs including, postcards, mugs and of course sticks of rock.

To celebrate how well the business was doing Dad went out to buy something for the family and took me along. Something for the family ended up being the purchase of a brand new sports car.

We returned home with our shiny new purchase and we instantly saw that Mum was not impressed. After lot of heated discussions that night, the next day another purchase was made; mum's very first automatic washing machine.

The first time she turned it on we were all so excited that we sat on the floor and watched it for one full load. We only had three television channels so this was an exciting evenings viewing.

The sports car was to bring plenty of trouble for Dad and, apart from breaking down most weeks, he managed to wrap it around the same big oak tree in the village on not one, but three occasions. A regular in the pub told him 'To tie a yellow ribbon round that old oak tree' to avoid driving into it again.

Suffice to say it happened once more, and with the car now in a concertina shape, he decided it was time

for a change and he downsized to a more family orientated Vauxhall Viva. He also purchased a Betamax
video cassette player and some pirate movies off a
bloke who drank in the pub called Billy-the-Fib.

Billy-the-Fib told Dad that he got the video cassette
player from a geezer down the fish market, but Dad
heard a few weeks later from John-the-Copper that
a lot of video players had been stolen from the local
branch of Radio Rental's and to watch out if he was offered any and, upon inspection, Dad hastily removed
the sticker that said 'Property of Radio Rentals.'

I didn't care where it had come from as I was now
able to tape programs straight off the television. The
only problem was — there was fuck all worth taping.
The only things I watched were the selection of pirate
movies that included, 'Freebie and the Bean', 'Dirty
Harry' and 'Straw Dogs' starring the gorgeous Susan
George. The rest of the movies Dad brought home
seemed to have been locked away in his office for some
reason.

Dad's plans for the Red Lion Resort had one last
piece of his jigsaw puzzle to put in place and this was
to be the *big one*; the one he'd been dreaming about
ever since we had arrived in the village. He decided to
build a zoo. No, not just a small petting zoo, but a full
on mini Regents Park type of Zoo with wild and exotic
animals to boot.

We already owned a monkey (I think I may have
forgotten to mention that). I'm not sure what breed
it was, but it certainly was a dirty stinking little bastard and was caged in our living room. You could never watch anything in peace. He was a complete fucker

and drove me nuts – excuse the pun. So the first things to arrive were the cages and pens. Once the cages were erected and the pens penned (is that right?) it was time for the animals to start arriving and first on the scene were all the cuddly little creatures, that were to make up the actual petting side of the zoo.

The very first to arrive were the rabbits, just four to start, but that's not where that ends; as they were not all females and you know what rabbits are like.

Next up two cows — Daisy & Gertrude and then some chickens and a few sheep.

Then it was the turn of the real animals; more monkeys (they were cute and funny) no that's a complete lie, they were also little fuckers who masturbated a lot and threw shit at one another – I would meet quite a few bands in my foray into the music industry that were very similar to those monkeys.

Two llamas arrived called Bert and Ernie, but were quite quickly renamed Sid Vicious and Johnny Rotten owing to their desire to cover you in the foulest smelling spit-like substance when within range. The llamas would make us laugh when they got over excited and jumped around like the cartoon skunk Pepe LePew.

They were followed by the wallaby; he was basically just a miniature kangaroo and very bouncy so of course quickly earned the name Tigger — he seemed to love his very existence. Dad then added a goat, which he allowed my sister's to name and to nobody's surprise, they named Nanny.

The strange thing is nobody realised that the goat was pregnant and when it gave birth one of its kids had a horn in the middle of its head, so I convinced my sisters that it was a real-life unicorn.

Next up was a very angry looking big black bull with big black balls, which were always a topic of conversation, because the bull's big balls were so far away from his enormous penis. Then there was Ozzie the ostrich who was just completely fucking mental. He simply ran around his pen all day only stopping on the odd occasion to eat, shit and sleep; I just think he was upset that he was there in the first place.

Dad decided to add pony-rides to the attractions to create additional income, so purchased a couple, as well as a Shetland pony who under strict instructions; was not for riding. However, that didn't stop Dad and his mates when they had sunk too many gin and tonics, betting on how fast Garry-the-dwarf dressed in a little jockey outfit, could get from one end of the garden to the other riding the pony like he was a miniature Willie Carson – if there could be such a thing.

The Shetland pony seemed to be very sexually attracted to my little Sister Jill and would chase her around its pen with a large erection and Dad could quite often be heard shouting "Get off her you dirty bastard!"

Finally, last and by no means least, the deadly predators arrived — the big cats – two pumas. The puma is a large, graceful cat, although our two arrived as cubs they did grow quite quickly and, I won't lie to you, they were beautiful looking, but even then their little teeth were bloody sharp and hurt.

The female cub was called Elsa and the male Blue.

The day came when the zoo was finally complete, but Mum and Dad had one last arrival planned, in their infinite wisdom my parents purchased a huge St. Bernard, called Candy. She was a giant slime machine and never again would anyone go out of the house without being covered in dog drool. You never stood a chance!

The zoo had a grand opening with The Mayor coming along to cut the ribbon and the event garnered much local and national newspaper, radio and television coverage including features on both ITV and BBC news programs. The zoo proved to be a roaring success and became a must-see attraction bringing in customers from near and far. The Red Lion was on the map and Dad had become a local celebrity enjoying the limelight that he so richly deserved.

The zoo was a perfect place for families; mums and dads wanting a few drinks in the pub and at the same time giving their children a chance to get close (safely of course) to the animals. It was well maintained by three zookeepers; my three little sisters, Susan, Mandy and Jill – there was no way I was going to clean up the animal crap. I would wait until I worked in the music industry before I cleared up shit!

It did not take long before those four rabbits turned into about seventy, all bouncing around their pen humping one another like crazy, which inevitably attracted a new unwelcome and sinister guest to the zoo – the fox.

Dad decided he had to put out traps to kill the foxes, which were like bear traps and these things would snap a child in half, so a fox didn't stand a chance; they were gruesome and looked like medieval torture devices.

A few days later I saw Dad talking to a rather distressed villager and after a chat with Mum, I discovered that one of the traps had apparently beheaded their family cat. Suffice to say all the traps were removed and as an apology Dad got the local very drunk before going out and buying the family a new kitten.

All the fun and excitement of the zoo came to a shattering end the day I came home to find Dad in the cat cage playing with yet another new addition to the family — a baby puma. Dad always went into the cage to play with the pumas, but this was to be his very last time. Female pumas guard their cubs fiercely and the mother pounced, and started mauling him, leaving him in a fight for his life.

Dad somehow gathered the strength to get free and out of the cage, but was in need of urgent medical attention. He ended up with over one hundred stitches in his arms and shoulder — the truth is he was extremely lucky to make it out alive.

Of course, this meant that the zoo had to close and we were very sad and tearful when the mother of the cub had to be put to-sleep. But we were told that this was protocol after an animal attack. It was a dramatic and a sad time for the whole family especially, for my Dad, who I could tell was totally heartbroken, and to this day always blamed himself for what happened.

He tried to hold his feelings in, like it didn't hurt, but it was so bad he would just wander around with a blank expression on his face. Once the brewery delivery-lorry almost ran him over as he wandered aimlessly around the car park – I told mum that I thought Dad was in such a state that he wouldn't have even seen a 747 aeroplane if it was coming straight at him because his heart was breaking.

Arrangements with other zoos and farms were made to relocate all the animals and with much sadness, as well as plenty more tears, one by one the animals left — until all that remained were the rabbits. The rabbits were then offered to local pet shops and advertised within the community and were all soon dispersed to new homes.

Even that monkey in the living room found a new home and, as soon as the little fucker was gone, I started to miss him.

Chapter 8

Close Encounters of the Female Kind

It was approaching the end of the seventies and times would change in the coming months and following years, but memories of that era will remain with me forever including the new friends I made along the way: Jon Blane, Lewis-the-coppers-son, Ali and Gary Rush.

Everyone knew Gary as 'Rushy' so that helped on the name front and we became very close mates sharing a love of music and, in later years we would form Magnum Disco. As DJ's we would wear bright coloured Hawaiian shirts and false moustaches, in honour of the man who inspired the theme of the mobile disco, Mr. Tom Selleck, best known for his role as the cool private investigator Thomas Magnum in the hit television series 'Magnum, P.I.' and for possessing a magnificent moustache.

Magnum Disco was going really well, for a while and we retained some regular bookings, even playing at a five-star after-show party once. We did tend to use the disco as an opportunity to go out on the pull and thanks to the 6:08 minute version of Spandau Ballets 'True' we always found the time to pick a partner and join in the slow dances. Our Hawaiian shirts and fake moustaches seemed to have a magical effect on women and we were never short of snogs on the dance floor and so much more.

We also shared a love of bands like The Jam, The Specials, The Beat, Madness, The Clash and Ian Drury and the Blockheads and, whenever the opportunity arose, we would jump on the train to London and go to venues like The Hope & Anchor and Dublin Castle in Camden to see and hear live music.

I was really getting into New-Wave and Ska music, but my heart would always remain with Glam Rock. There was one band I loved and kept secret from my mates — The Dooleys, they had been around a while, but were only just having some chart success, my mates all thought they were too cool for this band, so it was easier to keep my mouth shut.

To many people, The Dooleys were a poor man's Nolan Sisters, but I loved the music and I'm not ashamed to say that I was passionately in love with one of the girls. She had a sexy little gap in her front teeth and when she was on Top of the Pops she never wore a bra just to tease me, as she stared at me through the gogglebox. Seeing her on television had this weird effect on me, causing what I called 'a pocket rocket.'

I fell head over heels in love with her and wanted to go to Top of the Pops to chat-her-up and ask her to marry me, but I never had the opportunity and even if I had I wouldn't have had the courage. But I did write a poem that I sent to the fan club, she never replied though — probably because it was a shit poem.

'Anne Dooley' you are truly the' Love of My Life' and

I've always 'Wanted' you to be mine because we are the 'Chosen Few' and 'I Think I'm Gonna Fall in Love with You' and 'Honey I'm Lost' without you.

Attending gigs were always up-close, sweaty and very personal. I got to meet a lot of the bands back in those days as they were always welcoming and appreciative of their fans. I got more bruises from being in a manic crowd watching The Jam than from any gig I've ever been to before, or since for that matter.

In the seventies at those small gigs, bands and singers would mingle with fans after the show and would stand around for ages, having a drink and chatting. I managed to get to chat to Paul Weller, Bruce Foxton and Rick Buckler of The Jam, The Clash's lead singer Joe Strummer, The Damned's Captain Sensible and even Poly Styrene, the lead singer with seventies punk band X-Ray Spex — those were the good old days.

There was none of that paying-extra for a meet 'n' greet ticket that there is today. Paying to meet your favourite band really gets on my fucking nerves and I've since been to conventions where you even pay for a photograph with an actor – it's total bollocks. I will admit I have worked with bands that have sold meet 'n' greet tickets even though I'm against it, but sadly, sometimes business takes preference over morals and you take the commission whatever the circumstances.

Those trips to London to see live music were always special —and one more so than any other —the one when I ended up backstage with the lead singer of Scottish punk band The Rezillos.

I was with Tight-John, Little-Willy and Gary-Rush. We'd been drinking most of the afternoon prior to the gig and for some strange reason Little-Willy had been stealing ashtrays from every pub we frequented. Not sure why as he didn't even smoke — he was however always a bit of a tea-leaf.

We got to the gig to find security searching everyone and Little-Willy now had an unusual amount of unexplained ashtrays upon his person and was trying to persuade us to help him hide his stash.

"What the fuck!" Tight-John said. "I'm not holding a stolen ashtray for you!"

"Bloody right!" I added, "What is fucking wrong with you mate?"

"My mum likes them."

After much arguing and not getting his own way, Little-Willy walked off to dispose of the ashtrays.

"Mate, don't get led ash-tray!" I shouted.

"Fuck off the lot of you!" he yelled.

He did eventually come back after he had dumped all the ashtrays in the River Thames.

The gig started, and after two shockingly bad support acts, The Rezillos took to the stage. The gig was fantastic and during the show I was sure I could see the singer Fay Fife (real name Sheila as I found out later) giving me the eye and was even more surprised when, as the band left the stage having done two encores, this chap came up to us and asked if we wanted to go backstage for a drink with the band.

We were escorted back to a tiny little room where a party was in full flow. The rest of the night was a little blurry, but what I do remember consisted of booze, weed, and the shit music playing on the cassette player. Tight-John getting-off with some really fat bird (and I mean somewhere in the twenty-stone region), Rushy getting pissed and some thieving little bastard stealing an ashtray – I wonder who that was?

As for me, well, to quote the title of one of The Rezillos albums, 'Mission Accomplished.'

The last thing of note that happen to us in the seventies — 1979 to be exact —was meeting up with my mates Terry-All-Gold and Little-Willy to see Hot Gossip at The Talk of the Southend night club, which apart from having a crap name that made no sense, was better known by the acronym TOTS.

Hot Gossip were a dance troupe of woman and men who became famous by appearing on the wonderfully camp 'Kenny Everett Video Show' on TV. They had scored a major chart hit the year before with 'I Lost My Heart to a Starship Trooper' when their lead singer at the time was a young Sarah Brightman.

A girl I knew called Mel, who was a smoking-hot hostess at TOTS managed to obtain some free tickets, so I asked Lewis the-coppers-son if he fancied going — as he had a car. Lewis drove a second-hand, very scratched, 1975 yellow Ford Capri II 3000 Ghia that had a fur lined dashboard and the ultimate seventies fashion accessories, black 8-ball gear knob and fluffy dice.

When we arrived, I introduced Lewis to the rest of the guys and we walked into TOTS and based ourselves not too far from the bar, but close enough to see the show and started downing pints of lager.

Hot Gossip was most noted for the risqué nature of their dance routines and, as they took to the dance floor you could smell the male testosterone in the air. The show began and immediately one girl caught my eye; she was a great dancer, very pretty and very flexible.

Much to our surprise at the end of the show the girls came out to mingle with the crowd and I made a fast beeline for this one particular girl who was called Donna and, much to the bemusement of my mates, we started chatting.

Things were going well, when the lights went low and the DJ announced in his smooth voice that it was time for the guys to grab a girl and hit the floor. So as the Leo Sayer's classic 'When I Need You' started up I asked her for a dance and to my delight she agreed.

Then Crash! Wallop! Smash!

Suddenly all hell broke loose as a fight started at the bar. We moved away and I looked over to see that the fight was between none other than my mate Terry and some chaps in suits. As the bouncers moved in to break things up I realised Donna had joined the other Hot Gossip girls who were heading back to their dressing rooms. I rushed over and after a quick chat she gave me her number and a little kiss on the cheek before vanishing back stage.

By this time Terry and the other culprits had been grabbed and roughly manhandled by the bouncers and had been thrown out like discarded bin bags out of the club and onto the street. The rest of us had already gone outside where I could see six burly bouncers scowling at the protagonists.

I instantly recognised one of them as Paul Smith, who had been in the football team with me at school and who also had a reputation as a real scrapper. I knew he was involved with the West Ham Green Street Hooligan Firm, so I said hello and he suggested that we all make a swift exit away from the club, before things got ugly and we happily obliged.

We all blamed Terry for buggering up the evening and then all decided to head back home. I did call Donna a couple of times and we had a few nice chats on the phone, but it never led to anything else, so I never did lose my heart or get anywhere with that starship trooper — I was gutted.

***

The eighties were finally upon us and these days the seventies seem like they were in a different century — hang on a minute the seventies were so last century.

Just last night I was trying to explain to my youngest daughter from my second marriage, Holly, that there were no mobile phones, no Internet, no video games, no iPhones, iPads, iPods and finally no computers, when I was growing up.

If you wanted to make a phone call to tell your mum you were going to be home late, you had to use a coin-operated public telephone. These were either the traditional red telephone boxes, which have long since become a British cultural icon or they would otherwise be located in a booth. The biggest problem with the box types, as anyone old enough to have used one will recall, is that the handsets were always sticky and the boxes themselves were damp, filthy and foul smelling. If you were enjoying a night out in London and needed to make a call the boxes would always be full of business cards and notes supplying the numbers of prostitutes.

I explained to Holly that if she thought getting out of bed was exhausting she should try lumbering over to the television every time she wants to change the channel and that sometimes when we walked across the room on the shag pile carpet we got an electric shock as we shuffled! That's right, an actual electric shock! And we only had three bloody channels to watch and one of them was full of strange men in brown clothing, discussing physics and math's most of the time — I'm talking about BBC 2.

Let's just say she really struggled to get her head around all of it and was totally mortified that there were no DVD's or Geordie Shore!

***

In 1981, I had met a girl and, after dating for a while we decided to get married. I felt compelled to get away from home as I was fast approaching 21 and I had visions of becoming like that character 'Timothy Lumsden' that the late and great Ronnie Corbett had just started portraying in the very funny TV sitcom 'Sorry'.

The marriage was doomed from the start. Even on my wedding day, I suffered from a bout of the dreaded wedding terrors and I told my Dad I didn't want to go through with it. 'Well, if that's how you feel then son, don't go through with it!' was his advice.

Well, I did go through with it, and yes, as predicted it was doomed, I just couldn't adapt to married life. We married around the time of the first ever London

Marathon and that's just what married life felt like – it was just like running a marathon with miles of nothingness ahead of me. I felt trapped and I couldn't see the finishing line. Sadly, it was a feeling I just couldn't shake and I ended up having an affair with some blonde girl I met in a nightclub.

In the short time we *were* married we had two lovely daughters, but eventually I couldn't take anymore and we divorced soon after. What followed over the next few years was an excess of drinking, staying out all night, chasing skirt and generally getting totally fucked-up. I even woke up in the gutter a few times – all of this was a pre-cursor to the horrendous situation I would get into years later.

Around the late eighties, Mum and Dad's time at The Red Lion would come to an abrupt end following a prolonged and quite bitter argument with the brewery, that could not be resolved in my Parent's favour.

Life had changed for my parents and things had not been the same since a fire ripped through pub in the early eighties, destroying everything they had built up and taking all those good memories with it. The fire devastated the bar and living areas and if it had not been for their quick thinking in getting my sisters out of the property — things could have been far worse.

The sad thing was that my sisters and I lost our childhoods in that fire. In my case, all my memories, photos, football trophies, school reports and much more. This was not the digital age, so when it was gone, it was gone forever – this shows the darker side of those times as there was no back-up, no restore button and no Cloud up there somewhere to save the day.

My parents were rehoused during the repair and refit and moved back in once everything was up and running, but as the next few years passed you could sense that they were just not his same.

My Dad, the man who would dress as Henry VIII and have huge Tudor based charity banquets every summer in the seventies, had changed and was a much more sombre man. He never rebuilt the stage and it appeared that the fire had taken a little piece of his love and enthusiasm for the pub along with it.

In the mid-eighties, my parents purchased a three-bedroom house in the village and their master plan was to turn all the rooms above the pub into luxury bedrooms, adding chalets to the outer grounds that could be used for providing a dedicated bed and breakfast service.

After many meetings and much debating the brewery refused them permission and within a year they had decided to move on. They retired from the pub trade and they moved into their house in the village.

Strange that these days The Red Lion, or just The Lion as it is now known, has been restructured and become a restaurant with adjacent luxury chalets providing a full bed and breakfast service — although this does prove that Dad was a visionary and had lived his life on his terms.

By the late eighties, I was working early mornings in London so I moved to Barking as it was located not far from the capital.

Barking always seemed like it was in London, but was actually in Essex. I think the fact it was on the

District Line Tube network made it seem close as if it was part of the city.

I was working for the aptly named, and musical referenced, 'George Benson Cleaning Company' as an area manager, which wasn't a bad job. I was based in London's West End, which most definitely had its perks; meeting lots of interesting people, including some quite famous ones was definitely one!

Every morning like clockwork, I would bump into Harry Enfield and then Jonathan Ross around the Wardour Street area, as they made their way to their relevant offices. After the first few times they would ignore me, but after a while they would nod their heads or say a polite 'Good morning'.

I have never had any problems meeting so-called stars or famous people. My attitude has always been that they are just people —like me, so why be afraid to say hello. I suppose in the modern age, they may not be so approachable as they are bombarded with people on their smart phones wanting selfies and the like.

One particular morning I was on my usual rounds checking on an office block in the West End. Entering the building I walked up the first flight of stairs whilst doing the dust test, which involved running your finger along the bannister as you climbed – it was dust free, which was a good start. I reached the first floor offices I saw two men standing outside, one of which was the very curly haired Brian May of Queen, the other turned out to be none other than the band's drummer, Roger Taylor. They had arrived for a meeting, but the offices were still closed, their associate being stuck in the dreaded morning traffic, which trust me is a nightmare.

I had the keys so I asked if they wanted to wait in the reception as I could let them in. I had to check on the cleaning anyway, which apart from the bin bags not being tied properly, was cleaned to the high standards the company required and charged those very high rates for. I did have a thing about bin bags being tied and not left messy – a bit petty, but that's how I wanted them.

As I returned to the reception, Brian and Roger looked a bit agitated, so I offered them a hot drink. Brian requested a tea and Roger a black coffee. When I returned, we sat chatting for a while about what it was like to be in the band with Freddie and that my Dad had been a drummer.

The owner of the company arrived and I went off to wash the cups, but popped back to say goodbye. The owner thanked me for looking after them and the two guys shook my hand and I left. I never felt the need for an autograph or to rush and tell anyone. It was just another day and they were just human beings. As I left the building, I could see a traffic warden giving me a ticket as my bloody meter had run out. Usually I would've spent ten minutes hurling abuse his way, but today I decided not to, as today I was in a very good mood and Ironically as I started my van the radio burst out 'Bohemian Rhapsody'.

Derek and Robbie also worked for the cleaning company and they were a right pair of scallywags. They loved an opportunity to make a few quid on the side, and I can recall the time we were cleaning carpets at the offices of an internationally renowned perfume company, whose name I will not mention, but who made the very popular 'One' perfume for men and women.

Grasping their chance while the carpets were still wet, they set about hiding bottles of aftershave and perfume about their bodies using cellotape. After one successful trip to the van they then returned for another batch of the lovely smelling cologne.

Robbie had made his final run and Derek was on his last one when, as he walking to the exit, a smallish and feeble looking excuse for a security-man tapped him on the shoulder. The security man looked like Sid Little from Little & Large fame. He wore glasses and his uniform was just a tad on the large size and hanging off him. His hat was too big and had slipped down onto his forehead.

"You Ok?" he asked Derek who at this time had starting to panic.

"Yes mate, just off to the van."

"Why you walking funny?" the security man asked. Without a second thought Derek replied "Me Farmer-Giles are proper playing me up!" Which, as any good cockney will know Farmer-Giles is Cockney rhyming slang for the medical condition haemorrhoids better known as piles.

"Sorry to hear that, I've the same issue mate." The security man went on in a sympathetic tone.

"By the way mate," he continued as Derek left the building, "you smell very nice."

I learned a lot back in those days and I believe some of the blagging skills I used in the future were first nurtured from my experiences with those two scallywags.

Chapter 9

The Not So Beautiful Game

Football has always played a huge part in my life, so it would be foolish of me not to share some of my experiences on and off the pitch with you, and besides, everyone loves the game and if you don't, well, you can either skip this chapter or just get in the game and read on.

The dictionary definition of Football: a game played between two teams of eleven players, in which the ball may be advanced by kicking or by bouncing it off any part of the body, but the arms and hands, except in the case of the goalkeepers, who may use their hands to catch, carry, throw, or stop the ball.

Well, that's just a load of bollocks isn't it?

For anyone that has ever kicked a ball, then you will know that I'm talking about — 'The Beautiful Game'.

'The Beautiful game' is the nickname for football that was first used by the Brazilian footballer Pelé, although football commentator Stuart Hall is the only individual to have claimed to have coined 'The Beautiful Game', but the less said about that perverted old fucker the better.

All the bands I have managed over the years have

loved football and the one thing about the beautiful game is that it brings with it —that thing they call banter —and life on the road touring was full of footy banter!

I loved football and I was once a pretty nifty player and, if I'd had a bit of luck I reckon I could've gone on to become a professional. When I lived in Southend it was tough to get to see Spurs, so my mates and I would go to see our local side — the Shrimpers. Who?

The Shrimpers... The Mighty Blues... Southend United Football Club.

We went to most home matches by bunking in under a gap in the rusty corrugated fence panels at the rear of the south stand, just to see our favourite players like Tony Taylor, Tony Hadley and Dave Elliott.

These were gritty, salt-of-the-earth footballers that were still allowed to tackle from behind, as well as slide-tackle the opponents on the hallowed turf of Roots Hall on Saturday afternoons, or sometimes Friday night; I used to love the atmosphere at the Friday night games under the floodlights.

Southend United would sometimes play their home games on a Friday night, if it clashed with West Ham United playing at home on the Saturday. You see a lot of our hooligans were also West Ham hooligans and matches clashing would affect revenue, so Southend would switch to the Friday evening.

Looking on the bright side of football hooliganism it meant that they got to have an extra terrace tear-up some weeks.

During 1974/75 all the Southend United players all started to drink in my dad's pub The Ship, so I got to sit and chat with them; I also helped many of them out of the door at the end of the night, as they staggered to their cars — and this was the night before a match. Some even popped in on Saturday lunchtime for a quick one — pre-match! Can you imagine Ronaldo, Bale or Messi doing that these days?

The problem was that they had a shit season, probably due to being half-cut most of the time and after a promising start, they failed to progress up the table, dropping like flies and finishing a very disappointing 18th just avoiding relegation by a mere four points – which as it turned out, ended up affecting my career before it even started.

Myself, Freddie-Fumble and another kid from our school football team called Tight-John had started training with Southend United Football Club on a Tuesday night and Thursday afternoon, and we all totally believed that we would go on to be football superstars like our idols; Jimmy Greaves, Rodney Marsh, and George Best.

In Tight-Johns mind, he wanted to be Gordon Banks or Chelsea goalkeeper Peter Bonetti — otherwise known as The Cat — Which wasn't a good choice, as we best remember him as being the goalkeeper who cost England the World Cup in Mexico 1970, when England, despite taking a two goal lead, thanks to Alan Mullery and Martin Peters, managed to lose 3-2 to bitter rivals West Germany —mainly due to The Cat putting in a pussy performance.

Tight-John was the school team's goalkeeper and had a very safe pair of hands when between the sticks, but he was also a little bit too handy if allowed anywhere near your girlfriend so you had to keep your eye on him. He was also as tight as a ducks arse and that's bloody waterproof. Once we all reached night clubbing age, the only way to get a drink out of him was to stick your fingers down his throat. I never once saw him put his hand in his pocket to buy anything, instead he would always borrow your albums or singles, eat your chips and on occasion borrowed money that he would never pay back.

I heard on the grapevine a few years ago, he became a merchant banker, which seems very appropriate given its meaning in Cockney rhyming slang.

Arthur Rowley was manager of the club when we started our training, and he was a really lovely man who seemed to see some potential in all three of us. We were sad to see him depart after the first team had a disastrous run of form, and be replaced with the, not so lovely and potential seeing Dave Smith, who took an instant dislike to Freddie and John bringing to a rapid close their potential football careers. Luckily though for me, I was allowed to stay for another season, and he even put me on the bench for a few first-team games and I managed to play about ten minutes in total, which was amazing – however, it was going no further and when an opportunity came for me to play in Norway — I grabbed it and went to Oslo for a brief time. I hated it and just as quickly I returned home ready to hang up my boots, when a chance conversation between my Dad and a customer in the Red Lion pub, led to the opportunity to play for the local village team and I put them back on again.

I really did believe in those days that I would be a

professional footballer and I certainly do these days have the physique of an ex-professional footballer – it amazes me how they seem to pile on the pounds when they stop playing.

Also, I had no 'plan B' in my life, so it's hardly surprising I would end up ploughing through endless jobs searching for that perfect career or opportunity – which I thought managing Koopa would be when the time came.

How wrong can one man be?

Through all the good and bad times there was always one constant; playing football on Saturday afternoons and Sunday mornings.

In the late seventies, I played for the village football team, Boreham and on a Saturday and I enjoyed being the centre-forward for the reserves. I scored plenty of goals during my time at the club and was somewhat a bit of a fucking bighead on the pitch (and off it too), back then, but I had the skill to go with it.

Why was an ex-Southend United player in Boreham Reserves? Was the first-team full of ex-professionals?

Well, the answer is no! It was simply the case that no matter how good you were, you would not get put into the first-team, as all the manager's mates were picked before you regardless of their talent, and this had led to much resentment in the reserve team.

In fact, I was a substitute for the first-team once — due to the amount of injuries and people on holiday and I came on in the second half, scored a hat-trick and then the following week I was back in the reserves.

It was total bollocks.

Better still was playing for the Sunday morning

team Quay Sports. Those times were incredible and while we never won anything we loved playing and had great banter.

Our home pitch backed onto a mental institution, which we crudely called the 'Insane Asylum'. We could always hear the odd scream and on one particularly cold December morning whilst warming-up, the screams sounded like someone was actually being murdered.

As the game kicked off the screams got louder and you could hear someone shouting "I'm going to kill every one of them!" The shouting and screaming was obviously disturbing the away-team's goalkeeper and I remember one of our players going up to him before a corner and saying "Last week some crazy man climbed the fence and chased the goalkeeper!" before walking away, laughing — the statement worked, and from the resulting corner, I headed the first of three goals in about fifteen minutes. The away team was totally freaked out and at half time we were leading about 6-0.

As the second half began, the screams became louder and then it happened — one of the opponent's players took a shot at goal, which flew not only over the goal, but the wall as well. Everyone stopped as a strange noise emanated from beyond; it was a strange gnawing sound as if someone was trying to eat the ball.

Quick as a flash I looked at the guy who had fired it over and said "Mate, you have to go and get that. We only have two balls!"

"Fuck off!" he replied being all macho.

"No, seriously, you have to climb over and get it," I

replied just as a loud scream emanated from behind the wall.

"No fucking way!" he said as tears filled his eyes and he started to shake.

By this time everyone had joined in and was gearing him on until the point, he literally broke down in tears and pissed in his shorts in front of everyone. His manager said afterwards that this was the first time he had ever substituted a player for pissing himself.

Playing for Quay Sports was always a laugh, but looking back at those days, one chap called Pete, who was part of the backroom team, seems to have had an altogether different agenda, he was the guy with the bucket, sponge and cold water waiting to deal with any injuries — but he seemed to enjoy this position a little too enthusiastically especially when he had a thigh injury to massage. He also loved squeezing out his sponge on you.

These days when we are discussing the old football days we tend to refer to him as Paedo-Pete.

Now there's a thought, there was only ever one bucket of cold water and one sponge. Imagine having your face wiped when the player before you might have had a nose bleed or worse. All that cold water mixed with someone else's blood running down your face, that's absolutely bloody gross. But that's just how it was back in those heady days of the seventies and eighties.

Quay Sports had a reputation for being tough and slightly arrogant, but it was just that we had a winning mentality and we knew how to look after ourselves. We took no prisoners and there was always the odd mêlée on and off the pitch. We would occasionally overstep the mark and I once famously took out three goalkeepers in one match with a series of sliding tackles, not with any malice, but with a desire to get to the ball before they did.

We would go out and have heavy drinking sessions and think nothing of turning up worse for wear the next day. Our team captain Gary Rush or 'Rushy' as you now know him from the magnum disco days always set a good example, well not really, and on one occasion arrived literally just before kick-off where he took thirty seconds to get changed, ran onto the pitch and within another thirty seconds was sent off for calling the referee a stupid cunt.

Sunday morning football in particular could be brutal; half-drunken men trying to break one another's legs waiting for the half-time whistle to blow, so they could have a quick cigarette – yes 'the beautiful game'.

On the odd occasion, our passion would of course overflow onto the pitch and get the better of us — leading us to obtain 9 yellow cards and 3 red cards during one local match which left us with a hefty fine from the County Football Association. Unsurprising I got a straight red during this match for punching a fullback who called my girlfriend – 'a right dog'.

Even our own players would turn on one another sometimes. I have grabbed one of my teammates by the throat before and a couple of our players stood toe-to-toe throwing punches after one had got in the way of the other – but at the end, we would shrug it off and get on with the game, then head off to the pub after the final whistle.

Belgium held another legendary tale from my football days I had left Boreham F.C. due to the politics and had been offered the opportunity to sign for Broomfield with the added bonus of being paid £10 per game boot-money. The term boot-money originally being derived from the fact that the manager left the money in your football boots although this rarely happened.

The club directors had arranged a trip to Belgium to take in some culture, hit the duty free superstore and play against a local team just outside the Belgium capital, Brussels.

Before the trip Ali and myself went to see our mate Kev-the-Snip who was working in the tailor's section of a very large, but to remain unnamed, department store to get kitted out with some appropriate clothing. Kev had initially started out as a barber, hence the nickname, and after visiting his store we ended up looking the dog's bollocks in our brand new blue blazers, cream trousers, smart button-down shirts and fancy ties – that Kev swiped through the till for the same price as a pair of socks.

I also should state than under no circumstances should a parent ever have asked us to keep-an-eye-on their sixteen-year old son on his first trip overseas — but someone did, needless to say that whoever's son it was; was pissed and throwing up by the time the ferry left England. He also returned from the trip having been involved in a mortifying glory-hole experience at what turned out to be a Brussel's gay bar.

The coach arrived at our hotel in the heart of the ornate capital city. The city really caught my eye with its gothic style buildings, including the intricate Gothic

Hôtel de Ville, which was the town hall with its distinctive bell tower. Now you should know that other than a small handful of us, myself, Ali and a brash, but amusing, Scotsman Jimmy (I know - it's stereotypical, but that was actually his name) the rest of the team were the boring types who had arrived in the city ready to take in the culture, museums and architecture.

There was not a cloud in the sky, allowing the beautiful sun to shine down making it a glorious day, but the only thing on our minds was to find the nearest bar and enjoy a glass of Belgium lager. The nearest happened to be only fifty yards from the hotel so we were soon sitting outside enjoying the sun with three lagers. The beers were served in curved stemmed glasses, the like of which I had never seen before and, after a short argument based on whether the lager had been served in a glass or as Jimmy would insist on arguing 'it's a chalice' we downed our delicious lager, ready for a second.

As the day progressed, we stayed in the same spot drinking beer after beer after beer. On occasion some of the other players would walk by and we would shout abuse at them before waving them off to their next museum. It soon became apparent that the same groups of people were going past time and time again leading us to discover six hours had passed since we enjoyed our first drink.

As the sun started to set, one of the other players came over to advise that we had been summoned by the manager to get back to the coach as everyone was waiting to leave to go to the Hyper Market. Barely being able to walk, let alone put a sentence together to have a conversation, we did what we were told and ambled back.

As we approached the coach you could feel the tinge of disappoint in the air. The other players were having a kick about while they waited and Jimmy ran over, grabbed the ball and booted it into the river, laughed and got on the coach. I boarded and took a seat near the front while Jimmy took the back seats to himself and then threatened to murder anyone who sat near him — before allowing Ali to sit there.

I fell asleep within minutes and awoke some time later to find that everyone except for Ali was sitting or climbing around the first four rows and there was a foul smell in the air that pierced my nostrils. Ali had projectile vomited all over the rear of the coach, and had managed to include the windows, seats, floor, the goalkeeper and the entire back-four, as well as a couple of the midfielders.

The driver had pulled over and was going mad, while all the time, Ali was snoring blissfully unaware of what he had done. After much cleaning it was time to move on and when the coach did finally arrive at the Hyper Market and much to everyone's bitter disappointment it was closed.

The fingers were pointing at Ali, but he was too pissed to care.

We went back to the hotel and everyone got ready for a night out in the city. I decided to go out as I was feeling fine, but Ali and Jimmy were both crashed-out in their rooms and would not to be seen again until the morning. The entire night was spent in a great nightclub and ended in a bit of a blur, but I do recall returning to the hotel to find it was already breakfast time and Ali was in the dining room having a coffee — so I joined him.

The rest of the team and management turned up shortly after and sat for breakfast, unaware and I'd only just returned and was still drunk. I would've gotten away with it too, if I hadn't decided to jump up on the table and start throwing croissants at the team — after one of them suggested I was still pissed before proceeding to nod off mid-sentence.

We had two hours until we left for the match so I went to my room to freshen up.

What happened next still mystifies Ali and, Jimmy in particular — as both being too hungover, dropped out of the match. I however, after one very stunning left-foot goal, a right-foot goal and a headed-goal — completed a perfect hat trick and ninety minutes later I was back in management's good books.

I'm still not sure how I managed that, but once we were back on the coach my hangover caught up with me and I slept all the way to the drop-off point at the clubhouse in Essex.

I never picked up a single injury at school, Southend United or playing in Norway, but during my time playing on terrible pitches in terrible conditions on a Saturday afternoon and Sunday morning, I have had two broken ankles, one broken leg, one broken wrist, three broken noses, one broken elbow, some broken ribs, a dislocated shoulder, almost lost a leg due to a blood clot and had a football boot metal stud go through a shin guard straight into a vein. Add to this, far too many concussions to remember and at least one hundred stitches and you'll appreciate why my body aches so much these days.

However, I wouldn't change a single thing; those football days were fucking magical.

I will never forget my playing days and although I never made the grade, the memories, the friends as well as the enemies, will remain with me.

In fact, I could write a book just about those football days alone.

I loved it and still miss the buzz from scoring a goal, the nearest I would ever come to that feeling again, would be when Koopa was making music industry history.

Chapter 10

It Comes in Handy in the Kidnapping & Extortion Business

The nineties were now fast approaching and I was still living in Barking in the rented house with three lovely girls.

We all had our own rooms rather like students have these days sharing the TV room, kitchen and bathroom. The lads seemed to visit me a lot in those days always trying to get the girls to go out on dates.

My housemates and I used to go drinking in one of the roughest nightclubs I have ever visited in my life — The infamous Ilford Palais.

In its heyday in the sixties it used to attract high profile celebrities and sports stars like West Ham United and England World Cup winning footballers Bobby Moore, Martin Peters and Geoff Hurst, but now was, let's just say, no longer the classiest nightclub in the county — some would even say country.

It's also infamous for being one of the places that Jimmy Saville started his DJ career. The Ilford Palais was indeed a rough tough place, filled with rough people, but the watered-down beer and spirits were dirt cheap and the music was always good.

I once got kicked out for literally no reason at all; I was in a great mood may be slightly drunk and I simply came dancing and singing out of the toilets towards the dance floor, when one of the bouncers just grabbed me from behind and led me out — to this very day I have no idea why.

Kim, was one of my housemates and for about two months was also my girlfriend, she was the lead singer in a band called the The Express and had a Debbie Harry look about her with the same iconic blonde hair. She was bang on trend with eighties neon prints, provocative leopard skin short skirts and Doctor Martin boots; she also had a great body. We had a short, but very energetic relationship and I suppose, I kind of managed the band a little, by helping them arrange gigs in the local area and sometimes in the heart of London along with helping with promo stuff, handing out flyers and unloading and loading the van, which I even drove on occasion.

She was exciting and sexy and I liked the idea of dating a rock singer. But our relationship was short and sweet and strangely enough, so was her singing career.

***

Not long after the opportunity to get onto the mortgage ladder arose and I became the proud owner of my very own flat; in the not so sunny Grays area of Essex. I worked hard and made sure all the bills were paid on time – life was good, I was content and I fucking loved that little flat.

The perfect life was mine and just to cap things off nicely, I had three girlfriends on the go; Jane, Kim and

Paula. It actually became hard work and on occasion just remembering to say their correct names would prove tricky. Jane was rich, Kim was super sexy and dirty, but eventually Paula was the lucky girl that I proposed to and we got hitched in 1993.

In hindsight, I got that game of 'Snog, Marry, Avoid' very wrong!

The first few years of marriage were full of surprises — some good, some bad —and we survived it all, but eventually I again just drifted into becoming a husband and doing all those normal things that were expected of me.

We had two beautiful daughters, Amy and Holly. But life from that point just became much the same old routine day after day, working hard to help raise a family and sometimes having to work harder to keep our heads above water. This would also be the time that I would drift away from most of my childhood friends for various reasons.

I had made it in life. Life was great! No, not really; I was merely going through the motions. I had a family, responsibilities, bills to pay and the need of a secure full-time job to keep me fully focused.

The years just kept rolling by and in the end it would be the music industry that would save me from my mundane existence and then betray me, becoming the catalyst that would bring yet another marriage to a crashing and bitter end. I would discover that managing a band is just like a marriage; me adopting the role of the faithful wife at home baking, and the band being an unfaithful sociopathic husband whose cheating is fueled by lust.

In a band's case — it was the lust for success, which would eventually expose the naivety and ignorance in my very own nature as a human being. When a band and their manager finally split — if not handled correctly, it bloody hurts, especially when you have helped mastermind their success. You nurture and connect with them only for them to leave a deep and painful void where once there was once respect — it's like experiencing a messy divorce and I should know! – I truly felt this pain when the Koopa bandwagon crashed around us all.

***

Being made redundant from the cleaning company lead me to try my hand at a few other skills: Selling life insurance, unpacking frozen food containers from lorries, and working in a record store; all of which I hated, so I ended up starting my own company supplying prestige cleaning services to office buildings in London. It was going very well, until I got bored. I sold it for the measly sum of one pound to my wife's brother Graham to start up an import company selling these shiny new discs containing movies that were called DVD's.

I started off importing mainstream movies before moving on to adult movies and sex toys, but I got greedy and eventually the company went bust.

I was living the lifestyle I wanted, but I had no business sense, and as the money was coming in, I was spending it on cars, holidays, first class flights to meetings in Los Angeles — all of which of course, weren't even needed.

Finally, it would all catch up with me and during another outlandish family holiday in Greece I got *the* call from my bank advising that they were closing me down. We were forced to sell our house to pay off the bank debts and worse, some rather nasty people within the sex industry, which became the reason why I went out and bought a gun from some shady chap down the pub and kept it loaded under my pillow — until everything got sorted.

I was bankrupt and my life was now in tatters as was my health, my marriage and, rather worryingly, my personality. I had changed and not for the better. For a while I was very dependent on my daily intake of the antidepressant Celexa and the beer Stella Artois, as they seemed to help me get through each day a little easier.

I did manage to freshen up my attitude and stopped taking them — the pills not the Stella! But it would not be the last I would see of the pills — I was at a real low, deep in the darkness and I felt my mojo fading away, I just didn't feel that I had a purpose in life. I was in such a dark place that I considered ending it all and taking away the misery that I had selfishly inflicted on everyone around me. I recall sitting in the bedroom crying with a glass of water in one hand and a pile of whatever pills I could find in the other. I sat and contemplated for hours, but thankfully in the end I bottled-it.

This may be the first some people will have heard this, as I wasn't the kind of person to cry out for help, and to be honest, in the dwindling relationship I had with my wife — I doubt it would have been heard by her anyway.

Wait, let's backtrack from the doom and gloom... Did I say adult movies and sex toys?

Well, who hasn't dabbled in the adult movie industry at some time?

Let me elaborate on this subject for a while.

I find Porn Hub to be one of the best when searching for those special 'Office Secretary' videos – I can't be the only one that does – surely?

For a short time, I ran a most lucrative DVD import business selling adult DVD's along with the odd sex toy here and there. It was the late nineties and sex toys were in! The best sellers were 'black mamba dildos', 'love eggs' and 'spanking sticks'. Everyone loves a good spanking — don't they?

We also carried a good line in vibrators; The Magic Rabbit being a particularly good seller at the time.

These days, even sex toys come with a one-year satisfaction or your money back guarantee and are sent out via the postal system quite openly as sex toys. Just imagine being the person who has the job of dealing with the returns.

I have a friend who shall remain anonymous who ordered a 'Lover 9 Inch Realistic Dildo with Balls and Suction Cup' well, it might as well have arrived with a sticker on saying 'Dildo for instance use!' Back in the day we sent our goods out in discreet plain packaging. And in case you are wondering the above 'Lover 9 Inch Realistic Dildo with Balls and Suction Cup' was for use at a stag weekend in Prague. I'm not aware if his luggage was checked at the airport — but it would have been interesting and hilarious if it had.

This brief period in my life would prove to be very

exciting, risqué' and eventful. The adult movie business and the sex toy industry, while proving lucrative, was most definitely not for the faint hearted and is full of some of the most unsavoury people I have ever met; it was a real eye opener and a mind-blowing experience.

Importing, offered me the opportunity to visit my favourite city in the World, Los Angeles. I did quite a lot of Air Miles travelling to and from The City of Angels for business meetings and talks with suppliers, which really hit the Barclaycard Gold and business bank account hard, but I loved the city and it was a place that would play a big part in the Koopa story in the years to come.

I was invited to visit the offices of one of the top suppliers of the adult entertainment industry and attend an adult movie and sex toy exhibition held at The Los Angeles Convention Centre. Seeing as they were also offering to pay for my flights and hotel I agreed without giving it a second thought.

A week or so before I was due to fly out to LAX my tickets arrived and I was both surprised and delighted to find that they were for Virgin (somewhat ironic in this case) Business Class. On departure day and with great excitement I headed to London Heathrow to catch my flight. The flight itself was an incredible experience and the comfort, food and service were exemplary.

After landing, collecting my luggage and passing through US Customs (which was a chore in itself, so many forms to fill in on the plane and God forbid you had gone over the line on the form or used the wrong colour pen!) I cleared customs and headed for the exit. As the automatic doors started to open, my eyes were immediately drawn to an attractive blonde woman dressed as a sexy chauffeur holding a card that read Mr. Gary Raymond.

She wore a grey jacket over a very mini miniskirt, fishnet stockings, knee length boots and a grey chauffeur's hat from which her long blonde hair crashed over her shoulders. Her jacket was unbuttoned to the perfect point where it exposed her more than ample bosom. I have always been very easily embarrassed and became red faced as I approached her and said "I'm Gary Raymond."

She said, "Follow me."

I thought to myself what man could refuse a lift to his hotel from a woman wearing such a lovely chauffeur's hat and followed her to a shiny black limousine, where she informed me that I would be staying at The Beverly Hills Hilton, which again came as a very pleasant surprise and she handed me an envelope with my schedule for the next few days.

We chatted a little about this and that and upon arriving she said she would wait in the lobby, while I checked in and freshened up for the meeting with her boss later that day.

Hold on, I was staying at The Beverly Hills Hilton. Fucking result! The place that hosted all those award shows — and I was staying there!

It would also be the place I would have the night of my life drinking with a very famous American actor.

I freshened up and went to the meeting, which was

all pretty routine before returning to the hotel to chill out and get some sleep. I thought I'd grab a nightcap to help, so I headed to the bar. It was not very busy and I ordered a beer. For some reason all the beer in the USA is of the Lite version, Miller Lite or Coors Lite. I ordered a Miller Lite.

I don't think Americans could handle a few pints of the old Stella Artois, they would be legless after two or three. Anyway, Miller Lite it was and, let's just say it went down just a little too easy, so I had to order another one which once again went down all too easily.

I was tired, but I now had the taste for it. A fellow drinker at the bar turned to me and said "You, thirsty man?"

"It's been a very long day," I said as I looked up to see Charlie bloody Sheen!

"Just 24 hours same as all the others!" he said.

I laughed a little at the not-so-funny joke and said "Cheers!" as I sipped another lager.

We chatted for a while longer and I moved on to drinking vodka and coke. I bought him a drink and he returned the favour and then returned it again and then again and then again, you get the picture.

We kept drinking until we were both so off our heads that the barman suggested that we should call it a night. Charlie suggested that we should go clubbing, but I was so drunk and so tired that I said, "Sorry mate count me out," before shaking his hand and staggering off to find my room. He was a really nice chap and top bloke that Charlie Sheen.

The day of the exhibition was upon me and with a

very sore head, I got up, showered, dressed and left my room. I took the lift to the reception to meet my chauffeur at 1pm as per my schedule.

I couldn't believe my eyes when I arrived at the exhibition centre; I'd never seen anything like it.

Sex sells and there is seemingly nothing that sells better than sex. Here I was in the middle of the adult sex industry at its most flamboyant. This had been billed as a smaller event on the sex industry calendar, but it was a scary place for a Cockney lad who was always a little bit shy discussing anything pornographic. This was a veritable smorgasbord of sexual smut ready to be purchased for the right price.

Sexy cocktail waitresses walked around offering free shots, scantily clad go-go dancers danced, and naked pole dancers 'poled' as it might be called.

And then there was the dildos — fucking thousands of the things all whizzing, vibrating and moving around like a field of dildo wheat swaying in a strong wind. There were so many other items, toys, gizmos and other cutting-edge sexual devices on show as well.

There were even dildos that you could attach gadgets too that enhanced your dildo experience! I bet these days there is a dildo that can also charge your smartphone, plays your favourite mp3 track or an app that lets you control it from your phone, to save you even holding it yourself.

And don't even get me started on the private rooms. I only visited one which held two girls testing out sex toys in a very enthusiastic manner with each other.

I had seen enough and needed some air. I was genuinely in a state of shock and I still had the end of exhibition party to attend later that evening. Phew!

The party was being held at the Viper Room on Sunset Strip. I was invited as a VIP guest so after a change of clothes at the hotel and a long conversation in my room with my lovely chauffeur (cough! cough!) I headed off to the party.

On arrival I was greeted by one of the hostesses called Teri. She had long legs and was so stunning looking that I couldn't take my eyes off her as she showed me to my table. I was sitting with some of the guys from the film company who supplied me with DVD's. They introduced me to some of the biggest stars within the adult movie business — problem there is once you have seen them in a movie you can't look at them in a normal way.

A few bottles of champagne and some vodka shots later I was shit-faced and decided to head off back to the hotel to crash. I staggered out of the club and my feet felt like rocks. Suddenly I felt the inside of my mouth begin to feel moist and the next thing I knew I was throwing up on the pavement — sorry sidewalk. I believe I threw up in the exact same spot as River Phoenix, but I lived to tell the tale.

The adult movie and sex toy industry was OK, but the business was seedy and full of obstacles, especially UK Customs. My Mum also discovered my new found profession and was more than less pleased so she disowned me for a while. I use my mum's disapproval as the reason for getting out of the business, but in reality it was probably those fellas with guns.

Let's not dwell on big-breasted ladies and 12-inch

sex toys as I would prefer not to discuss any further part of that weekend, so let's move on to the reason I'm writing this book in the first place: the music industry.

So where were we before you dragged me through the porn importing, Los Angeles partying days, the scantily dressed adult movie stars, that were oh so terrible. Yeah… really terrible!

Oh yes, I remember. I was ploughing on through life and was working for a company selling gaffer tape. For those of you that have never needed the use of a roll of gaffer tape, here's what you need to know: It is also known in some circles as cloth tape or duct tape and it has hundreds of uses. It is invaluable for use in the music industry, garages, workshops and even the home.

Apparently it is especially good for use in the kidnapping and extortion industry.

The office where all this magical tape selling took place was situated in a tiny village in Essex and the first thing of note about its location was that it was accessed via some very dangerous roads, especially in the winter when there was always the danger of the dreaded and potentially deadly black-ice.

This was also the dangerous wildlife. The cows were like a four legged street gang that you could see in movies like 'The Warriors' or 'Boyz in the Hood' and, if you dared to look at them in the wrong way, gave you the sense that they were telling you to fuck-off in cow language, which I guess is called mooing. Quite often the cows would escape from the adjacent field and start eating the cars parked outside the offices — they did seem to love a soft top.

We even had an evil gaggle of black swans that sometimes showed up looking all menacing and were totally ready to rumble. In my boredom, I actually gave them nicknames like Quentin (Tarantino), Harvey (Keitel), Steve (Buscemi) and Tim (Roth) in honour of the greatest gangster film ever made. One of the fucking geese attacked me in the car park once and I got so pissed off with it, that I went hand-to-hand and tried to punch its fucking lights out, however, it was a tough bastard and I ended up running away as it chased me into the office reception.

I also always had the distinct feeling I could hear dueling banjos playing a few hundred yards away, just like the movie 'Deliverance' and I lived in fear that I would feature in the real life 'Squeal, Piggy Squeal' scene and that there would be no Burt Reynolds with a bow and arrow to save me.

The office was painted white and contained about eight desks and without being too cruel, the people that worked with me in there were a little on the strange side. They were all born and bred in the area and some may have been related in that special 'country-way' that we hear about from time to time!

I hated this job more than Sinead O'Conner hates singing 'Nothing Compares to You', as it was all about a selling phenomenon known as 'cold-calling' and I loathed the cold-calling with a passion; I just hated everything about it.

But needs must and I had a family to feed. There is nothing worse than having to chat to some pretentious wanker on the end of the phone pretending to be their friend whilst persuading them to buy sticky tape.

Those inane chit chats would drive me to despair

and sometimes I guess the people on the other end of the phone were feeling just the same, but it was part and parcel of the job. I had one customer who was so boring that the minute you put the phone down you felt like you needed to scream out loud or just punch something to help restart your brain. The problem was this particular guy ordered a lot of sticky tape — so I had to call him a lot. One morning, though after spending ages with him discussing the football, last night's television and fishing, my ears switched off and my brain was telling someone to please shoot me right now, straight through the head. And after listening to him fucking going on and on he ordered no fucking sticky tape.

I suppose you could technically say that selling gaffer tape was one of my first forays into the music industry, as I did sell some to a few music venues and my old friend 'the roll of silver gaffer tape' would eventually come in very handy when I needed a musician or one of those annoying fans to shut up!

My tape selling career (trust me it was no career) came to an end when the owner of the company, I shall just call Mr. D. who was by the way always immaculately dressed in a Savile Row suits and was one of the most articulate, savvy, intelligent and honest men I have ever encountered, offered me the opportunity to work at the newly formed entertainment company in which he had just invested.

He had been impressed by my work contribution in organising a charity football match and the charity auction that had followed, and this was an opportunity I would grab with both hands.

No more trying to hit unachievable targets to earn decent commissions and no more selling sticky tape for me.

Unfortunately for me though — it was out of the frying pan into the fire.

Mum and Dad, Brian and Sheila on their wedding day with their parents. They were married on 7th May 1960 at the registry office in Bow, East London.

My lovely Mum Doreen Sheila Raymond. She has been known as Sheila all her life owing to the amount of Doreens in the East End area when she was young.

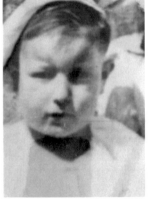

My inspiration and the man who I owe my maverick spirit too - my Dad Brian Victor Raymond.

Nan & Grandad Raymond behind the bar in their beloved East End pub, The Five Bells.

Grandad Raymond looking like a true landlord sitting outside The Five Bells looking all splendid.

Nan and Grandad Wotton celebrating their golden wedding anniversary with a glass of bubbly.

My lovely baby sisters, from left to right, Mandy, Susan & Jill

Mum and Dad out for a stroll around London's glorious East End.

Me in my baby stroller or push chair as they are known these days. Notice the fact that I am eating – no surprises there.

On holiday at Butlins in Clacton. I had just recovered from chicken pox hence the plasters. Mum & Dad made me wear the glasses and cowboy hat so people would not notice.

At Lands End with auntie Em – my favourite aunt. I miss those shiny green trousers.

Check out my rollerskating skills. I was a bit hippy at this stage with long hair and a liking for rainbow clothing.

In my bedroom with my first ever football trophies a cup winners medal and a man of the match trophy. Behind me is my lovely poster of Raquel Welch – she was a stunner and perfect eye-candy for a teenage boy.

Ladies and Gentlemen I present the best drummer in the world ever – my Dad Brian Victor Raymond.

My Dad on the maracas accompanie by the suave and very cool Johnny on guitar after they had just won a talent show at Butlins in Clacton, Essex They won a free holiday so we were back the following year.

My senior school Southchurch Hall High School in Southend-On-Sea looking like something from a Hammer horror movie.

The entrance to terror. The school had the most fearsome reputation and it was an all boys school so there wasn't a single girl unless of course you included Dirty Doris and Big Betty the dinner ladies.

My Dad in the Red Lion zoo in Boreham, nr Chelmsford in Essex with the llamas who I called Johnny Rotten and Sid due to their constant spitting.

When we lived at The Red Lion public house in Boreham, nr Chelmsford in Essex my Dad decided to build a mini Regent's Park zoo in the garden which included a number of wild animals.

Meet Elsa the puma who lived in the Red Lion zoo. We had her when she was a cub but she quickly became a full on scary jungle cat.

I met Paul Gascoinge when he played for my beloved Tottenham Hotspur after I was invited to an after match reception at White Hart Lane and he called me 'Gazza.'

Team photo from my time playing for Broomfield Football Club. This was before an ill fated European tour.

During a football tour in Belguim I manged to make it back in time for the pre match breakfast after spending all night drinking – I think I got away with it.

Here I am in action in this press clipping from the Essex Chronicle. This was in my days playing for Boreham F.C. The giant challenging the keeper is my good friend Lance Grant.

This is me playing 5-a-side football. I remember that this tournament always ended in a punch up – not bad considering it's a non contact sport.

My four wonderful daughters, from left to right, Amy, Kerry, Holly & Hayley.

This is me after the drinking and unhealthy living had taken its toll on me. I tipped the scales at 25 stone.

This is me today, happy and contented and with a magnificent beard.

Chapter 11

James Blunt or Merchant Banker

My new job was to sell music and comedy shows to theatres and other like-minded venues around the United Kingdom. I had the absolute honour to be booking shows for the likes of music legends Chas and Dave, Marty Wilde and the late and brilliant Cockney comedian Mike Reid.

But despite working with these greats, the job always circled back to one single constant — the single and most important thing — the sale. These renowned artists were just commodities to be sold to the highest bidder. The sale was everything and everything was about the sale, always trying to exceed your last monthly target and spread sheet expectations. It was all the same, just that standard company bullshit you see day-in day-out in every business that revolves around — the sale.

It literally drove me out of my mind in the end. But was much better than the alternative – selling sticky tape.

During my time I did the odd bespoke job for a client when they wanted some particular type of act for an event. On occasions I arranged for tribute acts to attend corporate events and parties. I was getting on well with the acts and began to think that I could do this for myself and so the seeds were set.

I was getting more restless in the office and things finally came to a head when I was asked to find a glam rock band for a seventies themed corporate event. I had contacted Rick Driscoll, the lead singer of a glam rock band called Kenny. The band had had many hits including 'The Bump', 'Julie Anne' and 'Fancy Pants'. Rick was a really nice guy and up for the gig. I was in the midst of arranging the final details, when I was called into the bosses' office only to be told to leave that particular event to her and to concentrate on the targeted bookings. Now this really pissed me off.

The final straw came when, after spending the day asking theatre owners if they would like to book a Queen tribute show starring that guy off of 'Stars in Their Eyes', and booking Mike Reid to perform his new stand up show in Margate, when his manager called me and ripped into me about how Margate was the shittiest seaside town in the UK, if not the entire world, and why was I booking Mike in such venues?

After getting a terrible earful of Cockney grief relating to me being a 'merchant banker' and a right 'James Blunt'. Yes, he called me a 'James Blunt!' I returned home in shock and decided that enough was enough and the following day, much to my wife's disgust, I handed in my notice. But not before I carried out a 'James Bond' type operation myself and stole my list of contacts.

Bollocks to working for other people, I thought, let's have another crack at doing something myself and, without much planning, the very next day I started my own booking agency.

I found myself dealing with popular tribute acts of the time such as Robbie Williams, Kylie, Britney Spears and Elton John, who was not only a tribute act and look-alike, but also behaved like the great man himself – it was tantrum central on occasions. Within a few weeks' things were on the up and the company that I named Booked In, Sold Out was making a small, but sufficient profit to maintain the family.

One particular day I received a call from a prospective client who was trying to hunt down a Stereophonics tribute act for an event. This was the very first time I chatted, via email to Joe Murphy, Joe would go on to be a part of my rise and subsequent fall in the music industry over the next few years.

He was also the Kelly Jones impersonator in the not so well known Stereophonics tribute act, The Stereophonies. They had actually once met the real Kelly Jones, who told them that they were the worst tribute act he had ever heard. Joe informed me his band The Stereophonies had split up due to differences of opinion (in reality, they were arguing over who the lead singer should be and I feel Kelly Jones had not helped).

He said he had recently formed a pop-punk, pop-rock or punk-pop band of some description and, although they had not given the band a name yet, they had recorded some demos in the studio and wanted to send them my way to get my opinion.

I have no clue why he wanted to send them to a guy who dealt in tribute acts and the odd seventies glam rocker, but I agreed to take a listen. I will admit I was a little bit excited to hear these tracks until I opened the package to discover it was on cassette.

"Who still uses cassettes these days?" I said out loud to myself.

I thought 'Oh bollocks' I placed the tape on the side and headed to the pub for a pint. The pub was kind-of my office when I started the new company and the barmaid gradually became my kind-of personal assistant.

Every few hours for the next week I received an email from Joe asking if I had listened to his demo, I eventually replied saying that I had been busy all week, but would give it a listen that night.

Before I could even try to listen I had to retrieve an old dust covered cassette player from the loft. I was lucky that I could see the required box I needed from the hatch so I very gingerly tiptoed barefooted across the loft only to tread on a piece of bloody Lego "Ouch! You James Blunt," I didn't think I had shouted that loud, but obviously I must have, as this was the question that I now faced "Daddy – who's James Blunt?" asked my nine-year old Daughter.

"Oh, he's just a singer I like," I replied sheepishly.

I climbed down the loft ladder and was setting up the cassette while all the time Holly was running around the house shouting at the top of her voice. "You James Blunt, You James Blunt, You James Blunt."

I composed myself and put the tape in for a listen. Now I'm not, or have never really been, a fan of pop punk, pop rock or whatever they label it these days, but I do like a good tune and, to be fair although the quality was poor, the tracks sounded pretty good. So I did what all good A&R men do and asked someone for a second opinion. I decided to call my brother-in-law Graham, who owned the very cleaning company that I sold him for a pound, back in the day.

Graham now drove a BMW, lived in a five bedroom detached house, went on golf holidays in Portugal and was a member of that secret-society that men in business join – let's say he had done very well for himself and if I was honest I was a little jealous.

He could be a bit of a 'merchant banker' as Mike Reid's manager would say, but back then we got on quite well sharing a love of lager and TGI Fridays. I also remembered that he had mentioned he was looking for some new ventures, so I thought 'what the fuck' and called him.

After listening to the demos together, Graham said he liked the sound of the guys and that he was interested in getting into the music industry — as a bit of a sideline. So right there on the spot, we discussed the possibility of managing this unnamed band from Colchester and with much excitement, I emailed Joe to arrange a meeting.

I think it was a Wednesday or perhaps a Thursday morning, that I met Graham for a late breakfast and then a quick pint of lager in the local Weatherspoons, in actual fact it may have been two, possibly three pints before we left the pub and headed to our very first meeting with the band. Where did this meeting take place? What bastion of the music industry was worthy of such a momentous first meeting?

There could be only one place — outside McDonalds on Chelmsford High Street.

As we walked down the high street, the morning sky had cleared and the scorching sun was shining brightly on our faces and I could actually feel my forehead starting to burn, the glare was hurting my eyes, which lead me to believe that the Ray-Ban sunglasses I was wearing, bought for five pounds off Tea-Leaf-Tom down the pub the night before — were not real after all.

We were standing outside McDonalds waiting for the band to arrive, looking like we were casing the joint, ready to make our move and snatch all those delicious Big Macs the staff were frying up and assembling from the selection of processed fillings. Suddenly and for no reason at all, I imagined myself dressed as 'Hamburglar' being pursued by Ronald McDonald in a sped-up TV chase scene followed by six scantily clad nurses — cue Yakety Sax the theme tune to 'The Benny Hill Show'.

That's just what happens when my mind wanders. That's normal male behavior isn't it?

It was around 10.30am and the McDonalds breakfast menu was just changing to the main menu as they prepared for the lunchtime rush. Suddenly, from nowhere a rather fat sweaty fella quite literally brushed us aside before bursting through the sliding doors almost taking them with him, such was his eagerness to get through them before they fully opened. He waddled as fast as he could to the counter and seemed to be mumbling something to the young girl serving. He seemed very distressed and started to wave his hands in the air like some kind of Tyrannosaurus Rex, who had tripped up and fallen on its back.

I wondered to myself had he missed out on his breakfast or was he after an early lunch or was he just having a snack, thus dismissing the breakfast or lunch debate that was going on in my head.

I guess he was late for breakfast, but the two Big Mac's, cheeseburger, fries and large milkshake he ordered seemed to be making up for him missing out and, most importantly of all, seemed to have calmed him down somewhat – all that sugar will do that to you.

In the hazy distance, I could see three people approaching. It turned out these three were none other than Oliver 'Ollie' Cooper, Stuart 'Stu Cooper and Joe 'Just Joe' Murphy, who would become, for a short while, the most talked about and famous band in the world, but for the moment, looked like three scruffy fuckers from the dole queue — but they really would have their fifteen minutes of fame.

So here we all were, was I about to, once again, throw myself out of the frying pan into the fire?

Instantly I was somewhat taken back by how shiny Joe's teeth appeared to be and how I had to tilt my fake Ray-Ban sunglasses to take a good look. They were very shiny and looked to be like a brand new set of pearly whites. With the initial introductions done, we all shook hands and decided to find somewhere we could sit down and have a proper chat, and after discussing a few alternatives we headed for the nearest pub just around the corner.

One other initial mental note was Ollie's weak and limp handshake. Now my Dad always told me never to trust anyone with a limp handshake and definitely do not do business with them — just walk away — so the alarm bells were ringing, but I chose to ignore them.

We headed off up Chelmsford High Street past the shop called Next where we turned left and headed up the street past Lakeland towards Yates Wine Lodge, which was situated opposite the river and next to Argos, these days it's called The Slug and Lettuce or Hungry Caterpillar or something or other.

I was still thinking about how Joe's teeth were so very white and new; I needed answers.

Graham asked everyone what they wanted to drink, which was lagers all round and headed to the bar to order. I grabbed the excuse of giving him a hand to ask the nagging question playing on my mind.

"Have you noticed Joe's teeth?"

"Yeah, looks like he's had some dental work done on them."

"They are whiter than white – he looks like that 'Angry Kid' off the TV."

"I wonder if these three are everything they say they are?" Graham quizzed.

Graham ordered five pints of Fosters and three plates of nachos, complete with all the trimmings, salsa, sour cream, guacamole and of course chillies. The barmaid who was quite ugly and covered in tattoos served the beers and we returned to the table. Graham carried two and I was doing that juggling act where you hold three, and hope no one bumps into you.

I got back to the table without spilling a single drop.

At first we kept the conversation very low key as we tried to get a feel of what these three wanted and were hoping to achieve. Then three or four pints in, I had to ask, I could wait no more, and my head was going to burst with the curiosity. I turned to Joe and asked, "What's with the teeth mate, had some work done recently?"

"Yes," Joe replied, "I was playing football and I was in goal, I rushed out to stop an attack and ended up getting my front teeth kicked out," he went on in great detail.

I could appreciate how much that must have hurt as I had some knowledge of the pain of playing football, having had two broken noses, two broken ankles, one broken arm, one dislocated shoulder and numerous stitches in my playing days, not to mention nearly losing my left leg after a collision with a goalkeeper ended with me in hospital thinking, I had broken it, only to be x-rayed and sent home with what the doctor described as minor ligament damage.

The next morning, I had been in terrible pain and I had pulled back the sheets to find my left leg had started turning black.

I cried for help, then simply cried and then cried some more before I was rushed to hospital where they discovered I had a blood clot around my knee that they immediately operated on, saving my leg — another twenty-four hours and it could've been far worse.

Back to the subject of Joe's teeth, I found out a couple of years later from Stu that a few weeks before our meeting he had deliberately ran out and head-butted the first tree he could find, after an argument concerning lyrics went against him. This would be something he would repeat in later years.

To describe the three guys in the band as a bit strange

154

would be an understatement. They all still lived with their parents who, it would appear, supported their desires to make it in the music industry – or did they?

Basically none of them had proper jobs or bloody income and they needed a mug – sorry manager.

Joe was about twenty-five years old and stood over six-feet tall, he was dressed in an Arsenal Football Club replica shirt, baggy and scruffy jeans with faded even dirty looking trainers. He had a very long face reminiscent of a horse and hair that reminded me of Rod Stewart back in his 'Do You Think I'm Sexy' days.

Unlike Rod, Joe did not exude any sexual charisma. However, this would not stop him having opportunities with the ladies as the band's career started to gather some pace —one rather attractive radio presenter, with an amazing pair of bosoms, definitely had a crush on him.

When he was younger. he was apparently a very good goalkeeper and told me that Colchester United F.C. were interested in signing him. I would be witness to this fact on a few occasions and have to admit that, when he played in a Celebrity Soccer Six tournament in 2006, he was in many people's eyes 'goalkeeper of the tournament' although that's not too difficult when you are up against reality show failures and soppy soap stars with white gangly legs.

Joe only got into the music industry in his quest to meet and shag Lily Allen, but the closest he ever got was when he shook her hand in Texas and came in his own pants, so I suppose he technically almost got half way in his quest.

Stuart 'Stu Cooper was slightly younger than Joe so

around twenty-three or twenty-four and always wore a cap when not on stage. I'm quite sure he may have been losing his hair. When on stage though he would have a range of strange hairstyles the most famous being The Rounded Mohawk. This hairstyle was a high raised thin style Mohawk that would run from the middle of his head around to one side and down to the back of his neck and when he turned his head to one side, his spiked hair was a spitting image of the Statue of Liberty's pointed crown. It definitely caught the eye.

Stu also had a piercing that looked very painful, it went through the bottom of his eyebrow and exited through the top of his eyebrow – it always looked sore! Stu was a decent sort from the start and we got on well, which cannot be said for his younger brother, Oliver 'Ollie' Cooper.

The biggest issue in the end with Stu would be the fact that the other two easily swayed his opinion.

Ollie Cooper, for the whole time I knew him, always seemed to be wearing the same few pieces of clothing, scruffy baggy jeans, long sleeved tops usually black, but sometimes grey all finished off with a black bobble hat that looked like it had been stolen from a sleeping tramp.

His attire was generally completed with a strange silver-balled necklace.

He must have only been sixteen when we first met. I won't beat about the bush or hide the fact that Ollie was obviously talented and he perhaps should have gone on too much better things, but he would never quite get the big break that he honestly believed he deserved. He wanted to be known as the best songwriter in the world ever and he was the best songwriter in the world — in his own fucking imagination.

In the long run he would have to shoulder a lot of the blame for all the doors that closed in our faces due to his twisted, control freaked nature and serious attitude problem with anyone in the music business.

He was a turbo weirdo and was also a little shit. I'm not sure he ever liked me, and certainly once the money ran out, he also quickly fell out with Graham. He obviously had huge trust issues and simply never overcome them. He always thought the worst of people and reckoned that they were just out to rip him off. Even, as he sat drinking the beers and eating the nachos that Graham had paid for, you sensed that he didn't have a shred of respect for anyone other than perhaps his two bandmates – no wait, as this story unfolds you will realise that he had no respect for anyone other than himself.

This is a typical scenario of Ollie's attitude:

We were all on the way to a radio interview and I could sense that Ollie was not interested in even being there as he was mumbling to himself and, when he did speak, it was with a vicious little snarl.

His mumbling reminded me of 'Mutley' the cartoon dog. Mutley was the sidekick to 'Dick Dastardly' in the cartoon series 'Whacky Races'. He had a wheezy snigger and a mushy, sotto voice. Mutley's character was always moaning and would grumble under his breath to his boss "Rashin' Fashin' Rick Rastardly!" but in Ollie's case would be "Rashin' Fashin' Fuckin' Manager!"

"Why the fuck do I have to be at this interview?" he said.

"Because they asked for the band."

Cue 'Mutley' style grumble.

"But Joe will do all the talking so I don't need to fucking be here!"

"They asked for all of you."

"That's fucking bollocks I was meant to be going out with my mates."

When we got there, he was right and had only spoken to Joe.

I got the train home that night, as I couldn't bear the thought of a journey back with him going on and on.

Chapter 12

Storm in a Teacup

As we continued downing pint after pint the conversation finally turned to music and they gleefully informed us that after initially calling themselves Elastic Flange they had finally decided to name the band Koopa.

The name was a derivative of Ollie and Stu's surname Cooper and proves that Ollie, although being the youngest member of the band, was already taking control of things. But it was a cool and original name if you excuse the similarity to 'Koopa Troopa', the fictional turtle like creature from the Nintendo video game series.

Still Nintendo never came along with any injunctions so all was well.

As in the case of all bands. each person had their own place. Stu was the drummer and a damn good one. I have managed some very good drummers including Sonny Watson-Lang of Twenty Twenty, Dean Lemon of Room 94 and Michael Bazzoni of The Promise and each of them have their own uniqueness. But there's a BIG difference between a good drummer and GREAT drummer and while the above are very good – my dad was GREAT.

Joe was a guitarist by nature, but played bass as he thought it'd look better as bass is bigger than a guitar and Joe was bigger than Ollie, so it made sense.

Ollie played guitar and was also the lead singer, he wasn't the best singer and in fact he wasn't the best singer within Koopa, but that's what he wanted, and as usual, he got what he wanted; he was a very good songwriter though.

The boys led me to believe that before meeting Graham and I they had just turned down a huge record deal, which I was struggling to believe. They explained that after meeting with various producers, publishers and record labels they were offered the opportunity to record some demo tracks for both B-Unique down in Brighton and a few weeks earlier at EMI Records in London. Both companies had apparently really liked their demos and both had offered them a huge deal - which they had decided to decline in order to record for themselves in their own studio.

Are you thinking what we were thinking... cough... cough.... bullshit!

We should have got up and walked out there and then, but stupidly we let that load of bollocks ride.

It would turn out that they did do some demos for a label, but it never went any further than that, and indeed no offer was ever made. All the warning signs seemed to be there at the start and like an idiot I missed them all because I was having such a good time drinking.

Graham was very drunk, and I was well on the way

when without any discussion and much to my surprise, Graham suggested to the three of them that we would manage their band and release a single. All on his own, he confirmed that *he* would cover the costs of producing and pressing the physical single and, even though he had no idea of the procedure at that time, or how much it would cost, he told them that we would get it in the record shops.

He would also cover the fuel costs of getting out and about doing some gigs in order to build up the fanbase before releasing anything. We then all agreed that we would split the revenue fifty/fifty after all the initial costs were recovered.

The band would be responsible for the recording of whatever track we decided to release and be responsible for building up some kind of fan-base on the only social networking site worthwhile in those days — MySpace.

I discussed some ideas about playing gigs and, after Stu revealed they had already bought a van so he would be willing to do all the driving, we all shook hands on the deal and continued drinking to celebrate our newly formed and exciting partnership. So that's it on a handshake and nothing else, I was suddenly the manager of a pop-punk band and about to serve up music industry history. I was also part owner of a record label.

We signed the band with no written agreement, no lawyers, no paperwork, just an honest understanding between the five of us and the willingness to give it ago. The whole time we worked together there would never be any management agreement — that handshake was all that we needed.

Well, that's what I thought anyway and it did serve well, until others got their sticky fingers in the pie.

As time passed, I would discover that the band was not at all motivated by the desire to have a career in music, but only by the rush they got from the fame, the thrill from the drugs, the binge drinking of copious amounts of alcohol and quite simply the fun of just having a good time no matter at whose expense.

Looking back, I'm of the opinion that Ollie Cooper, who was just a fucking spotty-faced teenager, barely out of nappies, slightly illiterate and with an air of arrogance about him that you could cut with a knife, played all of us like a damn fiddle from the very start — well done on him for that, perhaps it was us that were the idiots.

With all the usual issues I had with the band — the biggest was that the whole project became like a drug to me. It dragged me in, to the point where I was totally dependent on my daily-fix, no matter who I affected with my selfishness. There were some great times and even amazing times, but eventually the band would drag me right down to the bottom and, if I hadn't of got away, I would have most certainly ended up locked away in an asylum, in prison for murdering the fucking three of them or even worse, killing myself just to get away from it all.

There were a few times I narrowly missed the grim reaper, mixing alcohol, drugs and the music industry is a naughty cocktail of extreme excess and if you're not extremely careful, or are even slightly naïve like I was, it will toss you head first into the belly of the beast and eat you alive — I for one was totally unprepared for any of it.

Times would now start to get very tough financially and, with only my wife Paula working keeping the family afloat, while I was off chasing the dream of managing a successful band, I would also end up sinking some of our life-savings into the process, which when the time eventually came, would be tougher getting back than I imagined.

I was to become something I would later live to regret as it had an adverse effect on family and friends alike. I ended up acting fucking crazy, wondering how I could have done this to them all. I was as fucking mad as a hatter. I would almost ruin my own life, my children's future and most of all I would eventually need to seek help for both health and mental issues.

Was the band to blame for any of this? No! Just me – but at times it felt like it was their fault.

We stayed in Yates Wine Lodge for a few more hours drinking to our futures. The booze was flowing freely and the drinks ranged from lager, vodka shots, Jägermeister with Red Bull, and even a bottle of bubbly made it in along the way. Not once did any of them put their hand in their pockets or even offer to buy us a drink back.

I looked at my phone it was only 3.30pm in the afternoon and I was tipsy, no, sorry, I was fucking ratarsed, pissed as a newt, drunk as a skunk! And when drunk I believe that everyone else in the world is as deaf as a post so therefore I felt the need to shout as loud as possible instead of speaking normally. I also felt the need to urinate at least every fifteen minutes.

The music was blasting out on the jukebox, which led to some impromptu singing.

'Storm in a Teacup' by The Fortunes came on and I was instantly transported back to the time I purchased my very first vinyl single. I have such fond memories of driving the record store girl mad, as I couldn't remember the title correctly or the band's name and I thought it was called 'Pitter Patter.'

She mentioned that she had not heard the song so asked me to sing a little bit of it.

I coughed to clear my throat and began,

"One drop of rain, on your window pane."

She looked at me like I was some sort of idiot.

I went on and on through the next verse and then the next as she, my mates and all the customers in the shop just stared at me.

Then just as I was about to sing those six words that would reveal the actual song title everyone in the store shouted out "It's a storm in a teacup," before bursting into fits of laughter.

The girl behind the counter sniggered and then turned and walked toward the wall behind her to the numbered slots where the chart singles were kept before coming back to me to say "Sorry it's out of stock Elvis," whilst obviously trying hard not to burst into laughter.

So here I am, drunk and dancing to Bruce Springsteen with Graham, Ollie, Stu and Joe all as happy as bunnies and it's still only 5.00pm in the afternoon – I had been drinking since breakfast — when 'Night Fever' by the Bee Gees came on and I was up doing my best John Travolta impression. For the next three minutes and thirty-two seconds I was strutting my funky stuff as well as, bumping into furniture and knocking glasses all over the place whilst all the time crossing my arms and then throwing them into the air to replicate that famous Travolta stance. The song finished, I collapsed on the chair and within seconds the manager politely asked us all to leave, so we headed out, but not before finishing our drinks and calling the manager a wanker on the way out.

Ollie, Stu and Joe decided to call it a day, even though we insisted on going to The Cave; Chelmsford's only lap dancing club. They decide not to join us, as they needed to do something. These days I know that the phrase 'need to do something' means smoking exuberant amounts of weed in the back of their van.

We hugged our goodbyes out and I told them that I would call to set up a 'going-forward' meeting. I actually said something in gibberish, but that's what I meant. The guys left and we decided to grab a burger back at McDonalds.

As we walked in I saw the same fat sweaty fella sitting eating a burger. Had he been there all day, surely not! In hindsight, this may have been a warning from the Gods showing me how I would become if I didn't take more care of myself. The warning sign was spot on, as I would eventually become that very same fat sweaty fella sitting, consuming burgers like they were going out of fashion. Bollocks!

I scoffed down my food and went for yet another piss. This one was a challenge as the toilet was upstairs, but I managed to negotiate the stairs without falling over and pissing in my pants. I was in Newcastle once and got so drunk that I fell over outside a kebab shop and shit myself. Yes, you just read that right. I shit myself.

We headed off to the lap-dancing club, as we knew it opened early to catch the rush-hour city punters off the trains; we were up for some fun.

The first thing you see at a lap-dancing club is not a pair of beautiful breasts, but a pair of burly bouncers ready to eye you up and down to assess whether you are worthy of seeing those breasts in the first place.

They are the guardians of the breasts and none unworthy shall get to see them unless they deem it so.

It was now early evening and getting dark and cold. The daily commuters were starting to arrive home and everywhere you could see flustered men in suits rushing through the gates of the railway station heading for the nearest bus stop or car waiting to pick them up. Some, however, headed straight for the pub opposite or joined us in the queue for the lap-dancing club, eager to let their hair down after a long day in the office.

The whole entry process is somewhat creepy. The bouncers loom, staring at you, while all the time radiating an air of ultra-violence. One of them was short, which is always going to be an additional issue, as short bouncers seem to have some kind of Napoleon Bonaparte complex going on. He knows damn well he is a little on the short side of life, but makes up for it by having a big aggressive nature. He stood with his arms crossed, looking mean.

Standing next to him and compared to shorty, was a bloody giant of a man. He must have been six-feet six at the very least. He was bald with a sloping forehead.

After checking us over a further few times and much to our surprise shorty said, "In you go chaps."

The Cave is what they call a gentlemen's nightclub situated in the very heart of Chelmsford. You can have a drink and just watch, or you can get yourself a lap dance. It's not bloody cheap though, and it's also a bit of a misnomer as there's not really any dancing involved – it's more dry humping than lap dancing.

We sat down and ordered a couple of large vodka and cokes and looked at all the gorgeous woman walking around half naked. The music was all R&B and was very loud. We were busy discussing which dancer best took our fancy when, I stood up and without seeing our waitress behind me, I crashed straight into her, flipping her tray in the air and causing her to spill the drinks all over herself. The glasses smashed as they hit the floor, and within seconds two bouncers were upon us both.

We received the usual bouncer glare as they looked us up and down and then the shorter one looking for a reaction shouted "Calm down lads," we didn't give them any verbal – although I really felt the urge to say something, I ultimately knew it would lead to a kicking in the alleyway, so I kept my mouth shut while all the time thinking to myself, 'what a muggy little cunt.'

"Sorry lads, you'll have to leave," the taller bouncer said.

They escorted us out of the club and, after noticing the wet patch on my trousers from the spilled drinks, we decided to call it a day after all it was getting a bit late. It was about 6.30pm! But to us it had been a very long day so we headed for the taxi rank and went our own ways. I fell into the taxi, gave him the address, nodded-off until we arrived at our destination, and I fell out the taxi at the other end.

I fumbled with my front door lock, but ended up knocking instead. My daughter Amy opened the door, took one look at me and said "Mum will not be happy with you."

I decided that the best course of action was to avoid my wife and go straight to bed, I drank some water to help me rehydrate in the hope that I wouldn't wake up with a bad hangover the following morning.

As a rule, I do the same every time I'm drunk and not once do I recall it ever helping. I must have drunk about two litres of water on this occasion before heading up to the bedroom.

I got undressed and fell into the bed, but as my head hit the pillow I began to get the strangest feeling in my stomach. It was like my entire stomach was shouting abandon ship. I felt the inside of my cheeks go moist and I knew what was about to happen and as I jumped up, I tripped and fell flat on my face.

I managed to gather my thoughts and just get to the bathroom to drop to my knees before all hell was unleashed from within my body — as I projectile vomited with the force of an exocet missile. If you have seen that truly terrifying movie 'The Exorcist', then you will surely understand what I'm talking about – it was disgusting.

The fluid just flew out of my mouth. It was horrendous and like nothing I had felt before or since!

Now there was just one little thing that I had forgotten to do and that was to lift the toilet lid and the vomit hit the toilet seat with such ferocity that it just rebounded back straight into my face causing me to vomit even more.

It was bloody everywhere!

Everyone in the house rushed to help, but they immediately recoiled whilst retching at the horrible sight of vomit dripping from my forehead, as well as being plastered all over the bathroom and to cap it all off I was stark bollocked naked.

It was everywhere, on me, the toilet, in the sink, in the bath, on the floor, up the walls and all over the freshly laid out towels and the cherry on top was that as I stood up and turned around there stood my daughters sleepover friends — staring at me in all my vomit coloured glory.

It was a right mess and I had to clean it up all on my own, but on the bright side, whilst vomiting I realised that we hadn't paid for that round of drinks that I knocked over in the lap-dancing club — get in!

The next day I woke up thinking it was just another normal morning. However, I wasn't one hundred percent sure where I was or even who I was at that moment in time, which was most disconcerting.

Then suddenly I realised — fucking hell, what have I been drinking was my first reaction. Then the thirst hit me, followed by what appeared to be a bullet to the head causing the most crippling headache. My eyes screwed up and I put my hands on my head. "Dear God, please help me," I said out loud. "Please not this!" I continued.

What the bloody hell did I do to deserve this I wondered? Then out of my daze, my memory hit me like a ton of bricks, the lager, the shots, the bubbly, the John Travolta moves, the lap-dancing club and worst of all the puking. As I recalled the events of the previous day I closed my eyes and pulled the covers over my head in shame.

The wave of shame that engulfed me briefly distracted from the physical pain I was starting to feel.

"Shit!" I murmured softly under my breath.

I pulled back the covers and sat up, I needed a drink as my mouth felt like I had been eating sand all night. I got out of bed and realised I was stark naked. After slipping on my dirty vomit smelling underpants I went to the bathroom to get a glass of water and that's when the nausea kicked back in.

"Fuck me not again!" I muttered to myself.

Suddenly it felt like my actual brain was bouncing around like some demented seventies space hopper inside my swollen skull. I was thinking it would never stop. I managed to stumble into the bathroom and that's when the stench hit me, the smell of vomit is like nothing else; it's quite like that of fermentation, a kind of sour smell you never forget. It was also freezing cold in the bathroom, as someone had left the windows wide open. The smell crept up my nostrils before hitting the back of my throat, my eyes opened wide, my cheeks went moist and my body started to shake uncontrollably.

I knew what was coming, I dropped to my knees and, with the holy throne of vomit collection, otherwise known as the toilet bowl before me, I unleashed the remains of my stomach. At the time I thought that my kidneys, liver and whole stomach had come up as well. I flushed the toilet and headed back to the bedroom.

I found that the best position to deal with my condition was horizontally so I returned to bed and dozed back off to sleep for a while before eventually waking up and trying the upright position again.

Sitting upright sucked like hell and I could feel the rest of my body calling to me to be disconnected from my head. I knew that I needed to get up and out of bed in order to survive this ordeal.

Somehow I managed to manoeuvre myself out of the bedroom and down the stairs to the kitchen. The house was deathly silent, not a soul in sight, which was probably for the best. Somehow I got to the fridge without dying and opened the door, I stood and stared at the contents hoping to discover some bacon to make a sizzling sarnie or perhaps some left over pizza from the kids. But alas, nothing!

I still felt the cloud of shame resume its position above me as I sat down and rested my head on the kitchen table. It was all getting a little bit too much at this point, I needed food. I decided to give the fridge another try, perhaps it had magically restocked since I last took a look a minute ago. I opened up the fridge door and to my surprise… Nothing has changed! Except one thing that hadn't been a minute ago, I decided.

Staring lovingly back in my direction was one single bottle of lager, standing there in all its glory, the distinctive 'crown' logo calling out to me – it was of course a bottle of Corona, my favourite of all the lagers in the world.

I heard the bottle speaking to me, requesting me to grab it, to pop the bottle top and push a wedge of lime into its bottleneck. My brain suddenly cleared, I forgot the trauma I was going through, and I started to think. 'That's it, that's just what I need right now, a nice cold bottle of beer.' I was sinking into the abyss. I looked at the kitchen clock on the wall above the table it was 9.30am.

Because sometimes we humans can be fundamentally stupid, I decided that no harm could come of it — in fact it might even take away the cloud of shame that was still choosing to hang around. I reached for the beer when, suddenly, my brain obviously had decided enough is enough and it sent a shudder through my entire body that started at my feet and made its way up to the very top of my skull — I shut the fridge door and sat down.

After a while I decided to look for some real food. I was in need of stodge, something to take the hangover blues away. I opened the cupboard door and there it was 'the king of snacks' waiting to save the day – its green and white packaging shining like a beacon of light at the end of the hangover tunnel – The very 'fuel of Britain' itself a delicious Chicken & Mushroom Pot Noodle. "That's it, the solution to all my problems," I said out loud. "I'll have a Pot Noodle sandwich," I declared.

The art of a making a great 'Pot Noodle Sandwich' is not merely pouring some hot water onto the dried noodles and buttering some bread. Oh no! The process is complex and involves many different clever moves. You need to be a Pot Noodle connoisseur to get this process and the timing spot on to deliver the perfect sandwich, oozing flavour and buckets of joy to your taste buds.

Follow the cooking instructions and you'll be having a food orgasm within minutes.

Cooking instructions:

1. Boil the kettle.
2. Rip off the lid and remove the sachet. You will need this later.
3. Add the boiling hot water to the fill line. Do not overfill!
4. Leave it alone for two minutes. Do not be tempted to stir!

Try to entertain yourself for the duration. Perhaps have a little dance, I usually do.

5. Stir thoroughly, then leave for another two minutes. Don't be tempted to stir!

Dance!

6. Stir again and then add the contents of the sachet.
7. Pick out two toppers from a loaf of white bread and butter thoroughly.
8. Carefully add *half* of the contents of the Pot Noodle to the slices of bread.
9. 'Hey Presto' you have a Pot Noodle sandwich. Lovely Jubbly!

Now remember that after finishing your sandwich you still have half of a delicious Pot Noodle to enjoy so grab your fork and get eating.

Now eating food after such an event as a binge drinking session and whilst recovering from a severe hangover can go two ways, either you will be sick again or, you will keep it down and the road to recovery would have begun. Luckily for me it was the latter and an hour or so later I was starting to feel slightly better. The kids were at school and the wife at work so I settled down to watch some television.

I reached for my James Bond DVD Box Set and carefully selected my favourite Bond movie. I loved all of the movies, but 'The Man with the Golden Gun' is my absolute favourite. Even Lulu's theme tune would put a smile on my face, especially the line 'He's got a loaded weapon…'

I watched James Bond while scoffing down a whole packet of Jaffa Cakes that I found hiding behind some tins and pondering as to whether the orange tasting middle bit counted towards one of my five-a-day and, and after deciding it would, I then devoured a whole Terry's Chocolate Orange for the very same reason.

The day would turn very sour and the air very blue later, when my unforgiving wife returned home from work and after our huge row, I was so pissed off that I decided to go back to bed, but not before emailing both Joe and Graham to set up meetings to plan the next moves for the band.

Chapter 13

Dropping the C-Bomb

Next morning feeling fresh as a daisy I headed up the A12 towards Colchester to meet with the band to further discuss the release schedule, and for the guys to give me a tour of their studio, that they had been bragging about so much. This would prove to be an eye opener!

I was late arriving due to the high volume of traffic after a lorry had apparently jackknifed and shed its diesel tank, along with its load of industrial hand wipes.

I arrived outside Joe's parent's house just outside the town centre and I presumed this was where we would all meet before going on to the studio. How can one man be so wrong?

I got out of the car and adjusted my jeans, which always seem to slip down when I drove, and headed up the path before ringing the doorbell. Moments later a plump woman opened the door and introduced herself as 'Joe's Mum Ginny'. She asked me in and then shouted up the stairs at the top of her voice "Joeeeeeeeeeeeeeeee," causing my eardrums to almost shatter.

Seconds later, Joe appeared and ushered me up the

stairs to his bedroom. I was instantly taken aback by all the Arsenal Football Club replica shirts on display dangling from the decorative picture rail covering every inch of wall space.

Joe proceeded to describe various shirts as "This one is the double winning shirt of the 1972 season…" and "This one is the shirt they wore in 1986."

Being a Tottenham Hotspur supporter this rather disturbed me and I was quickly losing the will to live. Luckily the doorbell rang again and within seconds Ollie and Stu had arrived and joined us in the room.

The room was a total mess and needed a good clean — as my OCD cleaning head took control for a moment in time.

It was very dusty, so dusty in fact, that I childishly drew a cock and balls in the dust on the top of the desk where the computer was stationed. I did a thorough job too, including some pubic hair and a stream of man juice splurging out of the top. I sniggered to myself thinking, God, how old am I?

I could not help but notice the DVD collection stored in a dusty dark wood cabinet in the corner. There was an extensive collection of television comedy and extremely large collection of pornography, of course, something I would easily spot given my history in the industry. I think that Joe may have been a good customer back in the day.

The floor was covered in all manner of stuff, football programs, guitar leads, lighters and much more. Next to his desk was a very strange looking object that I had never seen before, but was rather Dildo looking in design.

No, surely not I thought.

It was in fact a bong – which as I came to understand was a device used for smoking cannabis.

The device uses water to filter the smoke so that no chunks of the weed get into your mouth. You light the filled bowl and breath through the end, inhaling the smoke until it starts to hurt your throat upon which you release, causing shit loads of smoke to go down your lungs to give you the hit.

Then you start coughing like a bitch.

Before we even began to chat about the plans, the three of them insisted they needed a hit and there in front of a relatively complete stranger, they got down to it. The stench was awful and almost made me gag. I was thinking what the fuck is going on here.

After getting their hit of weed from the bong and then discussing an old episode of Jasper Carrots 'Goldenball's, which was showing on the television, I finally had their attention and we discussed getting on the road to play some shows, which they were very eager to do, along with building an online fan-base.

"Do you want to take me now, to show me your studio?" I asked.

Joe looked at the other two and they all sniggered.

"Something up?" I asked.

Joe stared me straight in the eyes and said, "No."

"Yeah, good idea, let's go to the studio!" Ollie said sarcastically.

"Follow us," Stu added.

I could sense a strange atmosphere, the kind you feel when you know you are about to get scammed – you know when some Prince of a country you have never heard of, emails you and wants to give you all of his money and all you need to do is send your bank account details – well, I had that kind of feeling.

I followed them as they headed out of Joes bedroom expecting them to head downstairs, but instead they turned left on the landing and stood outside a closed white door.

"Welcome to the place where the magic happens!" Joe proudly announced as he opened the door to what an estate agent would describe as a small third bedroom and low and behold there it was — their very own home recording studio. The words cramped-space would certainly not do the room any justice, it was fucking minute and for a moment I just stood there in total disbelief.

This was no recording studio, surely not, this was a confession box, it was so fucking tiny.

However, it did have all the elements to record music, including mixing desk, microphones, speakers, leads, more leads and a scattering of Joes soiled underwear and socks that looked like he used them for more than just footwear.

It also had one small window that was slightly ajar to obviously mask the smell of cannabis.

Once again alarm bells were sounding, but once again for some reason I didn't act upon them. We had a brief discussion about getting some tracks recorded and then I left the three of them to further fill the air with that sweet smell I would get to know so well in the coming months. As I said my goodbyes, I felt slightly intoxicated by the weed myself such was the frequency of its use while I was there.

I started arranging gigs to get the band out performing and to build up the live side of things and while we were out and about gigging the online fan-base was also growing as well. I could sense there was a small swell of support online for the band after a few new tracks had been posted on MySpace.

In the early days of hitting the road we kept it close to home trying to keep the costs down. We limited the venues to a fifty-mile radius, so that we could always get back home afterwards. I was attending every gig, which was the start of me joining Ollie and Joe in drinking as much beer and spirits, on the way there and back as possible and, in their case, coupled with constant hits on their bong.

I avoided the bong at all costs.

Stu never drank as he was always driving the van, but Ollie or Joe would constantly lean over from the back and offer him up a hit on the bong, which was most disconcerting to me, and probably why I drank more to hide the fear of dying in a horrible crash. Come to think of it, I must have always been as high as a kite myself as the battered old ford van was always filled with smoke from both cannabis and cigarettes.

I would get home stinking of fags, weed and booze, which would always lead to an interrogation from my wife who was adamant that I was smoking weed, taking drugs and also turning into an alcoholic.

I suppose two out of three is still bad though – isn't it?

The band had started to spread their wings a little further afield and we received an email from a booking agent about a big gig in Grimsby. He was after an unsigned band to add to the bill that one of his clients was putting on at the Grimsby Auditorium and, without even hearing them, he asked if Koopa wanted to do the show and that he was happy to cover any fuel costs — so I got him to email me the details.

This was a show in front of two thousand people and on the bill were Son of Dork, Simon Webb ex boy-band Blue and Westlife. I thought it might be tricky to get the band to agree, but I went ahead and said ok anyway. It was nice that he had thought of us, as booking agents are usually looking for some buy-on or show contribution, but not on this occasion.

Now, everyone will tell you that you can only get the right gigs if you deal with a booking agent, and it's true a booking agent will promise you the world for a price (or buy-on as it's known).

Most of them are like foxes and they have no morals – just commission on their minds and the artist I'm afraid to say are the chickens in the coop.

They are taking thousands of pounds in buy-on fees from vulnerable bands and artists in return for the offer of a twenty-minute opening slot at an arena show where the band end up playing to an almost empty venue, as they are on stage ten minutes after the doors open.

This is one practice that I would love to see stopped. Even unsigned bands are now taking huge buy-on fees from other unsigned bands – it's fucking immoral.

I know of an artist who got his mum to remortgage her house so he could perform with the first One Direction tour and did he get signed afterwards? Did he bollocks! It just doesn't work like that.

There are bands I have worked with that have paid 50k plus to buy-on to big tours and what do they get from it? A few more twitter followers and a bloody deep hole in their sky rockets – that's pockets by the way. Some don't even get bottles of water in their dressing rooms – it's a disgrace.

And if you're in a band, or you are a singer thinking it's not too bad and it's an opportunity to play to a large audience — then remember this; the audience are there to see the headliner, not you and they don't give a fuck who you are and in fact most of them will be at the bar getting pissed when you perform, so please at least think twice before you empty your mum and dad's hard earned savings account.

There are so many things wrong with this scenario that it makes me feel sick to my stomach and I'm deeply ashamed to say that I've been involved in taking a buy-on fee from some poor band in return for an opening slot and I claimed my commission to boot – when you're deep in the belly of the beast you sadly act like everyone else and that's a sad thing to say, but it's true – morals are best not used in the music industry. Booking agents and managers should be ashamed of themselves as this is pure exploitation and greed, but trust me, they don't give a fuck about you and care little for the quality of the show, it's all about who will pay them the most and their 10% plus commission.

Ollie, Stu and Joe would have not stood for any of today's nonsense; like paying your mates to load and unload the van, they would just fucking get on and do it themselves. They had an ocean full of flaws, but if I'd told them that some band wanted to pay to come on tour with them, their first question would've been; are they any good? Do they suit our sound? Not —how much are they paying?

But as I said before, this guy thought the band would be a good addition to the line-up – God knows why?

I was with the band that night as they had a gig in Colchester at The Twist. It was their hometown show and these were always fine as their families and mates, as well as a few fans would turn up.

I sat the guys down and said," I have some news —you have been asked to perform at the Grimsby Auditorium for a big radio promotion event."

They seemed genuinely elated and Stu asked, "Who else is playing?"

"Oh, just some bands, some signed some unsigned," I answered sheepishly.

"Like who?" Ollie asked starting to feel I was hiding something.

"Oh, Son of Dork and…" I replied, pausing for breath before whispering "Westlife."

"Who?" Joe asked.

"Westlife."

"Fucking Westlife!" Ollie screamed, "Go fuck yourself, I'm not playing a show with fucking Westlife!"

"It's over two thousand people, biggest crowd you have ever played to, so it has to be worth it," I explained.

After a short while Joe came over and said, "We'll do the show."

"That's great."

"But we will not compromise on our performance."

"What do you mean?"

"You know how we perform so let's just say we do it how we want to do it or not at all."

By this point I'd had enough so I just nodded and went to the bar for a drink. It would later come to light that what they actually meant; that they would act like complete dicks the whole night of the show.

The big day arrived and we set off on the long road trip to Grimsby. It was bloody freezing in the van.

What seemed like a fucking eternity passed before we finally arrived and, as I wound down the window to speak to a security guard about parking, a large cloud of smoke billowed out of the window.

"What are you doing in there?" He asked.

"Uh... n-no-nothing..." I replied.

He leant in and looked in the back.

"You guys doing anything suspicious in the back?"

"Uh...... no?" Joe replied nervously.

"I've been working here ten years and I know that smell."

As he and I spoke I could see the smoke from their last hit passing between us.

Then he laughed and said, "So load me one up and give me a hit .... then you can park up."

This was another world. There were tour buses parked at the back and inside the stage was huge with two big screens either side. Everyone, including Ollie, suddenly seemed excited.

The band had their very first dressing room with their name on the door and there were some beers in the fridge. Their first dressing room and they didn't even need it as they never got changed from the scruffy clothes they had travelled up in and they wanted to spend time in the van smoking more gear before the gig.

We settled in and then went exploring before our sound check.

As we walked past a tour bus Joe muttered, "We'll have one of these one day!" and as he did James Bourne, ex of Busted and now with Son of Dork and then of McBusted and now of Busted again, walked out and Ollie rushed over to speak to him like a child running off to buy an ice cream.

I have only ever seen him like this twice, on the other occasion he was barely able to speak, he was that excited – was this the real Ollie Cooper? – just an excited kid and not the one that could be a complete arsehole.

After sound check the three of them sat back in the van to get high and drink. I stayed in the dressing room on my own to avoid the smoke and the smell of farts. When stage time arrived all three looked nervous, which actually took me aback as they had always been pretty blasé pre-show.

They were introduced and went on to rapturous applause before belting out their set. Now do you remember when Joe said to me "We will do the show, but we will not compromise on the performance." Well, it was during the set that it suddenly dawned on me what they meant.

It simply meant that they would be as rude as possible to get a reaction from the crowd and to add insult to injury, they even dropped in a 'C' bomb – which basically meant that all those teenagers and their parents heard the word 'cunt' over the speaker system –

this is something you just don't expect when you are at a Westlife concert. They were acting like a complete bunch of wankers.

Even Johnny Rotten would've been shocked by some of the filth they were muttering on stage.

The stage manager first looked at me in disgust before coming over to shout that this was completely out of order and I should be ashamed. I just cowered in fear of my life. The bands finished their set with The Proclaimers cover '500 Miles' which to be honest the crowd seemed to have enjoyed. However, the organisers were less than impressed, as were the Westlife management team.

When I informed the band about the situation they just all laughed out loud. I explained the seriousness of it and suggested that we make a rapid exit, but once again, against my wishes, the band headed to the dressing room to collect any leftover beer for the journey home. Just in case of trouble, I decided I should go with them and as we headed up the stairs the Westlife boys were heading the other way and Kian, being polite and obviously having not heard a single word or song of the set, turned to the band and said "Great set lads," in his soft Irish voice.

As we passed Westlife's dressing room we could see it was empty and that there seemed to be a lot of food leftover. An argument then ensued over the morality of stealing sandwiches from a band who'd had numerous chart topping singles and I just watched in disgust as the boys entered.

While I waited outside and they began to grab the sandwiches, I heard someone approaching and as I turned my head, I could see none other than Louis Walsh coming up the stairs.

I ducked into the nearest door that was to a disabled toilet and with it slightly ajar, I peeped out as Louis approached the dressing room., as he entered I heard a bit of a commotion with lots of foul language then my three red-faced band members ran out empty handed and legged it out of the building.

I jumped out of the disabled toilet and legged it after them back to the van and I could hear all three of them laughing out loud.

"Louis Walsh just told us to fuck off!" Joe announced.

"Surely that's feck off!" Ollie declared, at which point we all fell about laughing; although my laugh was more of an asthma attack as I tried desperately to catch my breath.

The security guard that the band had spent all afternoon with in the back of the van, opened the gates and we made a swift exit and headed back to Essex.

The following day I received a nice email from the venue manager saying Koopa was banned from ever performing there again and that the other acts' managers were disgusted by the band's behavior.

Funny enough Louis Walsh would release a book a few years later and in it he complimented Koopa on their achievements – not bad when you consider he once caught them stealing his sandwiches.

The feedback from the Grimsby gig online was phenomenal and I could see there was a rise in fan growth. The band carried on doing gigs throughout the summer months and around August we met up to discuss what song they were going to choose as their first single, and they decided on a track called 'No Trend.'

"Good choice," I announced.

The following morning, I visited Graham's office to discuss the single and we set a release date of November 14, 2005, which was the 318th day of the year and was about the same position we reckoned the single would get to in the charts.

Graham brought some good news to the table and explained that he had sorted a small distribution deal with a company in London called Fullfill, and that the CD single would be stocked in a few HMV stores around Essex and, of course, it would also be available on all online music platforms such as iTunes. This was wonderful news and at the same time we decided that Mad Cow Records was to be the name of our label – the label was named in honour of our wives.

It was around the start of September when I set about getting the band a few new shows to get the ball rolling for their single promo.

Joe gleefully informed me that their 'No Trend' track was finished. It sounded very punky and raw and was just what we wanted. Koopa didn't bring anything new to the world of music, but they had something about them and with Ollie and Joe's Essex accents, they stood out, making them a little unlike anything else.

We still needed what everyone still called a 'B-side' and having already heard the bands recording of The Proclaimers classic '500 Miles' I decided that this would make the release somewhat cheesier and attractive to one-off buyers. People love novelty items and along with the single's artwork; a lovely looking pair of boobs lifted from an online photo of Caprice made the CD stand out even more — and in case you are interested, no, we didn't ask permission – remember this book is called Blag, Steal & Borrow.

Chapter 14

Do You Remember Myspace

I thought my teenage movie making years would come in helpful when we decided to put together a video for the new single 'No Trend.' I had, at the tender age of fifteen-years directed the epic that was 'Enter the Dragon 2', which was basically a remake of the Bruce Lee classic 'Enter the Dragon', but made on a shoestring budget of about £3.50

I loved this movie (Bruce Lee's – not mine) and these days I still put in on at least once a week. I have quite literally seen this movie hundreds of times before, but it never ceases to entertain me, and sometimes for a bit of fun I mute the sound and act out all the dialogue scenes.

My favourite lines being *'Don't think, FEEEEEEEEL! It's like a finger pointing away to the moon,"* and *"Boards don't hit back."*

The fight scenes are thrilling and I love watching Bruce Lee pull his pursed-lip expression, move his hands up and down in some mystical mesmerising movement before shouting his battle cry 'WOOOOOOO-OOOO-WAHHHHHHHH' and dispatching the bad guy with a roundhouse kick to the back of the head.

However, my epic movie would end up only being four minutes long after being fraught with problems from the very start; like casting issues, Tight-John dropped out after he got accidently head-butted in one of the opening scenes and the love interest, Janette Barnes, refused to kiss my cousin on the lips meaning we had to cut out the love-scene.

There was also much debate over the fact that I was directing as well as starring, because I had never actually had any Kung Fu, karate or judo lessons in my life, but had seen the movie numerous times; as Terry-All-Gold's grandad worked as an usher at the ABC cinema in town and used to sneak us in the side door.

We would sneak in for the first performance and stay until the last. Bruce Lee would kick, punch and quip at the baddies as he dispatched them in a series of exciting fight sequences. 'Enter The Dagon' was on a double-bill with the truly awful 'Death Race 2000', which we had to endure many times.

It's unthinkable now, but in those days' people could smoke in the cinema, but there were rules; smokers were required to sit on the right-hand side of the auditorium as apparently in the seventies smoke never drifted, but we on the left-hand side, still managed somehow to go home coughing and smelling like an ashtray, which always caused our Mother's to question us every time.

"Have you been smoking?"

"No Mum, I've been to the ABC cinema with Terry."

"Well, you smell like you have been smoking," Mum would rage.

We would have the same discussion every time and

it didn't end until the night my parents went to see a film at the ABC Cinema and came home coughing.

"Enjoy the movie Mum?" I asked.

"No."

"Why not?"

"Instead of seeing 'Freebie and the Bean' your father took me to some sex film."

"What?"

"It was a comedy called 'Confessions of A Window Cleaner', it wasn't pornography," said Dad embarrassingly.

I knew exactly what film they were talking about because I had a copy of the Timmy Lea book under my bed along with a copy of Mayfair Magazine, that I'd swapped for a set of football cards that I had collected through buying Bazooka chewing gum.

"The film was very funny, but it was really smoky in there!" Mum said.

I sighed and replied, "See, I told you."

"Yes, you did so stop looking so smug and go to bed."

My mates and I sneaked into a late night showing of 'Enter The Dragon' once and the auditorium was filled with a loud and obviously half-pissed laddish audience.

The automated system started with the lights going down and the curtains opening, then suddenly the curtains closing and the lights went up again.

Then it repeated itself, lights, curtains and this time no film, just a blank screen, then the curtains closed and the lights went up again. The audience was getting restless. Finally, the lights dimmed, the curtains opened and the film started, but within seconds of Bruce Lee's first appearance, the screen suddenly froze.

By this time, the audience had had enough and began to chant "WE WANT BRUCE! WE WANT BRUCE! WE WANT BRUCE!" A few minutes later the curtains closed, the audience booed, the curtains opened, the audience cheered and Bruce Lee was back and this time with no further problems.

On our way out we bumped into Terry-All-Gold's grandad who gave us the lowdown of all the earlier evenings problems; the projectionist who had arrived for work slightly worse for wear after an early evening session in the pub, had sneaked off back to the pub for one last pint before last orders and had left the projectionist booth unattended.

We thought it was rather funny and running all the way home we practiced our fighting skills ready for any dangerous situations we may come across, as by now we were all experts in the martial art of Kung Fu, as taught to us by the master Bruce Lee. Bruce was one of my early inspirations and later in life I would embrace some of his philosophies like '*If there are no waves, make some*', which came in handy in the music industry.

Back to the making of our classic movie 'Enter The Dragon 2'. We filmed on a Sunday morning and the set ended up being built at the back of the pub where all the beer crates were stored.

The special effects department consisted of my eldest sister Susan and a bottle of tomato sauce, for use as fake blood; it was going to be an epic movie.

The morning was mainly filled with me kicking and

punching my mates around and with my sister splashing tomato sauce all over our heads. It was fun and going well until I tried to do a roundhouse kick and accidently booted my sister in the stomach, causing the tomato sauce to explode all over her face.

She ran off crying out loud that three-letter word that I knew would bring trouble…

"MUM!" she yelled at the top of her voice. Mum rushed out and seeing what she thought was blood on my sister's face screamed at me "Oh my God! What have you done?" This then caused one of the transvestite bar-staff to run out after hearing the commotion and, upon setting eyes on my sister, let out a shrill of terror so loud it made all the dogs in the local area start to bark.

"I'll call an ambulance Sheila!" he shouted out.

"Wait!" I shouted, as I and the rest of the cast also covered in tomato sauce ran over.

"Oh my good God it's a bloody massacre!" the transvestite shouted, before adding "Someone call the police!"

"No, wait!" I yelled as loud as I could. "It's ketchup, it's just tomato sauce!"

Mum turned slapped me round the head and then said something I had never heard her say before – she dropped the f-bomb on me.

"You stupid fucking idiot!" she shouted. "What the fuck goes on in your head?" she added before grabbing my sister and taking her off to be cleaned up.

The transvestite bar person (that's a bit more PC I think) strutted up to me lifted his hand to my head, ran a finger through my fake tomato sauce wound before licking it in confirmation and advising me that my Dad was going to kill me when he got home, and suggested that my mates and I should bugger off out of it.

***

So getting back to reality, I was researching on how to get a cheap band video made and I spotted an advert online that declared *'I will make you a music video for free'* so I emailed the guy, sent him the track, which to my surprise he loved and on the spot did agree to shoot a video for free. I called Joe, who also had some good news; the bands MySpace page was attracting a lot of new fans, which was good to hear. Joe was always hands-on and ran the MySpace site, but he did have a habit of over egging the numbers online. I don't think Ollie or Stu ever helped online in anyway.

The day of the free video shoot was upon us and we set off nice and early to a studio in West London. I was just expecting a guy and a hand held camera, but this was something else! This was a green screen studio that was full with film crew waiting for the band.

Warren, the director was the man shooting the video for free, and he passed me the days' schedule — so all excited I rushed over to tell the guys and as I pulled back the side door of the van I was hit by the bloody waft of weed.

"For fuck's sake, its only eight thirty in the fucking morning!" I yelled.

"Bollocks!" Ollie replied.

"If you want us to do this stupid fucking video, then we will do what we fucking like!" he snorted.

The other two just turned and laughed.

"They are waiting for you," I informed them.

"They can fucking wait then can't they, you cunt!" came the sneering reply from Ollie.

I slammed the door shut and walked away. Their arrogance would only help them get noticed initially, but eventually people would tire of this type of attitude and all the nonsense.

After few minutes they emerged from the van clutching cans of lager and wandered over towards the video director and myself as we stood with a cup of tea chatting about the shoot.

"What's happening then?" Joe asked.

Warren turned, smiled and introduced himself before explaining how the day would go.

"So, let's get you guys into make-up, then you can get changed into your outfits for the shoot."

The three of them looked puzzled and turned to one another before Joe announced,

"We are in our fucking outfits mate."

I could see the director was a little taken aback. They looked a mess, so trying to hide my embarrassment and release a bit of the imminent tension, I declared, "Shall we get the ball rolling then?"

The remainder of that day went as smooth as it possibly could without any outrageous undue behaviour; only for a few weeks later to be told that the director didn't have enough cash to finish the special-effects, leaving the video half-baked and not good enough to push to any of the music channels on television.

In desperation, I managed to get the footage from Warren, and Joe who knew his way around a camcorder, filmed a few extra scenes and edited something together that looked good enough for a broadcast. Then, to cut a long story short, I showed the video to all the music, television channels and I couldn't bloody believe it when Scuzz, Kerrang and Starz all agreed to play it!

Looking back now at the 'No Trend' video it looks awful and you can clearly see gaffer tape marks where effects, would have been (bloody gaffer tape – that stuff fucking haunts me!).

Back in 2005 things were so different than today in the world of the unsigned band, television channels and even radio stations were so much more helpful. These days to get a video onto one of the music channels you have to pay companies like Fastrax a few hundred quid to submit it for you and, as for radio, well they won't even listen unless you employ a radio-plugger to represent you.

The industry seems to have no interest in unsigned acts making an impact these days and unsigned bands are limited to late night plays on specialist radio shows.

Until recently I had managed a fantastic four-piece band from Hatfield in Hertfordshire called Room 94, and while being unsigned we managed to get two albums into The Official Top 40 Album Chart and even then not one label was the slightest bit interested in signing them.

Back in the middle of the noughties it was deemed cool to be unsigned, but now with so many unsigned bands vying for attention online, and with so many uploading their fucking awful music to YouTube and

SoundCloud, it's just a complete mess in the unsigned world.

Don't get me wrong, I love YouTube and it's a great platform for getting your music and information out there, but I've no time for all the pretentious YouTube wankers who just sit in judgment over everyone else in the world, as they go about their normal boring lives – they should all just fuck off.

I have to point out that amongst all the shit that YouTube does spews out of its big corporate arse, there are of course wonderful people doing wonderful things and they have to be applauded. I have seen some of these people in action and they are able to relate and discuss matters with their online viewers with humanity and with the offer of support for people in need. They are not driven by that desire that eats away at those plastic people seeking the pursuit of 'celebrity status'.

The likes of people like Zoella are an inspiration to the young —but don't be fooled into thinking everyone is in it for the love; they earn thousands of pounds in revenue from advertising and brand sponsorship.

Anyway, let's get back to the story, it was now time for the launch of our single and we were going to need a little help to get some radio play. It is an arduous task and as I said earlier usually requires the skills of a radio-plugger, something that unfortunately was not an option for us given our budget. However, we would find a friend in BBC Radio 1 DJ Steve Lamacq.

Joe, as well as being an Arsenal fan, had a big soft-spot for Colchester United and was friends with the guy who ran the club's website, having access to the best seats at matches it suddenly dawned on us that Steve Lamacq was also a big fan of the club. Joe had seen him there many times, so we hatched a plan for Joe to coincidently carry a copy of our CD to the game and given the opportunity try and get it into the hands of Steve.

One cold early October Saturday afternoon that opportunity arose and, after a quick chat at half time, Joe handed over the CD to Steve who said he would have a listen. Can you Imagine how we felt when he played the song on his show all week and told his listeners how much he loved the band. It's amazing what the power of a hot Bovril and a chicken & mushroom pie can have.

I arranged a Launch Party for the single at The Twist in Colchester and even managed to blag a model agency to send along three Page 3 girls to enhance the evening, which pleased Joe no end and he seemed to spend the entire evening focused on trying to chat them up — alas without much success.

The venue was full to capacity and increasingly became hotter and hotter, so much so, that you could see the beads of sweat on people's faces by the time the band performed their set. I had the promoter place two rather large fans (I do mean electrical ones) either side of the stage to keep them cool during the performance – so at least Joe managed to get blown by something that night!

The single was released and sales and downloads went well. After a lot of hard work, 'No Trend' entered The Official UK Charts at number 71.

For a while the band was a true MySpace phenomenon, unlike the record label spin that would state — Lily Allen was a MySpace sensation; when she already had a deal in place and a famous dad. Or how Sandi Thom supposedly recorded her number one single in her basement flat; which I know for a fact (as told to me by her producer) was actually done in a studio and that her label had pre-planned the whole thing.

This was a great result, which we knew would help the band get noticed within the industry. Then came my fatal error — I sat waiting for the phone to ring and guess what? — it never rang. The next week the single dropped away down the chart and we were back to square one having learned lesson number one in the music industry; never take anything for granted.

Next time we would have a much more cunning plan up our sleeves.

However, one good thing did happen though, the band got a small publishing deal with a £400 advance.

The publishing deal came from a little Essex based publisher called Impact Music owned by a very nice, tall, grey-haired man by the name of Paul, who would soon become known by the band as Boring-Paul; as they said it was almost impossible to engage in any kind of conversation with him, which I thought was a bit harsh as he was a rather nice chap and would always attend the band's gigs.

Still bang the drums and sound the trumpets and let the fanfare begin…. Whoop! Whoop!

I just made £40 commission. No, wait, bollocks!

Make that £20 as had I to split it fifty-fifty with Graham — the mansion would have to be put on hold.

Chapter 15

Don't Eat the Cucumber Sarnies

If you were to ask a classroom of eleven-year olds nowadays what they want to do when they left school, most of the answers would be very predictable. There would be a rush of boys wanting to be professional footballers like their heroes Lionel Messi, Cristiano Ronaldo and Wayne Rooney and the girls would dream of being famous movie stars like Jennifer Lawrence, Scarlet Johansson and Mila Kunis.

It is without a shadow of a doubt that some would say they want to be the lead singer in a band, guitar player or even be a drummer, though funny enough, not many would say bassist! They would gleefully express the desire to record songs, be heard on the radio, be high in the charts and sell out arenas filled with screaming fans.

However, it's very unlikely that any of the would-be pop or rock stars would get over excited and rub their hands together whilst declaring "I want to live in a cold, damp old post office van."

Yet, for the majority of unsigned bands starting out on the long and winding road to prospective success, the reality *is* actually that, to try and build a fan-base, you have to tour, and to tour you have to endure the arse-end of the music industry, where the cold can chill you to the bone and the smell can be somewhat pungent; unless you have lots money behind you of course! Which obviously we didn't.

I never once heard Ollie, Stu or Joe ever complain about all those hours spent on motorways in all those traffic jams – but then again I suppose they were always high and probably didn't even notice.

But me, I hated it, but I had to be there, or did I? Was I just kidding myself about my own importance or did I just need to be somewhere else, other than at home?

That old white van was the start of many adventures that we would have. The van was battered on each side had rust eating away at each wheel arch and had a side door that sounded like a prison cell door closing when it was slammed shut. It was an ex-post office or delivery parcel vehicle that had seen better days and, towards the end — bitter days. The band had customised the van somewhat, so that the equipment was loaded and unloaded via the rear doors, leaving the middle for them to chill on the way to and from a gig. They had even added a couple of seats ripped from an old coach and had put a little table in the middle.

Also installed was an extra battery and cables to allow them to charge their phones and plug in their plush, in-van entertainment system; a battered old television and a rather tatty looking and scratched DVD player that creaked like an old man's knees every time it opened and shut.

I did mention once that we could buy a heater to plug in, but that would've meant not being able to watch

'Bill & Ted's Latest Adventure', or 'The Office', on DVD so was met with much derision from Ollie and Joe.

KOOPA only needed ten things to make touring and playing shows happen:

1. Not to be sober.
2. Equipment.
3. Van.
4. Fuel
5. Drugs.
6. Alcohol. (Usually lager and cheap, white label brandy and vodka)
7. Comedy DVD's.
8. More alcohol. (More white label spirits)
9. The odd service station sandwich.
10. Some mug to pay for it all.

One of our first shows was at a pub that put on live music somewhere in Suffolk and was called 'The White…' something or other. That's not its actual name, it's just that I can't recall its full name. It could have been White Hart, Horse, House, Tom, Dick or Harry for all I cared.

It was another boring journey and it was bloody cold inside the van as the heating panel had busted beyond repair so we were wrapped up like Eskimo's inside. The sky was pitch black and we were driving along country lanes heading towards the venue. It was so cold inside you could see the breath in the air as you exhaled. Eventually though, the smoke from the bong and cigarettes actually seemed to warm the van up slightly, which I guess was a blessing, but then it meant I proceeded to cough my guts up; I was having a bad day.

We turned up late as usual to find that the poster listed Koopa as the headline band along with two supports — you do know I mean there would be two support bands, and that I'm not referencing a band called 'two supports'; although that would be a cool name for a band, but would also be utterly confusing for anyone reading the poster.

Another poster proudly stated that the venue existed to bring quality live music to the good people of Suffolk. But obviously there were no good people in Suffolk that night as the place was empty.

There was not a single soul, just the barman who had nothing better to do than polish the glasses and keep fucking telling us that we wouldn't get many in tonight because of the weather.

One of the supports had not turned up for some reason, so the time had come for the other support band to play and while the Koopa boy's rudely stayed in the van, I thought I would watch them along with their parents, who had shown up and were eagerly clapping along and singing to every word. The only other people in the venue were the barman and an elderly man who was sitting at the bar with his dog; a Jack Russell.

The support act finished and whilst the Koopa boys, set up their own equipment; a yellow and red drum kit accompanied by very badly painted yellow amps, I chatted to the supportive parents about how to do this and that in this very tough industry.

It was time for the Headliner to play and the crowd, which now consisted of the barman, the three band members from the one support act that actually showed up, their parents and one man and his dog, all clapped in anticipation, but it was blindingly obvious that the boys were looking a bit pissed off.

During the second or third song the support act had to leave so I escorted them out to car park to say goodbye and at the very same time the barman decided to go and change a barrel, whilst the man with the dog needed to relieve himself so scuttled off to the gents.

Leaving Ollie, Stu and Joe playing their top seventy-five chart single hit to a jack Russell tied up to the stool. Can you imagine?

To be fair, as I walked back in he seemed to be loving it and was wagging his tail.

I could feel Ollie's stare burning through my skull and I knew it was all going to get messy.

The band played one more song, which they dedicated to the dog and then scuttled about packing up the equipment and loading it back into the van. Everyone was strangely calm and eerily silent until Ollie, took the moment we were all sitting in the van, to unleash his wrath upon me "You fucking wanker!"

"Calm down," I replied.

"No, I won't fucking calm down!"

"Why do you book these shit gigs and make us look like pricks?" Joe asked.

"Do you think I would put you in that position on purpose," I shouted.

"Yes! You wanker!" Ollie snapped back.

"Of course I bloody wouldn't."

Ollie was breathing heavy and looked like he was about to burst into tears, for just a moment I thought 'Please go on punch me, give me a reason to kick the living-shit out of you, you little wanker.'

That's when Joe piped up, "It's your job to make sure we are not put it that position mate."

"It's a fucking music venue isn't it so how was I to know!" I replied with an angrier tone.

"Let's all calm down and get going," Stu added.

By now I had just about had enough of all of it. The constant moaning, the constant smoke-filled van, the constant smell of weed in the air, and the rolling of bottles every time we turned a corner. The three of them were difficult people to deal with and I finally snapped.

Without a thought I shouted "There is more to life than alcohol and drugs you know?"

"Is there?" Joe replied.

The van went deathly silent for a couple of seconds with everyone staring at one another, then we just burst out laughing. This is how the life with the band unfolded – one minute heated arguments, the next tears of laughter.

On the flip side, we got paid £50 for the gig, which was a right good result, but sadly the bar tab we ran up was £49.80 so we ended up with just 20p.

Oh well, I thought to myself, that's another 2p commission earned, the wife will be pleased!

The next gig would prove to be much more of an eye-opener. The band was booked to perform at a music night in a working men's club up north and even better, we were getting a fee.

The promoter was a nice chap, which was a bit of a rarity, as most are complete wankers and the bane of every band's very existence. They are supposed to be the person who actively works hard to promote the show. They distribute flyers, plug the show where they can and it's their job to get as many people as possible along to the gig, but more times than not they are the person who fails to communicate with you until the week before the show asking you... no telling you... no ordering you... to get the band to post on their social networks to promote the show.

I agree that the bands should inform their fans about their shows, of course they should, but it is ultimately the bands job to perform and the promoters job to promote. I would like a pound for every argument and punch-up I've had with promoter's who put up a poster in the venue, hand out a few flyers and then did fuck all else, but blamed the band for the poor turn out.

Sometimes the promoter doesn't even turn up to the show – but this guy was ok.

The venue was what we called 'up-north'. We were all big fans of the programme 'Phoenix Nights' and as we arrived at the club we got a sense that Brian Potter himself might come out to greet us. The outside looked like it was in dire need of a coat of paint and the inside had a smell of bleach probably coming from the toilets. The walls were stained yellow from cigarette smoke and covered in posters advertising all manner of things, including quiz night, monthly raffle, darts tournament, bingo, dominoes and the one that really got my attention was tonight 9pm.

"Strippers tonight lads!" I said, "Looks like you're getting naked!"

The first room we entered was small with a tiny stage in the corner.

"Bloody hell," I said, "You'll never get all the equipment on there!"

There was a double door with a sign 'Cabaret Suite'. Through those doors was a slightly larger room with a much bigger stage with another set of doors, which I guessed was the entrance to the room that was holding the live music night.

I introduced the guys to the promoter and the sound engineer and left them to set up and do their sound check.

One thing I admired about Koopa, which even applied when times were better, as well as when they started out, was the fact that they never felt the need for all the hangers-on or groupies that a lot of bands have these days.

Sure, one of their mates might come along and sell merchandise, but apart from that they would unload and load their own equipment and set up on stage themselves.

These days unsigned bands are too arrogant and have too many hangers-on, which means managers on net income deals are losing out on commission. While the mates of the band all get paid £50 cash to come and get pissed in return for carrying a bit of equipment to and from the van.

After the guys were all set up and happy, the promoter handed me the night's schedule, showing that we weren't on stage until 10.00pm, so I suggested we go and watch the strippers next door.

The club was full of old men in flat caps, with their whippets and kestrels – not really just old men.

The lights dimmed and the compere wearing a black

velvet jacket and bow tie took to the stage. Now there's a time and a place for everything, including telling dirty jokes and this was the time and the place; his jokes were so filthy I felt like I needed a shower afterwards.

He started gently with "What did Cinderella do when she got to the ball…?" pausing for comedic effect "She gagged on it!" causing the audience to laugh out loud and from then on it got filthier and filthier.

After twenty minutes of so he announced that It was time to see our first lovely lady; the crowd erupted into raptures of applause, wolf whistles and feet stamping.

"Please welcome to the stage the deliciously exotic Black Forest Doris."

The lights dimmed, the seductive music started and the stage curtain opened, revealing a tall slim black woman with a huge Afro, dressed in a leopard print bra, which could barely contain her ample attractions and matching leopard print knickers.

The crowd was cheering and whistling as she swayed to and fro across the small stage. Then suddenly the music stopped and she stood still for a moment cupping her hand across her breasts, she unclipped her bra and let it fall to the floor – the old men in the audience went wild.

Toto Coelo's 1982 hit 'I Eat Cannibals' ripped from the loud speakers and like a wild woman Black Forest Doris leapt from the stage to mingle with the audience with her breasts on show for all to see.

The old men were now in a complete state of frenzy as she sat on their laps and slapped anyone trying to cop a quick feel, she also put one old man's head between her huge breasts before squeezing them together — he loved it. We sat there laughing at the old dirty perverts.

When the song finished she returned to the stage and as the mood softened with mellow music, she reached for a brown suitcase on the left of the stage.

She's a ventriloquist as well? I thought. No, was the answer and it soon became clear why.

First she stood still and rubbed her hands over her breasts, she then ran her hands down to her knickers before sliding them off over her very high heeled shoes. Now it was as clear as the nose on your face why she had the nickname Black Forest Doris.

She was so hairy down there; that it looked like a nineteen seventies, Michael Jackson might be in hiding inside her with just the top of his head exposed. She lived up to her name.

As I'm actually easy to shock, so what came next hit me like a bolt from the blue. Black Forest Doris opened the suitcase and took out a long line of beads and proceeded to ... how do I put this... insert them inside herself, line after line, with very appreciative and frenzied applause from the crowd.

Then laying down, she put her legs in the air and proceeded to remove said line of beads until they were all back in the suitcase. After which, the even more disgustingly, she reached into the suitcase and pulled out a rather large cucumber and, yes, it went in the same place as the beads before she proceeded to push it in and out.

You could see that some of the old men were about to burst, have heart attacks and drop dead such was the excitement. It was more than I could bear so I went out to get some fresh air and was followed by the boys a few minutes later.

Shortly after, the promoter appeared and asked if we were ready.

There was a decent crowd and as always the band put on a top quality performance with everyone in good spirits even in the dressing room afterwards.

As we were sitting chatting with the promoter and enjoying a few beers he asked if we fancied a snack, obviously we weren't about to turn down free food, so off he went and returned moments later carrying a big plate of tasty looking sandwiches.

"Help yourself," he said.

"What flavour are they mate?" Stu enquired.

"Cheese and cucumber."

I turned and stared at the boys and all I could think of was where that cucumber might have been. Of course it was not the same one, but I for one was not taking any chances.

For a moment, Joes hand went towards the plate, but as I gave him the look of death his hand recoiled. Stu, however, reached for a sandwich and took a bite, while the rest of us looked on in total shock. Stu then proceeded to gag, then gagged some more before he pulled out what looked like a massive black pubic hair from his teeth.

I gagged a little, as I watched him gag and then stood silent for a few seconds.

"We need to be hitting the road," I said to the promoter, "we've got a long journey."

That entire journey back home was spent discussing Black Forest Doris, those cucumber sandwiches and what they tasted like. Stu didn't say a single word, however Joe insisted that he had shagged Black Forest Doris in the toilets —or how he described it — had put cream in her coffee (whatever the hell that meant).

Chapter 16

Someone Please Get Me Some Fruit

As the year progressed, I booked more and more gigs for the band and those round trip journeys in the battered white van seemed to get longer and longer. We had one great little venue in Cheshire that was a nine-hour round trip, but it always paid well, so the band was happy to do it.

I went everywhere with the band and, on most occasions, it meant leaving home around lunchtime and not getting back until the early hours the following morning. I was always tired, grumpy and miserable when I was at home, which was not really fair on Paula and the girls, but I was addicted to the thrill and the buzz.

The diet of a normal human being goes straight out of the window when you are on the road gigging and fast food outlets and dressing-room riders of lager, crisps and chocolate bars become your only source of nutrition.

If you're very lucky you may get some curled up sweaty sandwiches that resembled leftovers from the previous night. On many occasions we would sneak back in to steal the food and drink that had been left.

Forgetting to drink water regularly was a habit and that's bad.

The worst were the motorway services that offered limited choices like McDonalds or Burger King, both within our budget range and you could forget about the roast dinner for over a tenner. In fact, we used to wish for McDonalds, as it gave us the chance to use our loyalty cards containing the six stickers to redeem for a free coffee, tea or hot chocolate, which helped warm us up.

Along with the bad, high calorific food was the alcohol. I was easily pulled into the drinking culture of Koopa, as I liked a drink and the huge amounts of alcohol, coupled with the poor diet, caused me to gain over ten-stone in weight over the period of time I worked with all the different bands.

Sometimes I felt like crying out "Please get me some fucking fruit!" Just before I stuffed another quarter-pounder with cheese down my neck!

I feel sorry for myself when it comes to my weight and while I may have sorted the alcohol and pill problems, I still had a terrible time trying to lose it. I have just never had real determination; despite the support of the numerous slimming clubs I have joined. Perhaps having bared my heart and soul in this book I can finally focus. When my weight problem got the better of me and the stones started to pile I could sense that my wife Paula hated the fat horrible bastard I had become.

Then of course there are the health issues to consider and I always seemed to have a cold or a cough of some description. The strain of touring would take its toll on everyone and I still blame that fucking van for every disease I caught, it was always freezing cold and full of smoke. It stank of farts and sweat and was really noisy. It rattled as you went around corners, it rattled when you went straight, it was a total death trap and I'm not even sure it ever had an MOT or any kind of service.

Even though I'm moaning now, the whole time I've worked in the music industry, there's always been one thing I have totally refused to do — and that's go on a fully equipped tour bus. I fucking hate them – I would rather take that old white van over them any day.

Many musicians, entertainers, dance crews and bands travel in sleeper buses, commonly referred to as "tour buses." Imagine fifteen people sharing one of these for two weeks with everyone in one another's faces all day, every day. I would end up murdering someone if I had to do it.

Imagine the smell of sweat, microwaved food, sick, farts, empty beer bottles and the stench of the portable toilet, with the strong smell of Dettol trying to overpower the lot, after someone would decide every other day to have a little wipe around. Disgusting! No thanks!

Then you have to endure the large amounts of booze, all the partying, the arguments and the shagging that keeps you awake all night. There is always one bloke constantly shagging on board every night, leaving some poor woman to do the walk of shame, as he tells her she has to leave the bus as it is departing to its next destination.

Once in a while you will get some idiot who befriends the band and jumps on board for some beers in Glasgow only to wake up the following morning in Manchester having passed-out. And I've been on many of those badly routed tours, booked by so-called professionals, where they leave Glasgow, drive passed Manchester to Bournemouth, only the following day to return to Manchester!

In the Koopa days we just did the straight round trip and only on the odd occasion, if we were on an actual tour, would we try to get a room for the night. We therefore became proficient at finding the cheapest Travelodge, mostly positioned on the opposite side of the motorway or located in a noisy service station. We would then spend the night waking every 10 minutes because of said noise, so that by the morning; having felt liked we had slept on the floor instead of the actual pull-out beds, we would wake with our backs nicely cricked in pain ready to fucking kill one another to be the first in the shower.

Then to cap it all off, after ones refreshing shower one could pull back the curtains to open the window to the view of a massive truck filling up at the pumps, just in time to receive a good old fashion lung-full of emissions.

We once even had the pleasure of staying in a Travelodge that had dirty, stained sheets, bugs in the bathroom and some rancid food left in the bin, but we slept there anyway because we were so fucking knackered.

Staying in a fucking Premier Inn would have felt like we were sleeping in The Ritz.

Throughout the whole time that we were out on the road, we would constantly argue over the venues and about the band giving it their all regardless.

On one occasion I overhead Ollie screaming, "You should give one hundred percent, even if it's just a shithole in Liverpool like tonight!"

"Manchester," Joe replied.

"What?"

Joe then explained, "Tonight the shithole is in Manchester. The shithole in Liverpool is tomorrow night."

Shortly after arriving, Joe stormed off and in a very stroppy tone said, "This venue is a fucking shithole!"

"Yes, it is, but it's a packed shithole so shut up and get out there and play." I replied.

With no other source of income, the band seemed to be given pocket-money by their parents, which gave them the cash to fuel their drug habit. I doubt that's what they were given it for; as I can't imagine their mums saying, "Remember to grab some drugs on the way to the show darling."

There we were, club after club, dive after dive, shithole after shithole, all the while trying to build a fan-base around the United Kingdom and spending more and more time away and getting further and further from home.

There were lighter moments along the way, like the time I reversed the van over a fan's foot in Bristol, or the time when Joe was asked if he would ever fuck a fan? To which his reply was "It would be very foolish to stick your dick into an electrical appliance."

Most of the time, touring would be fine and we would have many exciting and comical moments, but sometimes you could find yourself in very dangerous situations that would only happen to a band on the road.

The first time I felt in danger was at a small club in Wigan. Just being in Wigan in the dark is dangerous enough, but imagine being in an inescapable position in the dark.

The band was playing their set of about seven songs, when a rather scary man with long hair and crazy looking eyes, jumped on stage and tried to start singing along to '500 Miles', the bands cover of The Proclaimers classic. He was very drunk and you could sense that this would not end well. I could see his mates egging him on from the front of the crowd and for a while Joe, seemed to be handling the situation with ease and was just letting him sing along. There was no security in sight.

I had the feeling things were going to get out of hand, and right on cue, Joe stuck out his hand and pushed the fella off the stage straight onto his mates at the front. This of course instantly caused a reaction and the air turned blue as he and his mate started giving the band abuse and gesturing for them to come down. I knew it was all about to kick-off and get nasty; Bollocks, I thought — here we go!

I'm not one for violence, but I'm always ready to step in when the situation calls for it. However, just as it appeared things would turn wild-west, two security men ran in and broke up the pending bar-room brawl. If it came down to the nitty gritty then I guess the boys in the band could probably handle themselves, but that's the last thing we needed right now. Having gone backstage we set about making a rapid exit, so as the guys packed up, I collected our fuel expenses and we all headed for the van.

As they packed the last piece of equipment away, I turned to the promoter and said my goodbyes then watched as he slammed the exit doors shut. We were in a dead-end alley at the rear of the venue that, apart from smelling of urine, was lit by a single bulb above the exit doors and suddenly I saw 'Crazy Eyes' and his mates heading down towards us.

Fuck, I thought – we are dead men and I started to prepare myself for the worse.

There were about five of them heading our way and one looked like a snarling rabid dog. I looked at the boys and we just nodded at one another, why we did that I have no idea, but in hindsight, it seemed like the cool thing to do.

I stood fast with my fists clenched as 'Crazy Eyes' stepped menacingly closer, so close I could smell the alcohol on his breath. Suddenly, without a word of warning, he reached out, slapped Joe on the back and said "Great fucking show chaps I'm sorry I fucked up your last song."

The band would over time encounter the odd moment of violence or attitude towards them and there would be times when people would throw things; bottles, ice cubes and even a fire extinguisher.

Ollie once suffered someone flicking a lit cigarette at him throughout an entire set, which he finally resolved by doing a special air jump manoeuvre, a twist, and then smashing the headstock of his guitar onto this chap's head, which seemed to deal with the situation, but left the chap seeking immediate medical attention.

Situations like this and worse would happen and

will always continue to happen to musicians on the road and it's probably happening to a band somewhere out there right now. It's a part of touring life and you have to expect it. Some situations are serious and some just hilarious.

There was a funny incident at a venue called The Hermit Club in Brentwood, the guys had left the stage to roars, whistles and bellows as the crowd of teenage girls and boys screamed for more.

"More, More, More!" they cried – but nothing, no sign of the guys coming back.

You could feel the crowd's disappointment and as their cries of "More" died down you could hear a banging coming from the dressing room at the back.

"What the hell is going on?" I said to the promoter.

"I've no idea., he replied.

The banging was now getting louder and louder. 'Thump, Thump, Thump' …

Then one of the staff shouted "Sorry I think I locked the band in the dressing room."

He rushed over unlocked the door and there they were, flustered, but ready for their encore.

Being in a band and being the manager of the band are strange occupations indeed, in fact there can't be any other jobs like it in the world, perhaps running off and joining the circus or a travelling fun fair would come close. Touring is bad for your health, bad for your relationships and most of all bad for your sanity.

But it's the one place you can be yourself — but beware — It's definitely not for the faint hearted or weak minded.

We had become a unit, albeit a dysfunctional, unstable and argumentative unit, but a solid unit all the same. In a strange way all those hours on the road had turned us into brothers, but not the cozy family who would share Sunday lunch with, no, think more Cane and Abel or Ronnie and Reggie Kray, so low and behold if you wanted to take the four of us on, you would be in for a war you could not win.

Being on the road touring, makes a band and its road to success not a particularly straight one. There are sharp bends called challenges, and junctions called confusion, speed bumps called enemies and red lights called failures. Your tyres — like your moods — will be deflated and inflated, but you will always have that spare called determination to drive you on to success. The problem was our vehicle, like our bodies and minds; was ready for the knacker's yard.

Being an underground-band meant that they attracted a certain type of fan who were not interested in mainstream bands. These were the fans that were deemed the loners, the misfits, the bullied, the weird and wonderful, as well as the overweight and the obese.

Combined, all these fans confirmed that Koopa had built up a loyal following of complete weirdos, but they were great supporters that would do anything to help their promotion. They were unlike any other fans I've ever met, which is a huge statement. There were not thousands of them, in fact you could count them on your fingers and toes and indeed they were all a bit odd, but they would just go that extra mile for my guys. Obviously we've had some fans that were just a little pesky and gave off slightly bad vibes, but we never had anybody that was utterly creepy or freaked us out too much. Most people end up being really cool.

The one thing to remember about your fans; never eat any homemade or unwrapped food items they give you. Joe was once given some home-made muffins, which we all thoroughly enjoyed, only to find out a few weeks later that the fan had put just a little too much love into making them – I thought they were very moist!

One Koopa fan gave Ollie a card where the fan had signed her name in pubic hair stuck with cellotape. They had another written in blood — I suppose all fans are harmless until one tries to kill you.

I hate being put in these kind of situations and to be honest, I prefer to avoid people as much as I can. When we turned up at gigs I would always do my best to plan how to avoid the fans, so I didn't have to talk to them. I just really fucking hate that thing they call small-talk. I would even sometimes do that old trick of pretending to take a call on my mobile if anyone approached me. I would politely put my hand up and whisper to them "Sorry I have to take this."

It works great until someone *actually* calls you, then you just have to accept the fact that you look like a right wanker.

Fans are a necessary evil though, and out of all the bands I have managed, I would say the last band before I semi-retired Room 94 have the most amazing fan-base of them all. These fans don't just go an extra mile, they go way beyond that and their loyalty and dedication to the cause is unlike anything I've ever seen – they would simply do anything– I actually believe they would kill for them, they are that obsessed. They travel thousands of miles a year just to watch them play and buy every piece of merchandise that goes on sale no matter what it is, and they buy their albums in every format in order to help the band achieve their goals. Some would say that the Room 94 fans are better than One Direction fans, even though they are outnumbered by about a million to one.

These kinds of fans are worth far more than their weight in gold – and back in the Koopa days, some of those overweight fans would have been worth a small fortune.

Chapter 17

Never Trust a Man in Flip Flops

It was a World Cup year, and a chance meeting in London would lead to Koopa being part of the England Squad's build-up to the tournament, and the nations anticipation of the up-and-coming World Cup in Germany.

While the band was busy in the studio recording some new tracks, I had set up some meetings with record labels and a public relations company, at Graham's request, to get their opinions of the band and an idea of what they could do for them promotion wise. Graham and I had decided that it would be great if we could get the band signed and cop a little signing-on bonus commission in the process.

I had previously emailed some labels, but as was usual never got any replies. This had become the norm with the majority of record labels, as they switched between not replying to you when you sent them a promo package containing a demo CD, to not reply to you when you emailed them with an mp3 attached.

I always reply to an email —so why can't industry types? The reply you get when you bump into some snotty faced, just out of university, A & R person is "We are always too busy, we get too many emails."

It's total BULLSHIT – The music industry is full of lazy fuckers.

For a label employee to take one minute to reply would be worth its weight in gold and would not lead to all the mistrust that artists, bands and managers have for record labels — courtesy costs absolutely nothing.

So with all that anger inside me towards labels, I headed off for a day of meetings in London. It was about April time and as usual it was raining. It seemed to rain every time I went on the train, was that just coincidence — yes of course it was how could it possibly be anything else.

The train was packed and seemed to stop at every bloody station between Chelmsford and London's Liverpool Street. The first thing I needed to do was visit the Pasty shop (it was a Gary Raymond tradition) and not a very healthy one to boot. Train to London equals large Cornish Pasty! Yummy.

I headed for the underground to my first meeting, I hate the underground; I always feel judged by those suited city workers for being overweight as I attempt to squeeze into the crowded carriage that would speed off causing everyone to wobble like they were having a seizure all the way to the next stop.

And please tell me — why is there always that one person who stands holding the overhead handrail with one hand who manages to sleep and snore until the exact time they reach their destination. How do they do that?

Then there's the inevitable fight for the one lone Metro newspaper lying on an empty seat opposite or on the back shelf behind you. You see a glimpse of a football headline and just as you lean over to grab it some city gent, in a pin-striped suit, snatches it and opens it on the latest and most exclusive property in London page.

I arrived at my destination and spent the next twenty minutes just trying to get out of the bloody station battling the jostling people with their rucksacks and pull-along baggage trying to race for the escalators, only then to be constantly buffered by someone running up the moving staircase, who is obviously late for something very important.

I eventually left the station, and headed to the given address, which was about a five-minute walk away. I was early – you should know this about me — I'm always early. I hate being late for meetings and I hate people who turn up late for meetings. It's never a good start.

I was actually very early by about thirty minutes, so I headed off to get a cup of tea from a small greasy-spoon café I'd spotted across the road; I sat down I checked my phone for texts.

No email in those days, people still carried laptops around to check emails and could only do that, if they could find somewhere with Wi-Fi, which usually meant McDonalds; being as they were one of the first to jump on the free Wi-Fi bandwagon. Good marketing for them, bad health for the lap toppers.

Is it me or was even 2006 in the technological Jurassic age?

I had a Nokia 3230 and it was my pride and joy. I could make phone calls, receive phone calls, send texts and receive texts. That's everything I needed. I checked my emails on my computer when I got home, I listened to music on my CD player and I watched movies and television shows on my television set.

There was no need to do anything else on your phone back then so one of its best features was the battery. It was like a long distance runner, it just kept going and going. I think it's still in a box in the loft and I wouldn't be surprised if I got it out and the thing would still have battery power and would burst into life and shout "I'm still here for you Gary!"

It was a true warrior and it had to be, as I dropped it almost every day, but it just jumped up, dusted itself off and was ready for action. Not like the iPhone, the first time I owned one I dropped it on the second day and, like a man with glass bones, it shattered right there before my eyes and I'll admit I burst into tears. The Nokia 3230 would have slapped me in the face and told me to stop being a girl and get on with it.

I sipped my tea I noticed out of the corner of my eye a chap sitting near me that I recognised, being near a major record label building, I wondered if he was in a band? or I'd met him before? Well I knew, I knew him from somewhere.

Then out of the blue it struck me, he was that guy off that programme about the Sunday league football team. I loved that show it was called 'Fash F.C' and was a weekly reality show/documentary that followed ex-professional footballer John Fashanu as he went back to the grass roots of football, managing a team of amateur players in a Sunday League.

"Hello mate, my names Gary, I've seen you on the footy show on TV," I said, "I love it mate," I continued.

"Cheers!" came his reply.

"My names Paul Baker, nice to meet you."

We sat for a while and chatted and he explained that he had a meeting with a record label; he wrote novelty songs and had written one for the England football team for the World Cup. Obviously never one to miss an opportunity he gave me a copy of the song on CD along with his business card.

He was a delight to chat to and really interestingly, aside from being a Chelsea fan, he had captained England's gay football team to World Cup victory a few years earlier, which made him only the second Englishmen to lift the World Cup after Bobby Moore had done so in 1966 – that's some achievement.

I explained my reason for being there and before long, time had caught up with us and I had to leave.

"See you again sometime," I added as I rushed out the door.

The meeting with this particular label was brief and boring and actually going nowhere, so I moved on to my next appointment with the promotion company. When I arrived a very attractive red headed secretary, wearing a tight sweater, showed me to the meeting room.

A man wearing a checkered shirt, jeans and flip-flops entered and reached out to shake my hand. This was a double alert situation as he was wearing flip-flops and had the dreaded limp handshake!

To cut a long story short, he told me that for around two grand a month on a three-month agreement, he could get us some plays on student-radio, interviews with online bloggers and all the usual bullshit that you can do yourself with a computer and an email account.

You see, the problem I seem to find with public relations companies is that for most part, they are useless tosspots. I can count the decent ones I have met on one hand and to be honest, that would be after I had cut at least two fingers off.

"Can you get the band's music Radio 1 or XFM?" I asked.

"I'm not sure the band's music is ready for national radio just yet," he replied.

Well, that was brutal, I thought.

He babbled on about online blogs and regional radio stations, but in my mind every time he opened his mouth, all I heard was; *"Give me your money, get out and let's see if we can get anyone to play your shit band's music,"* over and over again.

So I decided that this meeting was well and truly over. I said thank you, shook his limp wrist and left, all the time musing that his company would have taken our six thousand pounds as well as charging expenses, in return for a few plays on a student-radio station or some weird station like 'Shit FM' and we would need to get an awful lot of downloads to see any benefit – besides we didn't have that kind of money anyway, in fact we had fuck all.

I thought six grand would purchase a bucket load of flip-flops, as I checked-out the girl on reception and her tight sweater one last time on the way out. That had been a lucky escape and another massive lesson learnt. I realised that unless you have a huge budget, PR is an expensive way to try and gain exposure. I feel sorry for bands and artists trying to get noticed these days as all the PR companies and even most labels seem to be obsessed with the amount of followers you have on Twitter or how many likes you have on Facebook and yes, of course these matter, but trust me no band with 100,000k followers will sell that many singles or albums, and once all your teenage fans have spent all their hard earned cash on their smart phone contracts, alcohol and computer games, they'll have very little money left over for you and your music and they will just torrent your music off some illegal website.

All the way back home, I contemplated this new world I had chosen to step foot in.

I had quickly come to realise that the music industry had its fair share of wankers and it also had its fair share of people pretending to be in the business that were wankers, and that these wankers can be bigger wankers than the music industry wankers. It's one vicious, bloody cycle.

In fact, the music industry can get so nasty that It makes you feel that Satan and his minions are running the whole fucking thing, or maybe it's just a fact that it's such a damaged and sick industry, that it just brings out the devil in everyone that gets involved in its seedy, underhand, backstabbing ways.

I name no names, but you probably can guess who I'm talking about, and I'm sorry to say I might well have kissed their arses as I myself tried to progress in the industry.

When my journey reached its crashing crescendo; I felt like I had sold my soul to Lucifer himself.

Selling one's soul can be defined as allowing one's integrity, values and moral code to be defiled, in order to obtain riches and success. And there was a time I became so immersed in Koopa, that I would have given up everything to become a success and enjoys the spoils of fame within the music industry

I suppose I should make it very clear that not everyone is out to get you and there are some extraordinary people doing extraordinary things, but the industry has its fair share of dishonest, greedy people who are out to exploit your talent and your musical aspirations. There are con-men and scammers at every turn and I'm sure there may be some unsigned bands out there, that might want to tar me with some of the brushes that I now deplore them to stay away from, but I've been blagging my way along in the industry for the last ten years and while not everything I have done is of the highest morals, was it has allowed me to do is spot those who are just taking the piss.

To take my mind off all the bullshit I gave Paul Bakers CD a listen; I really liked it and it cheered me up after the horrible day I had had in London, meeting pretentious industry jerk-offs

The track was called 'Stand Up 4 England' and it was really catchy. I thought it would be a great song for the band, but I knew Paul wanted to get it released as 'Joe Public United', which basically meant Paul and his mates singing it.

I emailed him that night out of politeness to tell him that I'd loved the track, and I also mentioned my idea regarding Koopa releasing it under our label Mad Cow Records. To my surprise, he replied almost immediately saying that he was really interested.

He had obviously looked up the band and seen the potential from his side of the fence. Now all I had to do was convince my side of the fence; the boys and Graham.

Graham was easy after one phone call he loved the idea, so I then emailed the band a short message, along with the track and awaited. That was it for one day so I settled down to catch up on EastEnders, which I hadn't seen for a week; it was my favourite soap, in fact it was the only soap I watched. I always found Coronation Street to 'northern', Emmerdale too 'farmy' and Neighbours, well I just found that shit.

The following morning, I checked my emails for the bands reply, "Fucking hell!" I yelled to an empty house. "They are up for it!"

They had a couple things they wanted to change, but they loved the song, so I picked up the phone and called Paul Baker. I explained that everyone was on board and he was delighted. I arranged to meet him again along with Graham later that week in order to set a start plan, and told him that I would get the band to start on their version in the studio straight away.

Within a few weeks the band delivered the finished track and it sounded great. It was typical of all those novelty football songs; it was catchy and easy to sing-a-long to.

We decided to donate the profits to charity and decided that Barnardo's was a great and worthy cause. Now you would think that you can just crack-on and give them the profits at the end — but oh no — it's just not that easy. You have to have meetings and more meetings and then sign contracts before they will allow you to donate the profits; it's really tough to give to charity sometimes.

We also decided that a video would be a good idea and while Graham and Paul set about doing the deal with the charity, I started to think about the video and promotion.

World Cup fever was well on the way and I was ready to be a part of it. I was convinced that we could make our own video and our genius plan was to film the band performing 'Stand Up 4 England' with a local dance troupe. Joe used his contact at Colchester United to use the pitch for filming, which was fun and games and ended with me in goal trying to save potshots from the three boys.

The second wave of brilliant ideas came in the form of some postal workers, firemen, the local publican and the lollipop man. We filmed them singing along to the song throwing a ball from side to side, then along with careful editing it looked like they were passing the ball to one another.

The video was shaping up, but still it lacked a little something. We needed a famous-face to help promote it. The face that was staring back at me as I watched the local news on TV, was Essex cricket star Darren Gough. He'd be perfect, I thought. So after a fair bit of digging, I called the head of media at the Essex Cricket Club. He liked the idea and said he needed to first run it by Darren, but if he agreed, then he found no reason why not.

It was the very next morning, I received the call that confirmed Darren was on board so we headed off to Chelmsford, the club's home ground, and after a brief introduction we were out on the pitch ready to do some filming. Darren Gough was a good footballer and his keepy-up skills were second to none and, while the entire Essex cricket squad stood around egging him on and taking the piss out of him, Darren dazzled. That scene was soon in the can; as they say in the movie world.

The great experience with Darren Gough led me to think that we could get more stars involved. I pondered before shouting out loud to myself "Can we do it? Yes, we can!"

Sky hosted a football show called 'Dream Team', which was loved by the band, so I gave them a ring and after many rerouted calls, conversations and being put on hold, I finally got through to the production company. I explained everything regarding the football song, the charity Darren Gough's involvement, and the girl on the phone advised that there were a couple of guys that could help us out and we just needed to find a good meet-up location in London in the next few days. That not presenting a problem I told her I would call back and confirm the details.

I knew the perfect place, as I knew Paul the composer of the song had a swanky apartment in East London, which would be an ideal and within an hour I had it all sorted and, to nicely top it off, Paul had persuaded a couple of models to be there as well.

I always loved being back in the East End and this was no exception. The sun was shining and as we drove through Bethnal Green I could feel my childhood memories engulf me. I could almost smell the pie and mash and I could hear my Nan telling me off for eating her bread pudding.

We arrived at Paul's apartment; it was an open planned affair connected by an inner staircase. It was stunning and, as Paul showed us around, he described it as New York living — London style.

The additions of a pool table and grand old 1950's Wurlitzer Rockin jukebox sitting proudly in the corner, complemented his home. The jukebox was magnificent and two firework pilasters, that splashed red and blue across the speaker grill, lighted its front. It even played original 45rpm vinyl singles.

We were playing pool, drinking lager and listening to the old classics on the jukebox when the doorbell rang it was the 'Dream Team' guys. Everyone shook hands and I explained what we needed to do. Not long after, two stunning models arrived.

The afternoon was filled with fun and laughter and after filming finished, everyone enjoyed playing pool and consuming large amounts of lager and Jack Daniels. It turned out that one of the 'Dream Team' lads was none other than Rob Kazinski who would go on to much bigger things, including being in my favourite soap EastEnders, before he headed off to Hollywood to star in the vampire series 'True Blood' and blockbuster movie 'Pacific Rim'. He said he loved every minute of it and I'm sure he left with one of the models – I hope he looks back with pride at our 'World Cup video'.

We were definitely on a roll and having a good time,

perhaps too much of a good time, as I was now forsaking all husband and fatherly duties and had been drawn in lock, stock and barrel to the Koopa bandwagon. Little did I know then that the murmurings of discontent were gathering momentum on the homefront.

The following week, two telephone calls I was to make would up the ante. First, we contacted the chaps at Soccer Six, which was a charitable organisation that held six-a-side (hence the title) football tournaments in order to raise money for national and local charities.

Our main focus was trying to get the band to perform the World Cup single at their upcoming tournament at Upton Park, the home of West Ham United. And, after a lovely chat with one of the main guys involved called Mark, we were invited to be a part of the actual tournament itself.

I have a lot of time and huge respect for the guys that run Soccer Six, but over the years the calibre of stars playing would end up mainly being Internet-sensations and reality-stars — you know the kind of people I mean. It's a real shame that the big stars don't get behind such a worthy cause anymore, but I guess the more famous you are the more you are in demand or can't be bothered.

But everyone that attends helps to sell tickets and it's all for a very good cause —so long may it continue.

However, the crowds are always fantastic at these events so I tend to throw some of my acts at them for the day so they can show off their lack of football skills to the general public. It does really annoy me that they call these events Soccer Six, as football is our national sport and we invented it, so please use the correct terminology – but I suppose Football Six just doesn't sound right when you are advertising.

Pushing all the moaning aside, I quite like going as it has given me the odd opportunity to get a bit pally with the likes of Danny Dyer, Tamar Hussein and a few others from my love of football hooligan movies.

Chapter 18

Should We Audition for Britain's Got Talent?

There was to be a big charity football match at Reading Football Club's Madejski Stadium in aid of The Red Cross and The Bobby Moore Fund. The match was between England and Germany and would feature a host of legends from the football world, including the likes of Paul Gascoigne, John Barnes, Paul Merson and Chris Waddle as well as German 1990 World Cup winning captain Lothar Matthaus. There would also be a whole host of stars from television and film as well as many other top sportsmen. So of course I wanted to try and get the band to perform our football song there.

When I got in touch with the organisers I was pleased to discover that they had already heard about it! And that they also supported Barnardo's, so the band was invited to perform their World Cup song, live on the pitch at half time, with one added little bonus; the match was being aired live on Channel 5 — back of the net!

We were all excited at the beginning of the day, but that was nothing compared to the end of the night as we would have a whole host of international footballers, movie/television stars and even the future Lord Mayor of London, in our little music video.

We arrived early to receive our schedule and passes and all was well in our world; we had total access to dressing rooms, pitch, basically wherever we wanted.

We were given our own box to watch the match that included a free bar (a fatal mistake) and hot and cold food whenever we fancied some.

During the afternoon we wandered around taking it all in when we noticed Richard Ashcroft of The Verve and, after a brief chat persuaded him to film something for our video.

Right there was my light bulb moment "Let's make this our mission!"

"Mission?" Paul said.

"Yeah, let's try to get as many stars as possible to be in the video," I continued.

"How?" asked Graham.

"Well, we will just bloody ask them — they can only say no."

Paul piped back in and added, "That's a great plan, I'll help to get them all involved."

"We just need to be quick and not waste their time," I added

Everyone agreed and we went back to our private box for a drink to celebrate our master plan and raise a glass to the fact the band was going to be on the television. Although that didn't pan out quite as well as we had expected, as we hadn't factored in the advertising breaks.

It was match time and we took our seats for the forty-five minutes of football. Just before the interval Koopa prepared to perform and as the referee blew his whistle for half time the stage manager said, "Go!" and as the players trudged off the crew rolled the mini stage, housing the band's equipment, into the centre of the pitch. I was really excited and a wee bit nervous, so imagine how the band must off felt, but they could handle it and would indeed handle much bigger things in the months to come.

The announcer introduced them and they belted out (well mimed) their football song to the packed stadium and everyone seemed to love every second of it.

As they walked off to applause and cheers I patted them on the back and congratulated them on a job well done. I could see Paul was emotional, full of pride and the joy of hearing the song he had penned, actually performed and live! Paul, however would be another one who wouldn't be a fan of the boys for too much longer.

The second half started and we settled back down to have some more drinks and enjoy the match. The game was slow and boring, but was livened up when Boris Johnson came on as a substitute.

You could sense he looked bemused and ran around like a headless chicken for a while until he seized his opportunity and, to the bemusement of everyone in the stadium, the current higher education secretary and future Mayor of London, used his ample bulk to flatten one of the German players in a rugby style tackle that in hindsight was more of an assault.

The crowd erupted into cheers of joy and tears of laughter. I spat out a mouthful of lager over Ollie as

I gasped in shock at what I had just witnessed — he wasn't amused. Minutes later the game finished and Germany had reversed the 1966 World Cup final score line against England and won the match 4-2.

Now it was time for us to spring into action. We jumped up and headed for the player's tunnel, where for the next hour Paul and I would seduce the stars with charity chat and then quickly nip them into the medical room, where Joe had set up the camera ready to get them to sing-a-long to the song.

To our amazement everyone kept saying yes. First up we got Martin Offiah, the rugby league legend, swiftly followed by Danny Dyer and ex-Manchester United winger, Lee Sharpe, then our first real superstar of the day, the legend that is Paul Gascoigne. The man who called me Gazza when I first met him and said "See you later Gazza," to me on his way out after filming.

It was non-stop everyone was saying yes and we were on a roll and legend after legend spilled through those medical room doors. Then along came Boris Johnson and I was sure he would say no as I approached the one and only — Bojo.

"Boris do you have a moment, please?" I asked.

"Err, yes," he mumbled.

I explained everything and to my utmost delight he agreed to be filmed so I showed him into our makeshift studio and we very swiftly got the footage we needed. Once he had left the room we all fell about laughing at his bumbling mannerisms. We were nearly finished for the day when I had another super idea.

"Let's get one of the Germans to be in the video!" I declared.

"How's that going to work?" Stu asked.

"Let's get the band to sing 'Stand Up 4 England' and have the German refusing and remain seated."

"That's a great plan!" Joe shouted. "Gary, go get ze German," he commanded in a very bad German accent.

I headed off down the tunnel towards the German players' dressing room and knocked firmly on the door as I thought the Germans would appreciate an assertive and efficient approach.

As I entered I could see that only two German players remained; Lothar Matthaus and ex-Spurs favourite Steffen Freund. I explained our video idea and to his credit Lothar Matthaus immediately jumped up said "Count me in," followed by the order, "let's go!"

I was so chuffed I could barely contain my smile as we walked into the medical room, but I hung on in there with a business style attitude in front of the World Cup winning captain. The looks of disbelief on everyone's faces were fantastic, as I introduced them all to my new German best friend.

We filmed a very funny scene and then said our goodbyes to Lothar as he had to leave to attend the after-match party, which sadly, our passes did not cover.

As we were about to pack up ex-Spurs legend Chris Waddle came into sight, just one more I thought — but this was to be one step too far.

I rushed out towards him and explained what everyone had been filming and how well it had gone and without a thought he looked me in the eyes and said nice and calmly "Fuck off."

The world stopped for a few seconds before I gathered my thoughts and asked the question "Sorry Chris, what did you say?" to which he replied aggressively in his Geordie accent "I said fuck off."

I was totally shocked and took a step back. "No problem," I said, "but next time, perhaps just say no thank you?"

I could see his heckles were up and a punch in my direction was beginning to look likely. "Go away!" He shouted which alerted the door security man at the match-party entrance.

I turned and walked away, but couldn't resist turning back and waiting until he was just going through the door to shout "Thanks for costing us the World Cup in 1990 mate — I think that ball is still in fucking orbit!" before I ran off to find the others in the medical room.

"Chris Waddle just told me to fuck off!" I declared before explaining what had happened.

The gang were silently shocked, but then fell about laughing as we walked out, past all the autograph-hunters, to the battered old white van. On the way home to Essex Joe told me that the band had been smoking a few bongs in the back of the van with a famous footballer that afternoon.

"Who?" I asked.

"That would be telling and we ain't telling." They never did tell me and anyway I was far more preoccupied with my Chris Waddle incident.

It kept playing on my mind; that really was the worst penalty I have ever seen. Hold on, wait a minute... Hold the front page... Chris Waddle actually told me to fuck off. I tweeted him about this recently asking if he remembered the incident… he simply replied "Nope."

A few weeks later I was standing on another football pitch; this time it was West Ham United's ground in Upton Park.

Stu, Ollie and Joe were there to participate in the Soccer Six charity event. I remember it for four reasons, Joe being a half decent goalkeeper, Stu being a useless footballer whose gangly pale white legs reminded me Bambi. Ollie faking an injury so he didn't have to play and expose his lack of football skills, and the small matter of the torrential downpours that ruined the whole day and dampened the spirits of everyone involved.

Stu got to play for about 2 minutes in total, but still ended the day with a shiny winner's medal.

My biggest memory though of this event has actually nothing to do with the football, it was the moment I opened the van door to discover the former member of a massive manufactured pop group, sharing a joint and a few bongs with the band. Let's just say I doubt he was able to 'Reach for The Stars' that night.

The World Cup was almost upon us and the single was ready for release. The music video, filled with all those stars, with the exception of Chris Waddle, was getting shown on 'World Cup' specials on the music channels and Chris Moyles had even given the track a spin on his Radio 1 Breakfast Show, albeit about 30 seconds in a skit about the best football songs that had been released that year, but it was still there!

Paul Baker had kindly arranged for the band to be at the World Cup promo night in London and all the band kindly managed to do -was land him with a very expensive bar bill or around £300.

The band also had bookings for promoting the song at Butlin's Holiday Park the weekend before the first England match, and they fucking hated every minute of it. Ollie was being so obnoxious that even the other two had the hump with him all day.

But every piece of promo needed to be done to give us any chance of charting.

Paul Baker was himself running around London like a blue-arse fly getting anybody who was anybody to listen and help promote the song, good job he did because if he hadn't the single would've been dead in the water, cos the boys were doing fuck all.

Paul Baker business skills also managed to get 'Stand Up 4 England' on a compilation album, which was very exciting, as these types of compilation album always sold very well; right up until the moment England got knocked out of the tournament when, at that point they would be confined to the bargain bucket.

It was release date, for the single and it just missed out on the top seventy-five entering the charts two places lower at seventy-seven, which was a shame especially after all the hard work Paul had put in. Football songs just weren't selling this time around and the state of our national football team was undoubtedly not helping.

Golden-boy Wayne Rooney got himself sent off and David Beckham got injured in the quarter-final against Portugal, and after a dull 0-0 draw we once again got knocked out via a penalty shoot-out, courtesy of Frank Lampard, Steven Gerrard and Jamie Carragher all missing from the spot.

'Stand-Up-4-England' had run its course, although a few months later I received a call advising that we were entitled to claim a Gold Disc for the compilation album 'England the Album' as it had got to number one in the album charts and had also achieved sales of over 100,000 copies. As a surprise and to celebrate our involvement I commissioned Gold-Discs for the band, for Paul and of course one for myself.

Sadly, at this point the band discarded Graham as he was no longer willing to waste any more of his own money on them. Times were becoming harder and life with the boys, got more intense, so intense that it would cause me to take a sledgehammer to my Gold-Disc in a fit of rage.

The boys were back in their home-made studio finishing off some new tracks and things were ticking along, but we needed another angle to boost our press exposure and get some much needed industry attention.

I had heard through a friend about a new show starting on ITV called 'Britain's Got Talent' and considered for the briefest of moments of getting the band to apply – we were getting more desperate by the day and I would have clung to any crazy idea or any life-line that was dangled.

I suggested to the band that they should audition.

"Koopa don't do fucking auditions!" was the frosty reply from Ollie.

In hindsight, what the fuck was I thinking.

Years later I would discover a band called The

Loveable Rogues performing to nobody on a wet and windy Sunday afternoon, who would end up in the final of 'Britain's Got Talent' and were signed to Simon Cowell's Syco label before being dumped out in the street with the rubbish after only getting to number 9 in the singles chart — yes even a top 10 single is not good enough for some people — especially Simon Cowell and his disciples at Syco.

Now, despite the fact that the viewers assumed The Loveable Rogues went through a normal audition process to appear on the show – they most certainly did not!

We put them forward to the producers, by sending them a link to their YouTube video of them performing a very cheeky cover of the Scouting for Girls song 'Posh Girls' and straight away the program's producers were not just keen to have the band on the show – they were begging for them to be on the show. The band was not that keen, but the producers wanted them and went out of their way to make sure the band knew that — so in the end the band agreed.

So without any producer auditions, no meetings and just a few emails back and forth, they were put straight through to the live auditions. This is what the producers called a 'preferred contestant' and you knew from that point they would make the live shows.

These preferred contestants don't have to queue up with everyone else, they just turn up at the live audition and perform to Simon Cowell and the rest of the judging panel at a prearranged time-slot.

Surprise! Surprise! It is unbelievable that so many

viewers fall for this one-man's promotion for his own personal wealth and nothing else!

It's long been known that there is quite a degree of preferential treatment on these talent shows and every week that these shows run there will be another 'It's a fix' claim in the national papers and in fact The Loveable Rogues were making all the headlines after they themselves, let the controversial practice slip, when they were being interviewed about their success on the show.

It's amazing how gullible we can all be, especially when the time came and the first viewing of the band was seen on national television with cameras following them on their car journey to their so-called audition'.

You instantly knew that the band would get through given the amount of airtime they received and anyone with any sense would have worked this out straight away, as the video of them in the car was ridiculous.

The trip involved driving multiple times around a roundabout outside The Birds Nest Pub in Deptford, London, passing an Iceland at Trafalgar Road in Greenwich and finally parking in a Sainsbury's car park in Greenwich before we see them magically walking up to the Wales Millennium Centre in Cardiff – it's all smoke and mirrors.

It's official, 'Britain's Got Talent', 'The X Factor' and 'The Voice' get acts via management companies and doing research on YouTube. Let's get over that fact!

'Britain's Got Talent' take it one step further by allowing overseas acts to appear, some of whom have appeared on their own country version of the show.

Begging the question shouldn't the title be changed – it's called 'Britain's Got Talent' after all.

In the open auditions you have to be amazing or awful if you are to get through to audition for the judges. The audition process is most definitely not portrayed accurately and is an illusion, lots of acts are hand-picked to progress — if producers think they can make money out them.

It is not a fix or a scam to invite someone to audition, but perhaps the producers should be more honest and say what acts have been invited– perhaps have a section labelled 'hand-picked by the producers' and a section called the 'general public that turned up and stood around waiting all day' section.

I'm just kidding, but something needs to be changed.

Are these types of show fair? I fear not, yes the public vote, but the judges sway opinions with a carefully worded monologue. It seems your fate is chosen from the minute you audition. The ability to change the viewer's opinion is vital if you want to get the end result from telephone voting; the public need to be told whom to vote for and the judges who are skilled professionals can make this happen — with a well thought out whisper, comment or subtle tear.

It's the same for all reality shows, I have had other acts audition for 'BGT' and 'X-Factor' without meeting any judges, they just sang in front of a staff member in an office for about 30 seconds before their fate was decided. Sometimes it's all about luck and the right look, not talent – think Jedward!

These shows are telling you who to vote for and whom to make the next big superstars. For every superstar band or singer Simon Cowell and Co. claim are the next big thing, there are the losers; those artists that come out of the show and have a one-year career, playing to families at council town shows and doing shit personal appearances at nightclubs, and that's just the lucky few, as everyone else is simply dispensed back into normal life – it must be soul destroying when you're serving a burger or coffee and someone says "Aren't you that bloke of the X-Factor?"

And let's not forget that the companies behind these shows earn percentages from all the finalists.

Let's stop the freak shows that are 'X-Factor', 'Britain's Got Talent' and 'The Voice' where they wheel out the bewildered and the befuddled for our amusement, like some Victorian freak show, before introducing the real talent. Anyway, aren't these shows actually about people like Simon Cowell and the rest of the judges.

Finally, as a little side note — can we do-away with shows like 'Big Brother' before somebody murders someone live on air – or is that what we are waiting for?

Perhaps I will apply and be the first – just kidding!

***

Anyway, so there we were, the four of us desperate for some kind of break.

I was at Joe's when my next inspirational idea was conceived, as he watched that awful Challenge TV station, which aired a very old episode of 'Bullseye'. I still can't believe that a darts based quiz show was made in the 1980's! It looked like it was the late sixties or early seventies, and what about all those thick moustaches everyone seemed to sport – it was so fucking awful.

On this occasion darts legend Bobby George was on; the self-proclaimed 'King of Bling', the man who made his way to stage draped in jewellery, wearing a crown and cloak while holding a candelabra.

"He lives about five minutes away from here you know!" Joe mentioned.

Suddenly my head clicked into gear again, my ears popped and out came a suggestion "What about doing a dart themed CD?" I suggested.

"What?" Joe asked.

"You know a CD with a dart board on it," I continued.

Then came my moment of sheer genius, "We could call it…" I paused for dramatic effect and finished with… "three in a Bed with Bobby George."

Joe looked at me, laughed and then paused and said "Great idea!" before continuing, "would be even better if we get him to do some photos with us!"

Only one tiny problem stood in the way, how to get Bobby George to think it was a great idea too. I went home and looked up the darts legend online. I found out that his wife was also his manager, so I thought what harm could it do to ask? An hour when by when we received a swift and to the point answer, 'Yes, great idea, come around Monday to take some photos.'

We asked and we got! With all details exchanged, we were set to go.

That same Monday I met up with the boys at Joe's house and listened to their new recordings, which included the very song that would go on to become Koopa's download-only, history making single.

I remember complimenting them on the quality of their new recordings before we set off up the road and arrived outside Bobby George's self-built seventeen-bedroomed mansion.

As we entered we were greeted by his lovely wife and manager Marie. Their place was impressive with the grand staircase, dark wooden banister and beautiful expensive looking patterned carpet. We were shown to Bobby's pub; an actual pub built inside the house complete with full size snooker table and of course dartboard. It reminded me of the good old pubs I grew up in back in East London.

Bobby entered, larger than life and completely 'blinged' to the max, we all shook hands, he sat in his 'Game of Thrones' style throne.

It was a pleasant afternoon we chatted, had a few drinks followed by a couple of games of snooker and then Ollie foolishly challenged him to a game of darts — Bobby absolutely smashed him.

After a little while and with plenty of lager inside me, I politely asked if we could do the photo-shoot for the cover. I explained the idea of Bobby sitting in a bed with the band, which would be a good spin on the title of the CD when it was released.

"Three in a Bed with Bobby George!" Bobby said out loud, "I like that young man!" he continued.

"Follow me," he commanded — so we did.

We followed him upstairs and into a bedroom, it was like stepping into a palace; ornate decorations adorned the walls and the furniture was very grand. Bobby climbed into bed (fully clothed of course) and beckoned the boys to do likewise. You could tell he was a pro at this PR stuff, as he lay there quite comfortably waiting for the boys to climb in and stop sniggering. We got some great shots and with the job done, we took up the invitation of a few more beers before heading off back down the road. He is a proper gentleman that Bobby George.

We finally had our cover and CD theme. It was a non-chart eligible CD and featured the tracks 'Erin's Main Obsession', 'Pop Rock Factory', 'How True' and 'Unique' as well as 'Blag, Steal and Borrow.'

I needed to get the band back out on the road, but they were all skint and thanks to them, there was no more Graham to pay the fuel costs. I had covered the cost of producing the 'Three in a Bed' with Bobby George CD's, which was added to the growing pile of receipts the band had built up and would be paid back to me when they started to generate an income.

It was getting harder than ever to get promoters to put their hands in their pockets and stump up some fuel costs or, God forbid, a performance fee. I agreed to subsidise the guys a bit more and withdrew some money from my lifesavings and ordered some t-shirts to be made with the band's logo on. They were pretty cool; yellow with a huge red logo in the centre. We would sell them at shows and use the profits to cover fuel costs.

I eventually hooked up some gigs at the usual local haunts like The Hermit in Brentwood, the YMCA in Chelmsford and of course The Twist in Colchester and one of their mates called Chris sold the merchandise and CD's, which helped keep things afloat.

But these were tough times and they were compounded by the bleakness of the cold and dark winter nights we had to endure on our travels around the country at that time of year.

The van was in dire need of repair and would constantly break down, causing us to sit huddled in the back freezing cold waiting for one of the parents to come and help or, on the odd occasion for the tow truck to take us back to Essex.

Strangely, throughout these darker times the band always seemed to have a supply of drugs and alcohol that was making me a little paranoid and I felt as though I was being conned out of my life savings.

"Are they taking the piss out of me?" I would ask my wife Paula.

"Yes of course they are!"

I would have this same conversation with myself in the mirror every morning. In the end, I found out the answer when their mate Chris asked, "Gary, do you lend the band money for smokes and beer?"

"No mate," I replied.

"Oh," he muttered, "must just be me then."

"Don't be a fucking mug, and don't lend them anymore!" I told him which led to the band not talking to me for a few days after he ran off and told them what I had said.

It was when money was at its hardest to come by, that a certain incident took place in a pub in Camden, which could have ended with us all getting a good kicking-in from the bouncers. Joe, in his weed and booze, fueled state, walked up to the bar and ordered a double brandy and a pint of lager. When the barmaid bought the drinks and the bill over to his table, he downed the double brandy, followed swiftly by the pint and then came out with the oldest line in the book.

"I shouldn't be drinking that with what I've got," he said to her.

"Oh, you poor thing, why what have you got?" she replied sympathetically.

"£1.50," came his reply.

She called the doormen who enthusiastically grabbed Joe by the throat with the sole intent of throwing him out and was saved only by the promotor rushing over and paying the bill.

"You fucking idiot!" I shouted.

He just laughed and fell over.

Chapter 19

I'm Taking the Wife Dogging

As the cold weather of December approached, we had a gig in Romford in Essex at a venue called The Bitter End. It was a typical pub decorated with the usual dark wooden panelling with very worn furnishings and always seemed to have a musty smell in the air due to the mold on the walls and ceilings.

The venue, however had a great reputation for live music, they always paid the band a fee and gave them sandwiches, crisps, beers and best of all served up a rather smashing pint of cold Fosters lager.

I was with the promoter and the three boys as we walked to the dressing room for the evening when Joe, lagging behind, started playing about with his left foot in a strange manner causing him to stagger about and breathe heavier as he struggled with whatever he was trying to do.

"Is he unwell mate?" The promoter asked.

"That's just one of the euphemisms we use for him these days," I quipped as we all burst out laughing.

"I just had a stone in my shoe you wankers," Joe explained.

Before the band took to the stage I couldn't help

but notice the young ginger-lad who was part of the support act and was not that good. He was also very young, somewhere between thirteen and sixteen.

"You should sign him!" Stu joked.

"You three are more than enough for me, thanks very much," I replied.

Well, I'm guessing you are way ahead of me here… when I tell you that young ginger teenager was none other than Ed Sheeran. The ginger-topped singer/songwriter who would go on to be a bloody worldwide superstar and make some lucky manager millions of fucking pounds. I also remember, much to my embarrassment, someone who may or may not have been his dad or uncle asking me what I thought of him and replying that I thought his voice was a little bit squeaky.

I remember the night, ending in yet another band argument, which by now were starting to become more frequent and more intense. This one started after a very drunk Joe accused the brothers of trying to kick him out of the band in one of his ever increasing paranoid moments.

I told Ollie and Stu to fuck off and that I would see them in the van and then proceeded to calm Joe down by telling him to shut up and sit down.

We had a long conversation that night about our situation; how tough things were getting, how the strain of it all was putting us in bad moods and how it was making us all fucking unhappy. After our chat we joined the other two in the van, Joe shook hands with his band mates then all together we sat there and discussed our current predicament.

Our situation was now best described as desperate;

despite buying cheap fuel from supermarket service stations, eating rubbish low cost food, sleeping in the van or cheap hotels, we still seem to be spending a ton of money. It now also started to take its toll on their parents, who were lending them money and who were now starting to question what their sons were actually doing – and that's without all the money I had started to haemorrhage.

And if that wasn't enough, our health was starting to suffer as everyone was feeling ill and we were always catching colds, suffering from sore throats and coming out in rashes and spots.

Our constant drinking didn't help our fate either, as most of the time we drank to make ourselves feel better and to mask the fatigue from all the travelling. Sometimes I even had a drink first thing in the morning to help cure the hangovers, which only really resulted in even worse hangovers. I think at one point I was even drinking to stop myself from throwing up from too much drinking, which is fucking mental thinking back on it now.

We were all in a bad place.

The fun times were becoming fewer and shit times were becoming greater, but all of it would become non-existent if we couldn't find a solution to the financial situation fast. I was starting to believe that I was going to be a failure yet again. I knew that everyone was on the precipice of calling it a day and jacking it all in.

God forbid if my wife ever checked our savings account that I'd been freely dipping into; I'd be finished and she would have left me there and then. The lies and deceit were getting to me, I was ruining my children's future and now I was starting to feel guilt; this is when the pills started to help me get by and boy did they help.

A strange telephone conversation with a hospital radio DJ the following morning though, would change everything forever — history was about to come calling.

That morning, I was at home drinking a cup of tea when I got a phone call from Stuart, a contact of mine who worked at an obscure hospital radio station called Radio Horton, which was situated within Horton General Hospital in Banbury, Oxfordshire. Stuart was a lovely chap, a part time DJ on the station and he had called for a little catch up, which he was prone to do once or twice a month.

After exchanging pleasantries and chatting about the state of the music industry for an hour, he happened to mention the up-and-coming changes within the UK charts.

I listened with much intrigue, as he explained that, as of the 8th January 2007, the introduction of the new chart rules would mean that all songs purchased online will count towards chart positions, whether or not a 'physical' CD version of a song is available to purchase, thus making it possible for bands without the budget to produce CD's, giving the band an opportunity to get their music in the charts.

So as soon as our conversation was over my mind started to race, my head began to throb with ideas and all around me was still, 'We could chart a bloody single!'

I did some research and saw that The Official Charts

Company had issued a statement a few weeks before, but I'd read nothing in the music press, heard nothing on the radio and most definitely, until my conversation with Stuart, had not heard anyone talking about this rule change.

I also discovered that downloads didn't have to be *redeemed*, which made me think we could get our families to all buy a single and not have to worry about downloading it.

This was scratching at me, creeping up from the back of mind, I could almost feel the plan forming in my brain and my head was aching from the constant thinking.

Then it happened — do you remember like I do, the visual sound effects on the 1960's TV version of Batman starring Adam West? Remember how that every time someone got punched or kicked during a fight scene, a giant graphic was sure to follow?

Well, that's what it was like ... 'KAPOW!' It hit me!

Texts!

Yes, Texts!

Texts! Texts! Texts!

Going over and over in my mind…. What if we set up a short-code that people could text to order the single direct from their phone, and funny enough, I had only received such an email a few days before from a company asking if we would be interested in such a service.

I frantically scrawled back through all my emails. No, I don't want 20% discount at Pizza Hut — no, I don't want to listen to your band — no, I don't want the prince of somewhere or the other to deposit

$10,000,000 into my bank account — then finally I found it and it read it through *'Ditto music introduce the text short code... blah, blah, blah!'*

Wait a God damn minute – 20% discount at Pizza Hut!!

I picked up the phone and after a few minutes of clarification with a very nice chap by the name of Matt, I hatched a plan. We would self-release a single with no physical CD the first week of January 2007. Matt also informed me that sales were really poor the first week of January so if we could sell over 3,000 we could perhaps have a song in the Top 40 – how good would that be I thought.

We would have a pre-order text short-code and we could get everyone at our up and coming shows, as well as family members and friends to text for the single and because the song would be on pre-order, it would give us enough time to build up as many sales as possible before the actual release date – genius! Then, they could also buy the download online the week of release – sorted!

I called the band "I have some news... I'm coming over..."

I suddenly realised that I had spent the entire morning chatting to everyone stark naked, so I showered, got dressed and then headed off to see the band.

When I arrived, they were sitting doing what they did best, sucking on their bong pipe.

"Sit down," I said

"We are sat down," Joe replied.

"Oh yeah, sorry."

I proceeded to tell them about the new chart rules

and about the text-code and then explained that if we knuckled down and worked hard we could get another Top 75 single.

"We need to do better, we need a fucking Top 40!" Ollie stated.

"We can do that, but we need to get everyone to text for the single now to build up pre-orders and then, for them to all buy the download the week of release."

I then did my rallying speech, "Come on, let's do it guys! We have nothing to lose," I declared, "if we carry on like this the band will be finished by the end of the year anyway, so let's at least go out trying and not with a fucking whimper."

"Which song?" Stu asked.

"No brainer chaps, Blag, Steal and Borrow," I suggested.

"And remember those crazy Dutch people we met at the last gig?" Joe added.

"Yes, they were fucking mental mate."

"Well, they told us they would shoot us a video for nothing."

"They were fucking crazy though," Stu said.

"The one with big tits wasn't, she was hot," Joe added.

No matter how serious the conversation, we would always end up mentioning tits. I think we might have all been just a little bit over-obsessed with them.

We chatted some more and everyone agreed on 'Blag, Steal and Borrow' so I rushed home and immediately registered the track with Matt at Ditto, who would act as aggregators, and which basically meant the single would be available on the likes of iTunes on the day of release.

Matt gave me the text short-code, he had pre-empted my decision and had already ordered it. I remember that it was all very simple, all you had to do was text the word 'KOOPA' to '81330' and there you have it — that's one single sold, no need to log on and redeem the download to listen unless you really wanted to.

He told me that each text cost £1.50 and as the current rules stood you could text for the same single a maximum of three times and that we would get back just under £1 per track sold.

And even better I could log into the system and keep an eye on sales, so soon as I knew everything was registered, I text to make the very first purchase and within seconds came the reply Beep! Beep!

I clicked the message button and there it was, it read, *"Thank you for buying Blag, Steal and Borrow."* I logged into the system and there it was — sale number one. Just another 2999 and we have a Top 40 single.

I repeated the process to complete my three maximum allowed purchases and after logging back into the account I could see we had three confirmed sales on the scoreboard. I informed the boys and for the rest of the day they got busy with family and friends helping to build up pre-orders.

By the end of day one — we had over one hundred on the scoreboard.

Now those crazy Dutch people that said they would shoot a video really were fucking mental. We had met them at a gig at The Dublin Castle in Camden, which is a trendy part of London and a sea of cultural entertainment.

It overflows with a variety of colourful markets,

shops, restaurants, bars, pubs, clubs, music venues and, most of all, oddball people and on this night — all the oddballs were of the Dutch kind.

The Dublin Castle is a music venue I had visited many times in my teens, to watch bands such as Madness. Koopa was performing at the venue and got chatting to the Dutch after the show, where it turned out they owned a video production company and, after much drinking and smoking of pot with the boys, they said they would shoot them a video for nothing — well for just a few beers.

However, the evening had turned a bit ugly when one of the Dutch girls slapped Joe for touching her arse and one of the Dutch guys got so pissed he fell into Camden Lock and had to be rescued by a passer-by who was walking his dog, which ended up running away.

I don't know if he found his dog, but he did save a Dutchman.

However, it also turned out that the girl Joe had been slapped by earlier, ended up giving him a blowie in an alleyway, and I had been given some lovely pill that made me very happy indeed – so a good night had been had by all in the end.

I called Monika, who was a lovely Dutch woman I'd been trying to chat up that night, to confirm that they did indeed agree to shoot a video for free, so I arranged for them to come to the studio the following evening.

The Dutch guys came along with a pre-organised shoot idea; the band would re-create a practice session, and they would walk around filming, and after a few spliffs, bongs and a whole bottle of Jack Daniels, filming commenced.

With the shoot wrapped and everyone relaxed and in a happy state Ollie asked if they could teach him some swear words in Dutch; by the end of the night we had learnt neuken and kut, which we were sure would come in very handy one day! They also taught us the sentence 'Ga neuken zelf je stomme kut', which did come in useful a few times whilst touring in Holland some time later.

We even persuaded all the Dutch to text for our single that night. Monika advised that they would add some special effects and within a week the finished video was delivered and it looked fucking great.

From then on everyone we met, no matter who, or where, we encouraged to text for our single. I will admit that I even text on other people's mobiles without their permission or when they weren't looking, and Joe got his doctor to text whilst having a check-up for a certain little infection (enough said) – the pre-orders were starting to rack up.

It was December and we now had about one thousand pre-orders on the board, but we needed loads more. It was around this time that Ollie and Stu's dad Martin, who happens to be one of the nicest people I have ever met, and who was determined to see his sons do well, invested some money into the band so they could update their equipment and finally get the van serviced. There was a little spare left over to help with the promotion of the single, so I set about looking at the best ways it could be used.

That's when I had a chance meeting again with

Doggy-Dave a relation of my mate Little-Willy, Now Dave was the kind of chap who would sell his granny for a profit and always had some knocked-off designer clothes and perfumes for sale. I didn't trust him, but needs must.

He looked just like one of those blokes that wanted to give you advice when you're playing a fruit machine! You know the type I mean – everyone knows a Dodgy-Dave!

He would randomly burst into Del Boy quotes or say rubbish like "Stereo speakers, buy one get one free," – he was really fucking annoying and that's why I used to try and avoid him at all costs.

We were in the pub chatting about life in general and after I refused to purchase a knocked-off watch he was trying to sell, I got Dave and Willy to text for the single. Dave was fidgeting about and obviously itching to say something.

"What is it Dave?" I asked.

"I know a bloke called Wheeler-Dealer-Don, who told me yesterday that he knew a bloke who was a proper tea-leaf called Crusty-Chris, who was selling mobile SIM cards with £5 credit on for a pound each!" That's fucking ridiculous I thought, I must be in the middle of some comedy sketch, Dodgy-Dave telling me about Wheeler-Dealer-Don and Crusty-Chris, that's fucking ridiculous.

So I had to ask, "Why is he called Crusty-Chris?"

"Well, apparently he has a right shitty attitude, and when he was a nipper he had really bad acne — so now his face looks a loaf of tiger bread."

"Thanks Dave, I feel sick now."

"Can you get me the SIM cards?" I asked already thinking what we could do with them.

"No problem, how many do you want?"

"All of them!"

Later that night Dodgy-Dave called to say that Wheeler-Dealer-Don had confirmed that Crusty-Chris had 500 SIMS with £5 credit on, he wanted a monkey for them and that if I wanted, he could drop them off to me in a couple of days.

Now for those of you who just don't get the lingo and are wondering why would Crusty-Chris have any need for a monkey and where in the hell was I going to get one — let me clear this up.

Monkey is a Cockney term for £500 hard cash and not some tree dwelling cute jungle creature.

I woke up the next day all bright and early and I was buzzing with excitement, I wanted to tell the boys about the SIM cards, but it was only 9.00am in the morning and they didn't get out of bed till at least mid-day, so I sat there waiting and waiting and waiting.

Surprisingly, around eleven am Stu called and said they were heading for the studio that afternoon, so I arranged to meet them there, as I could wait a little longer. To kill the time, I sat and watched one of my DVD box sets 'Highway to Heaven' that never failed to make me cry.

I watched as the poor dying homeless man had been reunited with his family just prior to passing away, by the angel Jonathan and I blubbered all the way through. After blowing my nose and wiping my tears away, I set off for the studio still all excited to tell the boys my wonderful plan.

When I arrived the guys were busy pushing all the sliders on the mixing desk up and down. I sat them down and over a cup of tea for me and lagers for all three of them, they listened intently as I lay down the plan.

"The way I see it; it would be giving us a boost," I said.

"Sounds like a plan," Joe replied, "What do you two think chaps?" he added as he turned to look at Stu and Ollie.

"It's only a monkey, we could spunk that on some shit PR company and get nothing in return!" I exclaimed.

"This way we get one thousand, five hundred extra downloads and maybe get in the top fifty this time round," I continued.

"Fuck it!" cried Ollie, "let's do it, it's what a punk band would do!" he added.

"No different to a record label sending out buying-teams to buy up all the albums on the week of release!" I said, before adding, "that still goes on today you know. I know a couple of people employed by two of the biggest labels in the UK that have set up teams to go around purchasing albums for new artists the week of release."

"If it's fucking good enough for them, it's fucking good enough for us," Ollie added.

And there you have it, four guys with a plan to help enhance a small release from an unknown band who were totally unaware that we were about to send a shiver down the spine of the music industry.

Two nights later I'm in a creepy dark car park just

outside Chelmsford waiting for Dodgy-Dave and Crusty-Chris to arrive, with my engine running and my doors locked, sitting on a paper bag containing a monkey eating the packet of 'Percy Pigs' I had just purchased at the petrol station.

Moments later a car approached and pulled up alongside me, I recognised Dodgy-Dave in the passenger seat and presumed that the man driving must be Crusty-Chris. There was also a woman sitting in the back hidden by the darkness.

Dodgy-Dave jumped out of the car and tapped on the driver's side window.

"Hello mate," he said.

"Hello Dave."

Meantime the other man and the woman had gotten out of the car and were walking over, so I turned off the engine and got out.

"This is Chris," Dodgy-Dave said as he introduced us, "and this is his wife Maureen," he continued.

I said hello to both and shook their hands. Maureen was a very large woman with lots of curly blonde hair and looked like she had dressed up for the occasion, she was in full make-up complete with bright red lipstick; obviously out on the town later I thought.

Crusty-Chris was dressed in an eighties-style shiny track suit bottoms and a black Slazenger zip-up top, all finished off with shiny plastic looking trainers. It was true what Dave had told us; his face was not in the best condition, but he seemed like a nice chap and after a brief chat we got down to business.

"There you go mate," he said as he handed me a bag of SIM cards.

"Cheers," I replied and took them from him.

"I suppose you don't mind me testing a couple?" I asked.

"Not at all fella."

Thinking ahead, I had bought with me an old fully charged SIM-free mobile and selected one SIM at random, then turned the phone over, removed the back, removed the battery, inserted the SIM, put the battery and casing back and turned on the phone. I text 'KOOPA' to '81330' and bingo, within a few seconds I got the *"Thank you for buying Blag, Steal and Borrow"* reply.

I repeated the process two more times to make sure there was a full £5 credit on the sim and indeed there was. I asked if I could check a couple more and Crusty-Chris nodded. About ten minutes later and with nine confirmed sales I handed over my monkey for him to count and he said "Cheers."

"What you up to tonight?" I asked him.

"Oh, I'm taking the wife dogging."

I had absolutely no idea what he meant so stupidly I replied, "What taking the dog out for a walk in the dark!" or something along those stupid lines.

Crusty-Chris laughed and Dodgy-Dave covered his face in embarrassment and Maureen looked at me with total disbelief on her face while Chris explained what dogging was all about.

"No, you twat," he said, sniggering, "it's a car park me and the missus go, to have sex and watch other people having sex," he explained

In utter amazement, I said "What, you have sex in a car park — what the fuck is that about mate."

Dodgy-Dave was pissing himself laughing and Maureen just stood there in silence.

"It's fun mate, it's naughty, risky and we fucking love it!" Crusty-Chris continued.

"It's a national hobby," he declared, "you should try it, you can come with us if you like," he went on.

"I'm sure the missus would enjoy you!" he added.

I could see Maureen had a glint in her eye.

"I've things to do mate, but thanks for the invite," I replied sheepishly

I shook hands with Crusty-Chris and Maureen and said "Goodbye."

I told Dave I would call him later and as he got in the car with them I jokingly asked him "Dave! are you off for a bit of dogging too?"

"Yes mate," he replied "just off to pick up the wife on the way."

I'm still not sure to this day if he was joking or not.

Chapter 20

The Blag Is On

Everyone was in high spirits and the pre-orders were building nicely, so we arranged a little get-together to celebrate Christmas and in true traditional Koopa style — it ended with an argument over yet again something trivial.

I went home that night to spend Christmas with my wife Paula and daughters oblivious to the person I was becoming. I was sinking back into an abyss of alcohol abuse, over eating, poor health, and again I was heading to that dark place I had luckily escaped from years previous. The only difference this time round was the addition of the large amounts of painkillers I was knocking back to help make me feel better.

I should have stopped right there and then, if I could've only seen the woods for the trees, but nobody said anything so I guess I just carried on. Sometimes I was so fuzzy headed that I would just walk around in a daze to the point that people would move away from me in fear that I was a real life zombie!

I spent most of my spare time over the Christmas holidays inserting and removing almost five hundred bloody SIM cards into my old SIM free mobile and texting 'KOOPA' to '81330'.

I was so self-obsessed that I almost forgot to make sure that the carrot and milk the girls had laid out for Santa had been eaten and drank – by Santa of course!

Quite a few of the SIM cards actually turned out to be blanks, but as the new year dawned the pre-orders were building nicely reaching the two thousand mark.

It was now looking highly likely that the band would get a 'Top 50 hit' at this rate, so I was very happy. I had never heard of the midweek charts so we were sitting there blissfully unaware that history, and a wave of media attention, was about to hit us like a ton of bricks.

It was January the 8th 2007 and something very bizarre was about to transpire that would create a worldwide media buzz around the band, and make us wonder if we had gone too far.

The 'single' had been released and we were all working our nuts off with the promotion. Joe was hitting up everyone on MySpace and I was emailing and phoning around asking people to download or text.

The music video was going down well on the music channels with one channel choosing it as their video of the week and another as their hot-pick of the week.

The day passed and I emailed everyone to congratulate them on a job well done and that the sales had crept up just a little so by my reckoning, and based on the previous week's sales supplied by Matt at Ditto, we could be around the mid-fifties by the end of the week and might even scrap into the bottom of the forties.

But an explosion came the following afternoon.

I was up early to check sales, not much had happened overnight so I settled down to catch up on EastEnders. Around 10.30am my phone rang, it was Matt from Ditto and he sounded ecstatic– in fact, he was so hyper he could barely communicate.

He was breathing intermittently. "Have you seen the mid weeks?" he asked.

"I've no bloody idea what you are talking about mate."

"The mid-bloody week chart, it comes out today!"

"No mate, I still haven't got a clue what you're talking about."

Matt then went on to explain, in precise detail, that the midweek chart is basically information that is exclusively prepared for the music industry so that labels and publishers can track their sales and chart positions during that week.

He went on to further explain that it's under an embargo notice and only available to music industry subscribers, it's released on Tuesday morning's and every consecutive morning until the Friday and that he was, as he put it, "Fucking staring at it, in total disbelief."

"What are you looking at Matt?"

"I'm looking the band's single sitting at number 16 in the official midweek chart."

Stunned, I took a deep breath and replied, "What did you just say?"

"It's bloody 16 in the midweeks, congratulations mate!"

"Fucking hell!" I shouted down the phone.

"I need to tell the band; I'll call you later mate. Bye, oh, and cheers."

I put the phone down on the table and for just a moment in time, both I and time stood still. Then I let rip, running around like I'd just scored the winning goal in the F.A. Cup final. I fist punched the air and in all good football style pulled my T-shirt over my head and screamed at the top of my voice "Fucking get in!"

I phoned Joe first, who in his dazed sleepy state thought I was having a laugh. But on the acknowledgment of the truth dropped the phone and ran off shouting to his mum and dad to return a few minutes later. I then phoned Ollie and Stu.

I tried both their mobile numbers time and time again. I even called the home number... nothing. I tried every ten minutes before I gave up thinking that the lazy fuckers must still be in bed.

As the morning drew on strange things started to happen. My email inbox started to ping, then again, then again, and again and again. What the hell was going on?

Then the phone texts started; industry contacts who I'd only ever spoken to once before were getting in touch. It seemed that everyone in the record industry had heard our good news. The emails, that I thought would just be courtesy congratulation messages, were actually requests for band interviews and even some for myself for my tremendous achievement.

Blimey! We've only released a single! I thought and I tried to ring Stu and Ollie again, but still no answer.

It was now nearly 3.00pm in the afternoon, "What a pair of lazy bastards," I said out loud, just as my phone rang, it still wasn't them it was Neil Jones, a reporter friend and a good supporter of the band from The

Colchester Gazette, "Mate, congratulations, I'm proud of what you and the guys have done!"

"Mate, it's just a single release!" I answered.

"Are you aware what's happening and the significance of the timing?"

"No why?"

Neil then enthusiastically explained and as he did, I collapsed to the floor clutching my phone in total euphoria. I just couldn't believe what was happening.

As it turned out we most definitely had chosen the right week to release the single. Entering the mid-weeks, being an unsigned band and coinciding with the new rule change that week, meant that the band was creating a buzz in the music industry, the like of which had not been seen for some years, and my guys were hot news all over the World according to Neil and he wasn't wrong!

After the chat with Neil and having promised him an interview with Joe, I tried to call Ollie and Stu again, seriously, I thought, the biggest day of their careers so far and they are fast asleep – the wankers!

I went back to check my inbox, there were emails from Sky, ITV, BBC and Channel 4 all wanting to interview the band as soon as possible, so I started replying.

It was mayhem, but I tried to stay calm and deal with it in a professional manner. Shortly after my email to Sky I received a call from their press office asking for interview times and addresses in order to send chauffeurs.

"What the fuck is going on?" I said out loud to no-one and with a fixed smile on my face I took a call from Channel 4 "Give me ten minutes and I will get back to you," I said.

I called Joe again to keep him updated and I could feel something was wrong the moment he picked up; his tone was soft and he sounded as if he was in shock.

"Have you spoken to the Cooper boys?" he asked. He never called them the Cooper boys, it was always Ollie or Stu or sometimes much worse, I immediately knew something bad had happened.

'No, What's up?"

"Their dad died this morning."

"Martin?" I said, choking back the tears, "you're joking?"

I could tell Joe was in tears "Apparently he left the house at 10.30 this morning and just collapsed and died there on the spot."

"Heart attack?" I asked

"Yes, they think it was."

We chatted for a while longer before I had to rather coldly bring him around to the band and what was going on.

I explained that lots of media wanted interviews today and, after metaphorically putting an arm around his shoulder down the phone, he agreed we needed to use the opportunity that had been presented. We decided to do all the interviews between the two us wherever possible, but in the main it would just have to be Joe.

I called Sky back and they arranged to send a car to collect Joe, and then Channel 4 arranged to collect him from Sky and take him home after they had finished.

I sat back for a moment to reflect on the sad news about Martin, he had been a stalwart supporter of his sons from day one and had never interfered in the band or given me any problems along the way. I had always liked him and his lovely wife Sheila, who together had attended as many gigs as possible supporting their sons as well as Joe.

In the years to come I would work with bands that were also family orientated and while this can a benefit, it can also cause endless trust and control issues.

Families can cause huge conflicts within a band and the time I would spend with Twenty Twenty would highlight why, as a manager, it's best to avoid family member's involvement outside of the band itself; it only causes pain and aggravation.

On the flip-side though, I have encountered the complete opposite; working with Room 94 in conjunction with their parent's was a sheer pleasure from start to finish, I would count this as an anomaly though. In general, and after hearing many stories from other managers, I would suggest never getting involved if family is already running the project.

We would all seriously miss Martin. And if I could turn back time, for just ten minutes that day I would. For Martin to die at 10.30am the exact same time our big news was released on that Tuesday morning and for him to never share in the success of his sons on that day, not even for a minute. sends a shiver down my spine.

The calls and emails kept on coming and the word was spreading online. I was trying to keep up with requests for interviews, the calls of congratulations and press offices wanting to book interviews. At one-point Joe and I was approached to appear on television and be interviewed by Jeremy Paxman – thank fuck that never happened, as he would have seen straight through us!

It was all a bit of a media storm and as I sat down to watch a rather uncomfortable Joe field questions from news reporters on Sky, Channel 5 and ITV, I noticed he had developed a bit of a twitch. I was a little concerned, but he just said it surfaced when he got nervous.

During the Sky interview a very intelligent young man by the name of Colin Roberts reporting for a blog site called Drowned in Sound, slated the rule change, complaining that it ruins the charts, as in effect every track released from this day forward, whether single or album track, would technically be a single.

I totally agreed with him and all these years later the singles chart is an absolute mess, and is full of album tracks, songs from adverts, any track featured on Now That's What I Call Flogging an Album Format to Death and everything Simon Cowell tells his puppets, the general public, to download.

The singles chart is finished – I'm not even sure there is one these days. There seems to be a chart for everything, there's probably a chart that lists how many times I have just used the word chart.

Later that night Stuart Cooper called and we chatted for about an hour discussing and analysing everything that had happened and how we agreed that no one would ever be able to forget the strange emotions of the events that had taken place. I also had to tell him to watch out for The Sun newspaper the following day, as they had got wind of the tragedy and were running a story on the band based around Martins sudden death.

I'm ashamed to admit that the only way they found out about it was through me.

What happened that sad and joyous day was typical of how things were for all of us on this journey and as usual nothing would ever be straightforward.

The following morning, I pulled back the curtains and although it was cold the sun was shining. I turned on the computer to find many more emails. including interview requests from as far afield as Japan, The United States, Australia and even bizarrely Columbia – perhaps a drug baron wanted to sponsor the band. I thought.

As I got on with the task in hand of replying to everyone, I started to get a nagging thought in the back of my mind, quite a big nagging thought; how the hell are we going to sustain the sales to make sure we finished in the Top 40 and create music history?

Surely I wasn't going to have to buy more bloody SIM cards and have another dirty hook up with Crusty-Chris and his wife, so I logged into the account to check sales and to my surprise they were on the up!

Radio 1 had mentioned the band on Newsbeat and Steve Lamacq had played the song on his show. XFM had emailed to say they were playing the song and shortly after I received an email from a good friend at the BBC, who said Radio 1 were going to give the single a few plays that week.

Perhaps we could do this, I started to tell myself. The general public was listening and buying.

The week had been hectic and had seemed to fly by in no time at all. I was feeling like a train had hit me and I was exhausted. Joe had become a media-whore and was shattered from all the running from interview to interview and God only knows how the hell Ollie and Stu were feeling – totally devastated I presumed.

Matt from Ditto phoned me on Friday morning to tell me that we had slipped to number 29 in the singles chart and I caved in and called up Dodgy-Dave to hook me up with Crusty-Chris to buy some more SIM cards – I needed to make sure we stayed in the Top 40. I then stayed up into the early hours of Saturday morning texting.

Joe kept himself busy promoting the single online and, with the help of a string of blogger friends, the Internet was buzzing about this unsigned band Koopa, who were on the verge of making music industry history, but needed a helping hand.

Finally, it was Saturday evening and the chart chasing was over. I slumped in my chair and opened a bottle of beer. This was it now there was nothing else I, the band or indeed anyone else could do that would have any impact on the final chart position.

I went to the local pub that night and got so drunk that I forgot where I was and ordered a taxi home.

When he turned up and I gave him the address he said "Mate. that's a one-minute walk away."

"Here's £10 drive around the block a bit and then fucking take me home," I replied.

It had been a long week, I was drunk again, and walking home was not an option.

The following morning, I woke up with a bad headache being made worse by the nagging from my wife who was, as usual complaining about something.

I had breakfast with my daughters and then just chilled waiting to hear some news about the single.

During the week I had spoken to a very nice chap at The Official Charts Company who promised to call me if the band made the Top 40. I waited and waited, then waited some more. This was ridiculous, I needed to know I couldn't wait any longer. I checked the download sales just one more time and was delighted to see that we had reached over four thousand, so I sat back and crossed my fingers.

This was it, the culmination of all those gigs playing to no one, endless hours in that battered old white van and hour upon hour of trying to build up the online fan-base all being pushed aside in the chase for glory, my morals were non-existent and it was all about the SIM cards, this was truly make or break time... The music blag of the century was on!

I knew that If our single ended up at number 41 the band and I were finished. Now that might sound a bit harsh, but to be honest, it was true not a single one of those record labels, 'A and R-soles as we called them, would give us a second look if this plan failed.

Then came the moment of truth; the phone rang, I jumped out of my skin then jumped up and answered it.... it was my Mum. She wanted to know if my sister had been in touch about going over to her house for dinner later that week.

Two minutes later it rang again.

"Hello," I said.

"Hello Gary, it's Dominic from the charts company."

"Hello mate," I replied, "come on then, let's not keep me hanging on."

"Congratulations, the band are a new entry in at number 31 this week," he announced. "and that is an historic moment in the music industry, so well done!" he continued.

I paused to catch my breath and then replied "Thank you so much."

"Goodbye and congratulations again."

I just stood there, mobile phone in hand, speechless, dumbfounded and emotional.

We had only bloody done it!

Koopa was, officially, the first ever unsigned band to get into the BBC Radio 1 Official UK Charts as well as the first ever unsigned band in the Hot 40, which was something of an achievement, given that it is the chart of all the commercial radio stations combined – both of these were what I called a right fucking result!

Surely now this will lead to bigger things.

I was elated and knew full well the band would be too, but I decided to make them wait until we were all together at Joe's house and they could hear it announced on the radio. That way I could invite the local press and gain their reaction.

I called Neil at the Gazette, and we were all set. I was lucky that one of my mates Ali offered to drive me to Colchester so I could celebrate properly with a few beers.

The house was full when I arrived with everyone

drinking downstairs, while upstairs, Joe, Ollie and Stu were hitting their bong and the brandy bottle. I spoke briefly to the boys about Martin, as I hadn't seen them during the week. We then spent the rest of the afternoon drinking vodka with red bulls and waited for the chart rundown to begin. Everyone could sense that I knew more than I was letting on, but I managed to keep tight lipped even through the drink!

The show started and Fern Cotton and Reggie Yates mentioned something about a history making chart entry and the countdown began. Spirits in the house were flying high and eventually the golden time was upon us. Fern announced a new entry at number 31 and there it was — the bands single 'Blag, Steal and Borrow', the history making new entry and as it blasted out over the speakers. The house erupted, the volume got turned up to the max and everyone jumped up and down and sang along.

However, those particular jollities were abruptly ended by one of Joe's friends getting so drunk that he stood at the top of the staircase, opened his fly and then proceeded to piss from the top of the stairs to the bottom before falling down them and throwing up over the welcome mat.

***

It was the Monday 15th January 2007 and, while nursing a mild hangover, I found myself again swamped with interview requests. Koopa, for just one day; were to become the most famous band in the whole wide world and the band's website would have over one million unique hits.

The BBC wanted another interview, but this time with the whole band, so they arranged for cars to pick up Joe from Colchester before collecting me in Chelmsford and for a car to get Ollie and Stu, from Sible Hedingham – this was fucking mad, but great fun!

We arrived at BBC Television Centre and were ushered into the newsroom — it was all starting to get a little bit surreal; three scruffy punks from Essex were at the BBC, to be interviewed by the news team, and there I was sitting watching my little band discuss being in the charts while the headlines roll underneath about soldiers being killed in Afghanistan.

Ollie was like a rabbit caught in a car's headlights totally bemused by it all and at one point he actually said live on air "I don't know what's going on!" before continuing "I didn't even know we were coming in!"

Ollie never really liked the limelight and even on stage was a little bit shy at times, he also had a really fucking annoying habit of slagging himself off to the audience if he made a mistake or something went wrong — he was insecure I guess, no, he was just fucking unprofessional and his drug habit didn't bloody help!

The band had started getting offers to play gigs around the country, as I guess every promoter saw an opportunity to make a quick few pounds off the back of the band's success, but it meant we could at last get some decent fees. I knew the band's live fan-base was virtually non-existent, but I booked the shows anyway.

By now we were the biggest blaggers of them all; I

also knew this would eventually prove to be the band's biggest undoing.

The whole situation was summed up on Wednesday 17th January, just two days after making history and becoming the most famous band in the world.

We had headed up to London to the head offices of Kerrang Magazine we arrived in the van with not even a £1 coin for the meter; we had to borrow a pound from the receptionist - that's how high we were flying! We were number 31 in the charts, all over the news and not a fucking pound between the four of us - we never did pay that receptionist back either thinking about it!

That same evening, we performed to an empty hall in Clapham and just as we were leaving, the fucking van broke down and we had to get the security guard to push us up the hill in the High Street, so we could do a rolling jump start back down; it was evident that nothing had changed for us superstars — just yet.

But there was lots of interest in the three boys and the band appeared in all the Nationals that week and one particular television news reporter declared that "'Blag, Steal and Borrow' was an anthem for unsigned bands everywhere."

I suppose it was with its anti-label lyrics…

The industry is ON IT'S ARSE! They're quick to quit, THEY'LL SHATTER LIKE GLASS...

Chapter 21

The Cockney and the Essex Boys
in America

Completely out of the blue I took a phone call from a promotions company working on the Brit Nominations Ceremony in London, who wanted to invite Koopa along as VIP guests. Of course I said yes and, with much excitement, informed the band.

Joe's parents decided to book a limousine for the evening and make a real night of it. The limousine arrived at Joe's and we were all enjoying a few bottles of the finest bubbly, when I got a phone call from the very same promotions company telling me that the band had now been banned from attending the ceremony.

Apparently, two of the major investment music labels for the evening had aired their concerns that the band was DIY, and had been shoving that fact down the music industry's throat ever since the single charted. They felt the boys might be overzealous with their comments to the music and media press at the event.

"What a total load of old bollocks!" I declared.

"All I wanted to do was meet Lily Allen," said Joe.

"Fuck them all!" added Ollie.

I ended up getting a lift home in the limousine drinking alone and Joe's parents didn't get a refund.

The show offers were flooding in and the band had also been invited to perform at the prestigious The South by Southwest Music Festival in Texas as long as we could cover our own costs, which of course we couldn't – until I had an idea.

I called Neil our friendly local reporter for some much needed help. If we would get a nice piece in the paper about the band and their plight, we may be able to get local sponsorship and get the boys to Texas. I also had emails from a promoter in the US who wanted the band to play at his venues in Los Angeles and New York.

Neil agreed, and wrote an excellent article which appear the following week in the Colchester Gazette, and courtesy of a kind donation of £5000 from a local scaffolding company we headed off to the USA.

Around the same time, I had a call from a well-known boot company (I'm not naming names, but they used to be associated with bovver and football back in the seventies) who had heard about the band's success and wanted to get involved somehow and, after some deliberation, they agreed to give us $1000 spending money in return for the band handing out flyers while they were performing in the USA. This was a no-brainer of a deal and they sent me the money and made arrangements for the flyers to be delivered directly to our hotels in the US.

I was used to blagging left, right and centre by this time and it was paying big big dividends.

Nearer home the band had also been invited to open

on the main stage at the Isle of Wight Festival. The offers were still flooding in and included everything from tour supports in Europe to big one-off support slots.

Then finally there was the cherry on top of the big fat cake *the* call from ITV asking for a meeting to discuss the making of a documentary. Oh, and I almost forgot, amongst all this madness, I also received messages from three major music labels.

Dressed in my finest whistle I headed off to see the ITV executives. They wanted to make a documentary based around Koopa, but one that also focused on the way the industry had changed. They introduced me to documentary film maker Paul Buller, who would be in charge of the project and would also be the one to follow the band around for a few weeks; filming, interviewing and get the opportunity to show all sides of their battle to make it in such a tough and ruthless industry. I liked Paul from the outset and was delighted when I was told he would also be joining us in Texas.

I rushed home and told the lads who I had met at the studio.

"It's like a dream!" Stu said to Ollie, who replied with "Stop being so gay!"

It is around this time that some competition entered our arena; another band also from Essex called Belisha who was trying, without success, to upstage us. Under instruction from their manager, they tried at every given opportunity to slag off Koopa and were calling the band, everything under the sun to try and grab the spotlight for themselves.

It was during a local radio show interview that their

self-proclaimed charismatic lead singer apparently announced live on air "We are going to kill those untalented cunts in Koopa." They had taken one step too far and I was now well and truly pissed-off. I decided it must stop.

It turns out that their stupid plan to steal our spotlight was conceived by their manager, Jon. Jon had slagged us off to anyone who would give him the time of day, stating that we were charlatans and blaggers and that Belisha, with their real music ethics, should be the band in Essex that everyone talked about and not those upstarts Koopa and their cocky cockney manager.

The situation came to a head when our paths crossed at a show, and I politely advised him 'that if it he didn't stop I would shove his mobile phone so far down his throat, he would have to stick his fingers up his arsehole to dial for an ambulance.' He apologised and said it was just management banter and strangely we became very good friends after that and even worked together on a few projects together years later.

Turns out that *all* other bands are out to get you. I find that most musicians in general are rather overrated sellouts and untalented posers, while most of the ones you meet personally through the constant touring of basement and toilet venues are, egomaniacs, backstabbers or just plain wankers.

In the end the real enemy will be your own inner circle. In our case, the band and their manager. Spending too much time together eventually causes you all to hate one another and destroy your very own project from within.

Typically, you start off as friends and soon become like a family. You love them for the successes and you hate them for the crushing failures and you never ever take any blame yourself as it's never your fault.

The cracks, strains and drunken arguments in the van and on the other side of the world, would really start to take their toll on us in the coming months. It was only a matter of time before things would get nasty as we couldn't and didn't cope. The success that the single had thrust upon us was intense, by the end of the year I for one, was more than ready to kill someone and I really do mean murder someone and bury the body in the woods – it was that bad. The band would go on and on and in the end, I would snap and shout things like, "I have to spend hours talking to fucking idiots like you! Give me a break! and shut the fuck up!"

We would live life on the edge, throw caution to the wind and eventually crash.

The band was busy and out and about playing shows and it was almost time to head for the USA. Thank the lord that those American state officials didn't know the band like I did or they would never have let them in.

My wife Paula was driving me to Heathrow to meet with the boys and we said very little to each other throughout the one-hour journey. I was starting to realise that she was tired from all my 'dream chasing' and that I had become an arrogant, selfish-man who was ignoring his family duties.

I knew that time was running out on our marriage and that I should at least attempt to heal the rift, but for some reason I just couldn't give up the chase and needed the fix that I could only get from the band.

I was still drinking and eating far too much; I was permanently tired, overweight and always sweating. I was mentally unstable and should have sought some professional help. My demons craved the excitement of the band far more than they did wedded bliss, and my new tablet friends (my painkillers) were helping to ease my tensions.

I was in an emotional trauma from which I had no escape.

I arrived at the airport and checked-in before clearing customs and meeting up with the guys at the nearest bar. Joe was tense and nervous and had announced earlier that he hated flying. I wasn't a great fan myself and the thought of being in a confined space with these three was not exactly my idea of a fun way to spend the next nine hours. So I decided to drink as much alcohol as legally possible before the flight, pop some pain killers and hopefully pass-out on the plane and sleep for the entire journey.

Joe joined me and pretty soon the drinks were flowing and we were on top form getting louder and louder. It was about 7.30am and I was already a little worse for wear.

Joe and Ollie, for some strange reason, had started singing the jazzy number "Fly Me to The Moon."

Stu, who obviously was used to always driving and definitely not drinking, was taking full advantage of the carefree situation by downing vodka and red bulls as if they were going out of fashion and, as the boys broke into song, Stu decided to stand on his chair and give us all a little dance, but after only a couple of minutes he leant back and his flamboyant dance gestures finally got the better of him, the chair tipped back and he suddenly disappeared under the table.

For a few seconds the whole bar full of people as well as passersby stopped., then without blinking an eye Stu jumped up, put his baseball cap back on, picked up the chair, sat down and said, "That's why I drive usually!"

It was fucking funny, and with that we immediately ordered another round of drinks and I took two paracetamol readying myself for the long haul to New York; our first port of call. Shortly after, the notice board announced our gate number and we headed for the departure lounge, trying to sober up a bit to make sure we were allowed to board.

We did manage to make our way onto the plane and within minutes of securing my seatbelt, I nicely passed-out and the next thing I knew we were landing in New York. Joe and Stu had also been asleep most of the journey and Ollie was miffed that he had been left with nobody to talk to for the whole trip. I can now advise you that alcohol, paracetamol and long distance air travel do not mix, because as soon as we landed I rushed to the nearest restroom to throw up. (See how I said restroom instead of toilet – we were in The USA now so the terminology must be correct).

We were queuing to clear Immigration and Customs and I could sense we were being watched. Ollie and Stu went through seemingly without any problems, but as Joe and I approached, we were suddenly stopped by two rather mean looking Customs Officers — complete with guns. We were told to follow them and then I started to panic and was more than a little scared.

Ollie and Stu watched in amazement as their travel companions were marched off into the distance.

"What the hell's going on?" Joe asked me.

"I don't know mate, but there's nothing to hide so no need to panic."

There was indeed nothing to hide, but you really cannot help, but panic when placed in a situation like this. I was sweating and that was making me think I was looking guilty of something; even though I knew I was guilty of nothing at all.

We reached an office door and was then escorted in to face a young woman dressed in uniform. The two men turned around and left us alone with her.

"Hello," she said before explaining why we were there, "gentlemen, the flight crew informed us that the two of you seemed suspicious so we thought we would just check your information."

"Suspicious!" I asked, "in what way do you mean?"

"They said you were drunk and dishevelled when you boarded and that alerted their suspicions that you may be hiding something," as she explained we looked at each other in disbelief.

"It's our job to just check these things out when the passengers land," she continued.

"Now tell me please, why you are visiting the USA?"

Now I was beginning to think we may have been rumbled, as we had not applied for any work visas as we hadn't enough funds to do so, and so we decided to say that the band was coming out to have a short holiday and maybe write some songs.

So I explained to the customs woman that after the bands huge success in the UK, they needed a much earned break and that the reason we had passed out was that we were both terrified of flying, had drank too much and had also taken some tablets to help us sleep prior to the flight.

She paused for a moment and walked over to her computer. I have to admit she was starting to look very hot in her uniform and her gun made her look even sexier. She leant over her computer and asked for the name of the band – now every move she made was getting me a little excited sexually.

"Koopa," I declared and she tapped away at the keyboard.

She turned to us and said, "All I can find is information about some kind of turtle."

Joe replied with a polite tone, "Try Koopa-the-band spelt K... O.... O.... P.... A."

She turned and tapped some more and after a few seconds she clicked enter and you could hear the song 'Blag, Steal and Borrow', emanating from the speakers.

"That's you?" She said to Joe, "I like it," she added, "I love Jimmy Eat World, you remind me of them."

"Thanks, that's a big compliment," Joe answered.

She gave us our passports and escorted us through to the baggage area where we found Ollie and Stu.

"Have a good trip," she said as she turned to leave.

"Thank you," I said.

"Have a nice day!" Joe shouted.

She turned, smiled at Joe and we went to explain what had happened to the others.

"Good job she didn't check up my arse!" Joe said

and, for a brief moment I believed him, but as I swiftly turned to confront him with a stern face he was laughing and put his hand on my shoulder and said, "Only joking mate!"

Thank fuck for that I thought before further thinking he could of course be bloody lying.

I was just happy to be standing there as for a moment, I was not sure if I had been through airport security or was auditioning for Guantanamo Bay.

So the band and I had arrived in the good old U S of A and after jumping into the obligatory yellow taxi and checking into our hotel, we decided to celebrate the fact that we had actually been allowed to enter the United States — by making some Skittles Vodka.

Making 'Skittles Vodka' is simple.

First, you need to drink some shots to make room in the bottle for the Skittles, and then all you do is place your favorite combination of Skittles into said bottle of vodka and wait for it to infuse, then in no time at all you'll be tasting the rainbow. We got through about two bottles that night before passing out.

Early the next morning I was feeling very tired and jet lagged; when there was a knock at the door.

I walked over and opened it and was greeted by the hotel manager. We had only been in the country for a few hours, so what could we have possibly done wrong already.

"We have a delivery of flyers for you, sir," he said.

Then it clicked, these were the flyers we were going to be handing out in return for the spending money that the boot company has given us. Now we were expecting a couple of boxes, but imagine our surprise when the manager said "We have 25 boxes for you sir, where would you like them?"

"Fucking hell!" I said out loud as the band looked at me in dismay, "Sorry, just put them in the corner."

The hotel staff huffed and puffed as one by one the boxes were piled into the corner of the band's room.

When they had finished, the manager stood staring at me obviously waiting for a tip so I pulled out a $10 bill and handed it to him, he took it from me and then looked at me in disgust and left.

I checked the boxes and there were 5000 flyers in each so that meant we had 125,000 of the fuckers that we were supposed to hand out, and how the fuck were we supposed to get the boxes to Los Angeles?

Well, I need not worry as in the attached envelope was a letter informing me that another shipment would be delivered to our hotel in Los Angeles, so in the end we needed up with half a fucking million flyers in total.

"What the fuck!" I declared as we all looked at one another in dismay.

"There is no way I'm handing out all these fucking flyers!" Ollie stated.

"Fucking right," Stu added.

Then I had an idea.

"Let just hand out a few everywhere we go and take some photos," I said, "that way they are happy and we don't have to spend all our time handing these fuckers out."

So that's what we did and every time we were at some landmark in the city the band would hand out some flyers and I would snap a few photos. We prob-

ably gave out about 50 flyers in total in both cities —
but we never got any complaints.

We disposed of all the other flyers in the hotel trash
bins.

New York is unlike any other city in the entire
world, as anyone who has been there can tell you. It's
diverse, exciting and can sometimes also be just a little bit scary – have you travelled on the subway after
dark? Well, it's somewhat on the eerie side, and eye
contact with anyone is a big no-no.

The one time we did used the subway this weird
woman went along the carriage asking everyone to have a smell of the perfume on her neck and
some dirty old tramp was asking people, in his gruff
voice, if they had any doughnuts. The final straw came
when some weird looking man sat next to Ollie and
looked like he was starting to masturbate under his
coat.

"Thank fuck we are getting off at the next stop," I
said to the boys.

From the point of view of a Cockney lad and three
guys from Essex; it was jammed packed full of wonderful extremes. It has wonderful architecture and tow-
ering grey coloured buildings that soar to the clouds
above you as you walk along its sidewalks.

Turn a different corner and suddenly you're in Little
Italy or Chinatown. There are so many different places
that are full of life. Times Square is breathtaking and
standing in the very centre, surrounded by its bright
lights and billboards taking in everything around you
is in itself a very special moment. But it's also very busy
and, as we found out, if you stop and stare too long

eventually you might get brushed aside by the locals walking very fast as they rush from place to place.

The city is mind blowing and for once we had time to take it all in, to enjoy being there and see the sights, even though it was pretty chilly outside with blustery winter wind that caught you full in the face not to mention the heavy snowfall; I also do remember it being a little bit dirty and smelly. The traffic is horrible and noisy and, in the wrong place at the wrong time, you can easily choke on the pollution.

There are *so* many people in New York all rushing around at the same time in the same place, bumping into one another as they make their way to and fro. Some are nice and others extremely rude. Some can be really pushy and on occasion very intimidating.

We did all the usual sight-seeing musts like Central Park and The Empire State Building and we even took a trip on the ferry to see The Statue of Liberty. She was much smaller than I had envisaged and to be honest the ferry trip was cold, wet and with the Manhattan skyline being the exception, pretty bloody boring. The best part of that trip was when a pigeon shit on Stu's brand new NYC baseball cap.

While in Times Square we decided to have lunch at the world famous Hard Rock Café.

We were enjoying our burgers and the surroundings when all of a sudden the mood changed and there was an immense sense of danger. Then we heard screams coming from outside, then the first shot, followed by more screaming and then more rapid gunfire.

"What the fuck is going on?" I shouted.

Then there was more gunfire coming from just outside the restaurant. The people inside started to panic when suddenly one of the front windows crashed; now we were all a little unnerved.

We heard the sirens getting closer, the staff in the restaurant ushered all the customers to the back exit, so we grabbed our stuff and ran out of the exit door into an alley at the rear. By this time the sirens were loud and you could hear shouting — then it all went quiet.

The manager of the restaurant came out and told everyone there had been an incident just outside the building and that if we waited a few minutes we would be allowed back in, but being the opportunists we were, we seized upon the moment to make a swift exit and not have to pay our bill – plus we were shitting ourselves.

When we got back to the hotel I switched on the news to see if there was anything mentioned about the incident, but nothing came on – there was a lot of shootings that day and apparently this one had been just another one on the list, and as no one had been killed the news focused more on the many murders that had occurred.

The one other thing that really unnerved me while we were in the city was a homeless man sitting outside McDonalds in the snow and freezing cold conditions. I had walked over and handed him my coffee, only for him to take it and pour it away.

"I prefer to be given money pal," he said snarling at me.

I was stunned; hang on I've just given you a cup of coffee you, ungrateful wanker. He had looked at me with mad eyes, so I thought best of replying and just walked away. That incident made me very wary of the homeless for a while, but then I tried again once I was back in London and I received a "God bless you mate," at which point my faith in humanity had been restored.

The band had two shows to play in New York and all I had received was an email with instructions on the locations and what time to arrive; I suppose that was all I needed really. The first of the two shows was in The Knitting Factory in Brooklyn and the second show at a club in Harlem.

We were all nervous about the second show, having seen far too many documentaries and movies about Harlem, so we all had reservations about actually going there.

The first show went really well and the band used it to showcase a few new songs, including 'One Off Song for the Summer', which would go on to be the bands next single release.

After the show Joe ended up backstage where he happily received the double whammy; a slice of pizza and a blowjob from a young lady he had been chatting to at the bar earlier.

"How was it?" I asked.

"It was a deep crust meat feast with chillies, not really my favourite," he replied.

"No, I meant… oh don't bother."

Chapter 22

I Have A Big Problem When I Sneeze

The following night we had the gig in Harlem and as the taxi pulled up outside the venue, we were all shitting ourselves. I'd say it took under ten seconds for us to exit that taxi, sprint to the entrance door, that was about fifty foot away, and get safely inside, without looking up, down or sideways.

"Fuck me, we made it!" Ollie said relieved.

"Yeah, and I didn't hear a single gunshot," Joe added as we all burst into laughter.

That night the venue was busy and, by the time the boys took to the stage, you could hardly move. The band was right on their a-game and put on such an amazing performance that the promoter gave us some extra cash, paid for all the drinks after and then took us out for a meal.

Before we left the venue Ollie and Joe decided to ask around to see if anyone had any weed as they were running low. They split up and randomly wandered up to anyone and simply asked if they knew anywhere they could get some –— a simple, but rather dumb plan given the fact that they didn't have a clue who they were asking in the first place, but this didn't deter them.

Ollie spotted a man drinking at the bar and started to have a chat with him, the guy mentioned how he had enjoyed the band's performance and that he was visiting England in a few months. I was standing with Stu just a few feet away and we were both watching Ollie as he went for it.

"I don't suppose you know where I can get some weed?" he asked the man.

Looking slightly startled the man turned to Ollie and without saying a word he pulled out his wallet and showed Ollie his identity card and at the same time pulled back his jacket to reveal a gun strapped to his waist.

Ollie went as white as a sheet and I spat out my vodka and coke. Fucking hell, I thought Ollie was in deep deep shit.

I looked at the identity and could see the FBI logo on it.

"Oh bollocks!" I said to Stu who also had a look of terror in his eyes.

"Can't help you I'm afraid," the guy said to Ollie, "and as I enjoyed your show I'll pretend that I didn't hear that," he continued.

Ollie was shaking in fear and then he gasped before saying "Cheers mate," and walking away.

The promoter seeing what had happened came over and laughed before saying "Shall we go get some food?"

"Fucking good idea," I replied and we swiftly made our exit.

Ollie had just had a very lucky escape.

In the early hours of the morning we left the restaurant and swiftly shuffled out of Harlem in another yellow taxi back to our hotel. It had been one of those rare nights when almost everything had gone to plan and we had even made it back alive and all in one piece, despite all the worry and concern that we were going to be gunned down on arrival or carted off to jail by the feds. Best of all, that night everyone in the band was pleased the show had gone well and we were all in an exceptionally good mood — for a change!

Again, I'd been drinking heavily all night and was once again ready to just pass out so went to my room, undressed, and went straight to bed. One thing I insisted on these days was to have my own room, as the Koopa boys would sit up all night and smoke from their homemade bong, which on this occasion, was made from a Coca-Cola can and elastic bands – very appropriate given its use.

The boys had also invented this amazing 'sock smoke blocker' as they named it, or the 'SSB' as it later became known, which was a plain thick football sock with some kind of putty inside which they placed over the smoke alarm, blocking any fumes from the homemade bong, setting off the alarms. It was very ingenious and certainly had been extensively tried and tested – it definitely worked. I even think that an entrepreneur like Lord Alan Sugar, or the Dragons in their den, would have been impressed — but I doubt it was ready for the mass market, investment or media campaigns just yet.

It was around this time that the band would invent some new games to amuse themselves; that would mainly revolve around how much they could torture me.

Every night without fail, they would somehow manage to sneak into my room and, when not putting all my clothes in a bath full of water or throwing all my underpants out the windows, would play some prank on me while I was in a deep sleep.

That night was to be the debut of some prank they called 'the squirt game', which involved them nipping down to the hotel restaurant or bar to steal all the condiments and sauces. They would then sneak into my room and proceed to colour me in, like they were playing some kind of painting by numbers game, squirting sauce all over my face and body until I woke up — at which point the game would be over.

The big problem for me was that I was a heavy drinker and therefore a heavy sleeper, I woke the following morning and I felt strange, hung-over of course, but my eyes and face felt sticky.

"What the fuck has happened to me?" became my regular statement.

I could barely open my eyes and my nose was tingling like I was about to sneeze. I had a problem with sneezing, four of more in a row, would cause me to get an erection. I have never really understood this and it's something that has become more common as I get older.

I have considered visiting my doctor, but just can't muster up the courage. I have however, discovered that it does have some benefits, as pepper is a lot cheaper than Viagra!

I crawled out of bed and walked slowly to the bathroom; I needed to pee, but was unable to focus properly – what was going on with my eyes I thought. I stood in front of the mirror and having managed to wipe my eyes with a towel and finally open them, I saw the true horror before me.

At first I thought something was seriously wrong as my face as it was yellow, red and brown and there were parts of it that looked pitted and sandy; I considered calling the hotel reception for help.

I blinked and looked again, all I could picture was the scene in the original 'Poltergeist' movie when the guy stares in the mirror as his face starts coming off as he scratches frantically at it.

Was this happening to me? Was I possessed perhaps?

I blinked again and then I could smell vinegar, I moved my right hand towards my face and touched it, it was gooey, I was fucking melting!

Then, as I looked at my hand... it was bloody tomato ketchup. What had I been doing the night before? I remembered that I had gone straight to bed after we got back, then the penny dropped. "Wankers!" I shouted out loud in the bathroom.

I started to clean myself up and discovered I had been painted with tomato ketchup, mustard and brown sauce and then decorated with salt and pepper before being finished off with a vinegar gloss – those bastards, I thought. I knew it was them the second I discovered the brown sauce as Stu had bought a bottle along for the trip. I laughed out loud and then stepped in the shower before dressing and banging on their door repeatedly to give them a piece of my mind.

When confronted, they simply laughed and said I should stop acting like a girl and man up, fair enough I suppose.

That evening we had to get our flight to Los Angeles, we arrived and cleared customs this time with no problems and we headed to our hotel that was to be our home for the next few days.

The hotel had a kind of Mexican theme and everywhere you looked there were sombreros and bull-horns, the rooms had tortilla shaped beds and sheets – it was Mexican madness.

The reception housed a parrot or mynah bird of some kind, which of course we try to teach some good old-fashioned English swear words like; wanker and bollocks, but the only words it did eventually speak was obviously in its native Mexican tongue. I swear it called me 'chingada madre' as I walked past it one day. You're off to look that up on Google translate aren't you?

By stark contrast to the coldness of New York, Los Angeles was bloody hot. So hot in fact that we could all hang out by the swimming pool and have a few cold beers or jump in for a dip, whenever the mood called for it —everyone was chilled and having fun.

As we did in New York, we visited all the usual tourist sites like Universal Studios, The Chinese Theatre and Venice Beach. I also showed the guys a few of the bars I had visited on previous visits and we stopped by The Whiskey a Go Go in West Hollywood and as we sat and drank some cold beers, we contemplated what it must have been like for The Doors performing there back in the late sixties and seventies.

Well, I say we all sat drinking, but poor Ollie was refused by the barman as he was too young. He was pissed off and got a little angrier when I asked him if he would like a bag of crisps with his lemonade.

Soon after Ollie got all cocky and turned to the barman who had refused to serve him and said "I'll be playing here one-day mate and then you'll serve me!"

"If you ever play here! I'll give you free drinks all night mate!" the barman replied sarcastically, those words would come back to haunt him the following year.

As we left, Joe noticed a short, fat man with a thick moustache and bulging stomach walking out of a restaurant with two blonde women who appeared to have legs that went up to their necks.

"I know that bloke," he informed us, "I've seen all his movies."

"That's Ron Jeremy, the porn star!" he declared as he rushed across the road.

Oh, yeah I thought, I've seen his movies, sold quite a few as well.

Stu and Ollie followed Joe and for a brief moment Ron Jeremy seemed to be in a state of panic, as he wondered what the hell was about to happen to him, as the three excited Englishmen approached; in the end they all shook hands and the three boys stood around chatting for ten minutes to the porn legend before we headed back to the hotel discussing their conversations.

"What did he say his new film was called?" Joe asked Ollie.

"I think he said it was called Homo Erectus," Ollie replied.

"I must order that from Amazon when I get back home."

"You won't get that filth on Amazon mate," I declared.

"But if you really want a copy then I can get you one – you know I have contacts in the porn world."

"You dirty old fucker," Ollie added.

The following day we packed our bags before checking out of the Mexican themed hotel. We headed outside to hail a taxi to take us to the airport, but not before giving the mynah bird one more chance to say 'wanker' — but it was no good, he just didn't understand English.

We were jetting off to the prestigious South by Southwest Music Festival that was being held as usual in Austin, Texas and everyone was excited. In addition, we were due to finally hook up with filmmaker Paul Buller, who was about to start shooting the documentary about the band for ITV.

The flight to Austin in Texas was one of the most boring I've ever been on, as we had to first fly to George Bush Airport in Houston before waiting ages for the connecting flight to Austin. I was bored and I felt a bit strange, a feeling I hadn't really encountered for a while, then I realised I was completely sober and wasn't sure I was comfortable with the feeling, so at the first opportunity I found the nearest bar and ordered an ice-cold bottle of Miller Light. 'Much better!' I said to myself.

This was also a sign that my dependency of alcohol was starting to take over again.

We finally arrived in Austin, and made our way to our hotel, which seemed to be miles from anywhere, but in fact was only about 20 minutes outside of the city and, after we had checked in, I went to the room, I would be sharing with Paul to unpack, leaving the boys chatting to a very strange man on reception called Will.

Turns out the first thing the boys were after was weed to fuel their ever increasing bong habits and Will, as it happened, was just their man; as he had a shed full of the stuff at the back of the hotel and was luckily the areas local dealer.

Paul Buller, turned up shortly after we arrived and it was nice to have someone to chat to aside from the band, but I did rather embarrassingly do a rather large yawn in front of Paul, and like a venomous snake I sprayed saliva all over him. It doesn't happen that often, but sometimes when I yawn vigorously saliva sprays out – it's gross, but it's not unnatural or unusual. I apologised and we moved on swiftly and we were catching up on everything the band had been doing in the States and chatting about his plans for filming, when we were eventually joined by the boys, so we decided to head into the city to register our arrival and pick up all our passes and schedules for the festival.

It is almost impossible to describe the chaotic, cacophonic spirit of The South by Southwest Music Festival better known by the acronym SXSW.

Thousands of bands, singer-songwriters, hip-hop crews and wannabe pop stars all dreaming of stardom take over every bar, restaurant, coffee shop, tattoo parlour and available empty space to perform for record companies, booking agents, managers, journalists, music fans and any number of complete fucking idiots. The industry types are searching for that something special and all the artists are trying to impress the music industry delegates and get the holiest of holy grails — the big break, that would lead to a long and lasting career in music.

The big problem is that the music industry delegates are just there for one big piss-up at their labels expense, and most are usually so pissed they can barely remember where they were the night before let alone who they saw play. In a way everyone at the festival reminded me of all those coaches full of pissed up loud-mouthed day-trippers that frequented my Dad's pubs.

In my honest opinion to any starry-eyed young band, the presence of thousands of music business and media professionals at this festival of music — promises a false opportunity to get discovered.

Bruce Springsteen, visiting for the first time, described South by Southwest as a 'teenage music junkie's wet dream' and he was so right. I looked around in amazement as we entered the busy main street; it was like a carnival of hope and dreams. It's not like a festival with tickets, security checks and barriers, it's a whole city and music is everywhere, in every bar, café and even the sandwich shops.

After registration we all sat down and chatted whilst sharing a bottle of Jack Daniels and coke, it was 3.00pm after all. Then we just wandered around for a while checking out all the weird and wonderful people. Joe caused a slight commotion when he slapped this guy — who had announced himself as (The Naked Cowboy) on the backside causing him to get all rude and in Joe's face before noticing the crowd had stopped to check out what was going on, so then made a joke of the situation.

After a long day of walking, drinking and filming

we were starving and took the opportunity to try out the local steaks as the flyers we had received offered us a 20% discount. We thought hey, when in Texas! The home of men and meat, let's give it a go — that's the meat I mean of course.

We walked into one of the typical western-themed restaurants that adorned the city and after being seated and examining the menu I ordered The Texas T-Bone steak while everyone else ordered the rack of prime ribs.

"How would you like that cooked sir," the waitress asked, "just knock the jockey off, wipes it backside and bring it to me." — I love old corny seventies jokes!

Nothing… she just stared at me like I was an imbecile. "Well-done please," I added rather embarrassed.

I was starting to think my wonderful way with the ladies was starting to fade, but then remembered; I didn't have a way in the first place.

I also begun to realise that I was becoming a little too obnoxious and maybe needed to rain it in a little before someone hit me. The warning sirens of excess were starting to sound in my head.

The steak was a massive 28-ounce T-Bone and came with a side of loaded mashed potatoes as well as one of those create your own salads, which with us being in the United States, meant going to the salad bar and loading your bowl full of fresh salad before covering it in a thick coating of blue cheese sauce, thousand island dressing or other assorted full fat sauces.

Half way through this marathon meal I started to get the meat sweats and although they're said to be real, the meat sweats are more of an old wives' tale, than they are a medical malady, but regardless I could feel my body temperature increasing, I was starting to sweat and I also had a stitch in my side.

I looked up at Joe, Ollie, Stu and Paul and who were covered in sauce from the ribs they were consuming.

I wiped the sweat from my forehead and declared, "I'm fucking beat," and stopped eating.

"Finish it!" Joe said.

"No way, I'm stuffed, I have had far too much meat inside me today."

Everyone burst out laughing and I sat there bemused before realising what I had just said.

"Fucking grow up the lot of ya!" I said before fixing my gaze on the passing waitress and making the international sign for 'can I have the bill, please' (right hand, formed as if holding a pen, writing across a raised left hand).

Full of grilled meat we returned to the hotel and, while the band slipped away with their weird new friend Will to visit his weed shed at the back of the hotel, I retired to my room and slumped onto my bed looking at my inflated stomach, asking myself when was it due?

I needed to sleep off the booze and the meat feast I had overindulged in so settled into bed with the plan to get good nights' sleep, —when it began — the old comedy sex scene; squeak, bang, squeak, bang, squeak, bang as the rhythm of next doors bed accelerated. I could then hear the comedy woman moaning out loudly and it was all too obvious what the couple next door was up to.

It continued, squeak, bang, squeak, bang, squeak, bang, squeak, bang......

It was going on for what seemed like hours and I began to think that maybe the fella has swallowed an entire bottle of Viagra pills – it was always so tongue in cheek, but it was getting on my tits.

On and on it went, squeak, bang, squeak, bang, it just kept going, on and on until eventually I was at breaking point and suddenly I cracked and the booze mixed with all that extra protein in my system from the giant steak caused me to jump out of bed and slam my fists on the wall shouting "Will you for fuck sakes hurry up and cum!"

There was a slight pause and then the squeaking and banging got faster and faster until I heard both of them let out one last elongated moan before it stopped. Suddenly there were two thumps on the wall behind me. "We're finished!" someone shouted in his American accent.

Now wide-awake, I got dressed and headed to the bar. The boys were sitting with Weird-Will drinking and looking like they were away with the fairies. So I told them my story just as a young man with an older looking woman walked into the bar; both looking a little flustered.

Thinking it was the couple in the room next to me I was about to say something when the man walked up to the bar and ordered a beer before turning around and saying "What do you want to drink, Mum?"

'No way!' I thought before downing double vodka.

After a while, Joe stood chatting to the fella and it turns out that he was a record label executive from

England, who had just got back from seeing some band in the city and had run from the taxi thinking it was last orders at the bar.

Thank God for that!

Joe, Ollie & Stu promoting their first single release 'No Trend' with some page 3 models.

Me and Joe checking out an interview in a magazine. I was piling on the pounds.

Ollie & Stu in the back of a mini bus on the way to play a show in Holland. We came home the same day.

The band getting ready for a press conference in Malta. The show was sponsored by a beer company and the beer and spirits they were flowing all weekend.

I sent Stu & Ollie to the Chris Moyles book signing in Chelmsford so they could slip him a demo CD.

The three boys in the band enjoying a beer and a laugh with a reporter back satge at a gig.

The band with those pranksters from the TV show Dirty Sanchez.

The band with Pete Doherty of The Libertines at Soccer Six. Pete looks a little worse for wear.

Ollie, Stu & Joe as usual with a beer in hand.

The boys at the England vs Germany Legends match held at Reading F.C – They are enjoyong a sing song with Verve lead singer and legend Richard Ashcroft.

Doing some promo for the 'Stand Up 4 England' music video with former England cricketer and now radio presenter Darren Gough.

The band promoting the Stand Up 4 England single release. I managed to blag a CD signing at HMV in Chelmsford to help push the single.

Somehow I managed to get the song 'Stand Up 4 England' on a compilation labum which surprisngly went to number one in the album charts. The band and me received a gold disc and I got Bobby George the legendary darts player to present the band with theirs.

The charts never lie. Koopa became the first unsigned band in history to have a top 40 chart hit when the song 'Blag, Steal & Borrow crashed into the chart at #31 – this caused a media storm around the band.

Following the historic chart entry every national newpaper wanted to feature the band.

Koopa won two Glasswerks Awards following the historic single. Unfortunately, during a drunken argument on the way home both were damaged beyond repair.

ITV commissioned a documentary about the band and cameras followed us as we made our way to the prestigious South by Southwest Festival held in Austin Texas.

Here we are all enjoying a beer at the South by Southwest Festival.
Left to right: Stu, Nathan Wacey (producer), Joe, Ollie, me (looking very fat), Paul Buller (ITV). This photo was taken a few hours before a punch up with a band back stage.

Me, Ollie & Joe waiting around somewhere on the streets of Austin, Texas.

Stu being interviewed for the ITV documentary.

Joe larking about outside a liquer store in the USA. But the truth is that Joe's drinking had become a big problem at this time in the bands career.

The band in the studio in Los Angeles with Blink 182 legend Mark Hoppus and his engineer Chris Holmes.

Stu standing along the famous green drum kit played by Travis Barker of Blink 182. In fact, Stu used this kit to record his parts for the 'Lies Sell Stories' album.

Mark Hoppus making a dumb face during the recording of the bands album in L.A.

Stu, Ollie & Joe enjoying a beer with Jaret & Big Chris from Bowling for Soup.

The bands name on the listings when they performed at the world famous Whiskey a Go Go club nightclub in West Hollywood, California. It is located at 8901 Sunset Boulevard on the Sunset Strip. The club has been the launching pad for bands including The Doors, The Byrds, Van Halen, Guns N' Roses and Mötley Crüe.

Joe being interviewed. He loved being the focus during the interviews but to be honest the other two were useless and hardly had a word to say – Joe liked to be the bands media whore.

This promo photo says it all about the labels plans for the band –
they wanted Joe out.

The artwork for the bands
'Greatest Hits' CD.

The artwork for 'Lies, Sell
Stories' album which was only
ever released in Japan.

Chapter 23

What's That Coming Over The Hill

It was time for the band's showcase. We had also been invited by a representative of the American cymbal manufacturers, Zildjian, to Stubbs BBQ in the city that hosted one of the main events of the festival; a huge gig featuring Brit artists Lily Allen, Jamie T and The Automatic.

The bands showcase was on the outskirts of the town, well, I say outskirts, it was rather like saying you had a gig in central London, but actually were performing on the edge of Essex; it was actually quite some way out of the main city. It was well attended and the band put on a great show that was full of energy and they totally rocked the joint.

I ended up chatting to someone from Sony Records who seemed keen to set up a meeting when we got back to the UK, so we exchanged details and afterwards we all headed for the main event at Stubbs BBQ.

It was packed to the rafters, but we had been given the all-important VIP passes, which allowed us priority views and the use of the free bar inside — although it only supplied beer.

Paul, finally had clearance to film after chasing

about all night trying to get certain permissions signed off and we all settled down for a night of beer and music. Paul would get some more than interesting footage that night — resorting in the theft of the tape from his room to stop it ever being aired.

The night was going well, and as The Automatic blasted out 'What's that coming over the hill… is it a monster' we drank the free beer on tap and sipped from the bottles of vodka and brandy that we had sneaked in using Paul's camera-case. We were getting very drunk, very quickly and Joe in particular was looking very shaky on his feet and I wasn't doing so well either.

Lily Allen wowed the audience with her performance, as did Jamie T, and as we waited for the main act to come on stage, two of the members of The Automatic came out and started chatting with Ollie. Soon after they were heading backstage to their dressing room and I noticed Ollie and Stu following them with Paul in tow filming their every move.

Joe was now absolutely paralytic and could barely stand on his own two feet, his dependency on alcohol was starting to make him more paranoid than ever and he was mumbling about spiders crawling under his skin and other weird shit, but I decided to leave him and tag along with the others. It was weird as there seemed to be no security on the entrance to the backstage area; as they were all dealing with a Lily Allen tantrum the other end of the corridor.

I walked through and in the distance I could hear someone shouting, so I went to investigate further. As I turned the corner, I could see a commotion had started and could see Paul standing back filming it all.

"Fuck off you four-eyed wanker," I heard Ollie shout at the top of his voice.

I went towards the ruckus and pushing Paul aside, I saw Ollie confronting the lead singer of The Automatic' who had apparently taken offence to him following him backstage.

The guy threw a punch towards Ollie's face that just missed and in return, Ollie lunged toward at the guy, but Stu grabbed him and stopped him landing his fist bang in the middle of the guys face just in time.

"Get out, you idiots!" some bloke screamed at us and then he shoved Stu in the chest.

"Why did you do that mate?" I shouted.

He walked up to me and stuck his face into mine, he was being a right old billy big bollocks and said, "Because he's a spiky haired cunt," he said.

I laughed at him and said, "Yes mate, but he's our spiky haired cunt."

He took a step back and swung at me, narrowly missing, now I was pissed off and I moved forward and grabbed him by the shirt and without a second thought head-butted him — sending him stumbling back.

"Fuck it! That fucking hurt," I shouted. But I was in a drunken rage and if I could have done so, I would have ripped his bollocks off and stamped on them.

Ollie had managed to get himself loose from Stu's grip and in a manner befitting 'Wile E. Coyote' and 'The Road Runner', was now chasing two members of The Automatic around the room.

I couldn't help but sing in my mind...... 'What's that coming over the hill... is it a monster?' as he chased them around and around, knocking everything all over the place as he continued his frenzied mayhem.

I shouted to the others, "Come on, let's get the fuck out of here, these are just a bunch of wankers!"

We turned around and left with the intention of finding Joe and making a rapid exit, but Joe was nowhere to be seen.

"Where the fuck is he?" Ollie shouted.

We looked all over the VIP area and couldn't find him anywhere, then suddenly I saw him. He was so drunk he was crawling along the floor of the venue towards the exit doors. We ran over and grabbed him before making our own swift exit and jumping in the first taxi we could hail and headed back to the hotel.

What the hell was wrong with us? Now *we* are starting fights, we were out of fucking control and it had to stop.

Once I calmed down I realised what I was becoming – a fat drunken lout who acted like a twat, and you know what? Right there, right then —I kind of liked it.

But all this was an emotional trauma that I needed to escape from.

Back at the hotel I contemplated what had just happened, more nights like this with all the boozing, arguing and fighting and I would probably end up in hospital, prison or on a cold slab with a toe tag.

We were off home the following day and it was definitely for the best. We would get back and start planning for the future. But first we had something we needed to do.

Joe would be no good to us as he had passed out after falling over a white picket- fence about six inches high whilst walking up to the hotel, thrown up and then abused us all as being traitors for leaving him on his own earlier, before finally passing out in his room.

I hurriedly rounded up Ollie and Stu to ask them to help me with something. I told them that we needed to persuade Paul to delete the footage of the fight backstage. They agreed, but after a little more chit-chat, we decided it would be best to just steal it and destroy it, so we hatched a plan.

Stu would lure Paul into the bar on the ruse to discuss something important while Ollie and I would go back to the room and get the tape, I was sharing a room with Paul so we had easy access.

So there we were, Stu was with Paul at the bar chatting and I was in the room waiting for Ollie.

It was all a bit like Mission Impossible…. Dun dun dada, Dun dun dada, Dun dun dada, Dun dun dada, Dun dun dada, Dun dun dada, doo de doo, doo de doo, doo de doo, doo do.

Ollie knocked and I let him in and for some strange reason he turned off all the lights in the room putting us in total darkness.

"I can't see a bloody thing," I said.

"We don't want to be seen," he replied.

"But it's my room as well."

"Oh yeah, I forgot about that."

"No problem, 007," I replied as we both started laughing before I suggested that he turned the bloody lights back on.

We started to go through Paul's belongings before Ollie turned and said, "I've found his camera."

We clicked play and checked it was the right tape, it

was and for a moment we were drawn in as we watched Ollie chasing The Automatic around their dressing room and laughing out loud. Suddenly Ollie's phone beeped.

He looked and said, "Shit, Paul's coming back."

We quickly put the camera back and Ollie rushed out with the tape.

When Paul arrived he said "Goodnight," and went straight to sleep. He never noticed anything as luckily for us he was too drunk and surprisingly he never checked the tape before we left.

Ollie says he destroyed the tape, but I often wonder if he kept it — saving it for a rainy-days entertainment.

Our South By Southwest adventure was over, but little did we know we would be back the following year. The band still had some meetings and interviews to attend back in the UK, shows to play and another single to set up and self-release.

***

After a short break to recharge our batteries and, in my case spend some time with my daughters to catch up on how their schooling was going, arguing with Paula about the monthly household budgets, and getting the car serviced, it was time to get back to all things band related.

First up was a meeting with Sony Records, who I had spoken to while out in Texas, who now wanted the band to come in and have a proper chat. The band decided to drive to London, so we set off early and parked up. The boys prepared for the meeting by jumping in the back of the van and chilling with some puffing on the bong.

Paul was also with us filming the final parts of his documentary, so we headed off for a coffee leaving the guys to get high. This habit seemed to intensify and they were constantly relying on smoking weed before doing anything work related and I could hear those alarm bells ringing.

They were spending the majority of their waking hours stoned or drunk or, in Joe's case, alarmingly both.

I went into the meeting with the executives at Sony feeling like; hey, we have brought the industry to its knees and now they want to sign the band. 'Who the fuck was I kidding?' I felt like we held all the aces and that the dice of chance was loaded in the bands favour, I simply was an arrogant fool.

Paul, with his camera in hand, was told to wait outside and we were shown into an office, we were asked if anyone wanted a tea, coffee or water and told to wait, everyone refused the offer of a beverage as we were all feeling too nervous. A few minutes later a man and a woman walked in and introduced themselves and after some initial chitchat everyone seemed at ease, the meeting was going well and the band was replying to the questions that were asked of them in a professional manner.

Then suddenly, for some reason the subject got on to football, I don't know what it is about men, but regardless of the nature of a conversation or the situation, it always gets around to football. I have a vague memory that Joe may have dressed for the occasion by wearing one of his Arsenal replica shirts.

The band was asked whom they supported and all replied. "Arsenal."

"I'm a Spurs supporter," the label guy said and right there the mood changed. I could feel that the boys were looking a little disinterested, especially Ollie. The conversation moved onto the subject of live shows and after discussing Texas the chat turned to their fan-base.

"We hear that your fan-base for live shows is not that good here in the UK?" the guy said.

I could feel the tension rising so I quickly jumped in and replied, "Like any band, it's hit and miss, sometimes it's great, sometimes it's not so great. Have you seen them perform live?"

"No, but we have sent our people to some of the shows and they reported back that they were pretty well empty."

There was suddenly silence in the room and before I could reply Ollie jumped in and asked, "Well, what could you offer us anyway mate?"

The guy began a speech about what they could do to help the band and it seemed to deflect the questioning about attendances at shows and football allegiances. Then he ended with "That's of course if we decided to do anything, you still have a very long way to go before we would consider signing the band."

Now even I know that's just label talk and really means, *'we couldn't give a flying fuck about you getting a single in the charts and you've upset us in the process, so we had this meeting just as a front so we could say — well they weren't quite right for us.'*

Well, that was it. Ollie looked up at him and muttered the words that probably killed off the chances of the band ever signing to any major label.

"I'm not sure you know what you're talking about."

My heart missed a beat as I thought 'Fucking hell you stupid little shit eating wanker.'

Within a few moments we had said our goodbyes and were on our way out and back to the drawing board. I learnt yet an important lesson that day; never have your first meeting with a label with the band or artist present — as they might just open their mouths and fuck it all up for you!

As we were leaving Joe piped up, "Don't panic, our time will come, we don't want to be like a manufactured band anyway, so fuck them!" he continued.

I couldn't bear to speak to Ollie as we left and if he hadn't already done enough damage, he even had the cheek to say how well the meeting had gone on camera to Paul. I said goodbye to Paul and thanked him for all his efforts as he was now off to the editing room to prepare the film for broadcast.

I decided to travel home on the train alone, although there was a tiny part of me that did agree with the band, that all labels were just full of wankers and people who are so afraid of losing their jobs, but at the same time I just couldn't help but wish he had just kept his big mouth shut. I put my head in my hands and literally sobbed.

Was it me that wanted this more than the band or was I just a bad manager? – Someone playing at being something he didn't have a fucking clue about and wading out into waters that were just too deep to swim in?

Back home, I chatted to Paula about things and for once, she was sympathetic, but then suggested that I give up and consider 'getting a real job' as she put it. This just got my back up and we ended up rowing over something trivial like the lack of pot noodles in the house.

The following morning I'd calmed down a little and emailed Matt at Ditto to get the next single release set up for the start of June. A few weeks later the band was due to head off to Europe in the battered old white van to play some shows with a Dutch band called Heideroosjes.

I had initially decided not to go on the European tour, as I'd only just returned from the USA and I wanted to spend some time with my family. But after a series of disturbing domestic arguments I had second thoughts.

I knew I had become a selfish bastard who had little care for anyone but himself, but the constant arguments with Paula simply made going away feel like the easy way out.

The day before we were due to leave, Paul Buller's documentary aired on ITV and I was shocked to see it had been given a prime-time slot just before Coronation Street. The documentary was called 'Koopa – Do Anything You Wanna Do' and Paul had done a marvellous job everyone seemed to come across well, apart from me. I looked awful and my weight was getting way out of control — I was obviously in total denial about my looks.

My Daughters were so excited to see their dad on the television and my wife's contribution was to comment on how scruffy, fat and sweaty I looked – I remember thanking her before fucking off out to the pub to reflect on the creature I had turned into.

As I sat there alone, downing shots and pints and popping painkillers and I contemplated my life and what I had become. Deep down I knew I needed some professional help.

To be honest when you punch a wall so hard that your knuckles burst and start to bleed profusely, just because the washing machine won't stop fucking beeping, then it's time to get help.

So the following morning I made an appointment to see the doctor to explain my lifestyle and how I felt sorry to be alive and that I felt totally and utterly helpless.

The thought of sanctioning myself there and then had entered my head, just to get me out of the Koopa madness, but in the end he gave me some medication, which made me feel better for all of a week, and then it was time to hit the road again. I had no self-control.

I guess in life sometimes you're the pigeon and sometimes you're the statue.

The European tour was under way and we played shows in France, Germany, Holland and Belgium. It was the first time the band had ever had a real rider as such and we made sure it was full of beer, spirits and enough food to stop us having to buy any on the tour.

The tour passed without any problems and the crowds were large, happy and always most welcoming. The headline band, Heideroosjes, knew how to rock the house and how to party hard.

I was almost permanently drunk, as was Ollie and

Joe. Poor Stu had to drive, but that didn't seem to stop him enjoying himself at the end of the day.

There was one unforgettable incident that took place in Belgium after the band had just finished another successful show. We all spent the rest of the evening drinking and the boys also decided to partake in some very nasty smelling substance along with the crew of the headline band.

The hotel was situated just around the corner from the venue, so Stu had packed up the van and had driven it back to the hotel so he could walk back and party hard like everyone else.

It's very rare that we have a night that actually ended well within our gang and this one was no exception; we were walking back to the hotel when Ollie became very agitated and aggressive. Joe tried his best to calm him down, but he just totally flipped out like a madman and started lashing out at Joe, his arms flailing around like a windmill and his legs kicking out, trying to boot Joe as hard as he could.

Ollie had become extremely loud now and quite abusive, we were right outside the hotel and it was becoming embarrassing. Stu tried to help, but to no avail, then he unlocked and slid open the side door of the van then shouted, "Joe get his feet and help me chuck him in."

Ollie was acting like a complete and utter maniac and I just watched as Joe and Stu picked him up and threw him into the back of the van. Stu closed the side door quickly and replaced the padlock. You could hear Ollie screeching and he was also kicking the inside panels so hard, you could see the dents appearing outside; he was like a bloody wild animal or alien was trying to escape.

"What now?" I asked.

"Just leave him," Stu said, "he gets like this once in a while."

And that was it — we just left him.

In the morning I went out to find the van was still locked and all was quiet, so I went for a walk into the town to grab a cup of coffee and take in some of the local sights.

I also needed water in order to take my painkillers for my fresh new hangover. I was popping a lot of painkillers and sometimes slipped in the odd bit of speed, when I could get my hands on some, to help me get through the day.

I went back to the hotel as Stu and Joe were walking out.

"Where's Ollie?" I asked.

"Still in the van," Stu replied.

"You left him there all night?"

"Yeah, it's the only way to deal with him when he's like that," Stu replied as he unhooked the padlock to the side door and slid it open.

As the door opened a whiff of various disgusting smells wafted out and smacked us straight in our respective faces, I nearly threw up on the spot.

It smelt like warm cabbage fused with bad eggs all finished off with the rancid smell of vomit. It was disgusting and would take some cleaning up before we would all step inside again.

Then out of the dark popped Ollie all bright, bubbly and full of life.

"Morning wankers!" he shouted as he jumped out and headed towards the hotel before stopping and saying, "Oh, by the way you couple of twats — I was sick in your favourite hat Stu and I shit in your rucksack Joe!" before walking into the hotel with his right hand aloft giving us all the two fingered salute.

Joe retched as he jumped into the back of the van and you could hear him rummaging around.

"Stu you *are* going to need a new baseball cap!" Joe shouted.

Then there was a moment of silence before he opened his rucksack and cried out in horror...

"He's fucking shit on my passport!"

Chapter 24

Getting It in the Rear

It's June the 8th 2007, we are at Seaclose Park in Newport on the Isle of Wight and Koopa are minutes away from being the first band on the main stage and officially opening the historic Isle of Wight Festival.

This was a momentous occasion for the three guys and, if I was honest, it was for me too.

Joe looked the most nervous as he was scratching away at his face; his nervous nemesis. The other two were silent and just stood waiting. The time arrived and as I peeked around the side of the stage, I could see thousands of people waiting.

The stage manager gave the wave and as they ran out onto the stage, the crowd roared their approval. The festival was underway and I walked down some steps as proud as punch to watch from the side.

The bands new single was being released the following Monday called 'One Off Song for the Summer', and the festival organisers, a very nice and extremely helpful man by the name of John Giddings, had his team put the text code for the single on the big screens right next to the stage. During their set Joe informed the crowd of their whole unsigned-story and did his best to encourage them to get their mobiles out and text right there and then for the new single, it was amazing as people all around me just started texting and, as the band played on, I could sense we had the chance of another Top 40 single.

Pre-orders had already built to around 3000 without any need for me to visit another dark dogging car park. Radio 1 were giving the song some airplay and two lovely chaps at BBC Essex called Mike and Ollie were pushing the single. It had also been arranged for the boys to be live on air at their studio in Chelmsford the week of release.

The band left the stage to a rapturous applause, and I swear I heard cries for more! But this was a festival and while Echo and the Bunnymen took to the stage we disappeared to the bands dressing room to start drinking.

We chatted with the other various acts and in particular with the guys from the band The Feeling, everyone got on really well and was on first-name terms within ten minutes, so it was with great disappointment when a few weeks later, while at a one-day festival, they acted as though they had never even met us.

We decided though it would be best to head off back to the ferry rather than get caught up in all the traffic later and as were loading the van, one of the crew told us that the festival organisers had had to erect a special semi-permanent structure to house a full sized snooker table for Keith Richards of headliners The Rolling Stones just in case as he put it. "Keith fancied a game of snooker."

On the odd occasion Koopa ever received a rider we

used to request a 'white seagull' just to test if they were paying attention. Once I got a phone call asking if that seagull was to be dead or alive? How fucked up it that?

Back at the hotel we toasted the success of the festival and then I drank on my own for a while as they all took their usual seats in the back of the van for their usual bong session.

I was left on my own by the band quite a lot, but I was fine with that, as I had my other friends, beer, vodka and painkillers to keep me company – eventually I went off to bed and passed out.

Chris, who was a friend of Joe and helped sell the limited merchandise we had, was meant to share with me, but he always ended up just crashing on the floor in their room. They all liked to share a room as they only had one smoke sock to fool the smoke detector. It was on this trip that another new game was invented; this game was titled 'Gary Buckaroo.'

Based on the classic children's game, the rules were simple, I was the mule and the players had to load as much as they could on top of me while I slept. The winner being the person who placed the penultimate object on me before I 'Buckar-ooed.'

Instead of plastic game pieces normally used like a blanket, saddle, shovel, canteen, pan, etc., the band members would find their own weird and wonderful items, starting with the small and building up to the large.

This was the first time they had attempted to play, but I found out later they had actually been plotting it for weeks. So while I'm practically unconscious the game began, first came the smaller items like bars of soap, mugs, teaspoons and sachets of sugar, then slightly bigger items like coat hangers, toilet rolls and bottles of shampoo, the bigger items were added while all the time they were trying to contain their laughter and film the whole thing.

Next a kettle, followed by waste bin, then an iron and finally a bloody ironing board! I buckar..ooed alright sending the lot crashing as everything flew all over the place. "Fuck off," I yelled.

They ran off giggling and I locked the door and went back to bed. In the morning my room looked like a bomb had hit it and, to cap it off, they had written 'Gary is a gay lord bender' in shaving foam all over my bathroom mirror.

"You're so childish," I said as we left the hotel.

They just sniggered; I don't think I said another word to them all the way from Portsmouth, back home.

It was release day for 'One Off Song for the Summer' and I wanted to just boost the sales a tad, so I called Crusty-Chris to see if he had any more of them SIM cards, but sadly he had just sold out to some shady looking fella who was probably 'up to no good' as he so eloquently put it.

"Bollocks," I said out loud, but then I remembered that I had forgotten to check the text sales from the festival. To my delight a grand total of 3500 showed up on my screen, we only had to wait until the following day for the midweek industry chart. Great!

We charted at number 12, so all we had to do now was hope we stayed there. My first call was to Neil at The Gazette to once again get his help to push it in the paper and online.

'One last push to help make history again!' was the rallying cry from the Gazette as they jumped on board the promo trail. Joe was busy promoting online and Ollie and Stu were doing their usual helpful bit, which was absolutely nothing – or fuck all, as some would put it.

I had a call from Essex Radio for an impromptu interview during their drive-time slot, so I seized the opportunity to announce live on air that just 1,000 more sales would guarantee at least a top 30 slot, beating the band's January position, which was 31.

"We really need people to go out there and download the single," I begged.

"This is a bit of a plea to everyone, even those who don't like us. Please go out and buy it, if only to stick it to the record labels," I begged some more. I had suddenly turned into Sir Bob Geldof!

We were in the lap of the single buying public and just had to hope that they wanted to be a part of our campaign to shove it to the man. After all, the general public always loves the underdog don't they?

It was the end of another full-on tense week and for me, Joe and Neil from The Gazette it was game up, we had done all we could. It was now time for me at least, to sit down, drink pop painkillers and wait for the final charts to be announced.

A sit down was one thing I definitely needed as I was starting to lose the plot, I was always tired, was continuing to drink far too much and was fat. Fat, sweaty and very unhealthy. My reliance on painkillers was far too high and my relationship with my wife Paula was at the 'hardly speaking to each other phase'.

But none of that actually still seemed to matter as I was on a one-man mission to make this band famous. Sunday arrived and just as before I got the heads-up from my contact at The Official Chart Company, and as he said those beautiful words I stood and let out a huge sigh of relief, the single had indeed charted and those hotshots Koopa was in at number 21. I rang the boys and they were pleased to hear the brilliant news.

On the following Monday I had another really busy day from the fall-out answering numerous emails and phone calls. But still not one call from any label – had Ollie really blown it for us all with his comments that day at Sony? In all honesty the answer was both yes and no. Of course, there was no way that Sony, or indeed any of the majors would sign the band, as they were too outspoken against the industry, and to sign to a major label would surely mean selling out. But in fact behind the scenes we really did need a major label or at least someone with funding, otherwise the whole band was doomed to failure — as was I.

Around this time, I moved my family into a rented house in a small village outside of Chelmsford called Great Leigh's and, best of all from my point of view, it was right next to a pub.

Funny enough, towards the end of working with the band and with an ever-increasing paranoia surrounding every move I made, I would be accused by the three of them of using their money to buy the new house — utterly ridiculous, but that's how things would get.

My girls were unhappy at first, but soon settled in, as they didn't have to change schools. I was frequenting the local pub more often in-between gigs with the band and my drinking was getting even heavier.

For a while things seemed to be working out a little better on the home front, but for me, normal life was very dull when I was away from the band, and I couldn't cope with the mundane duties of running a home. I loved being with my girls and always wished, if things were different, they could have accompanied me to some of the shows, but I wasn't about to expose them to all the dangers that that entailed.

I tried, in fact, I tried very hard, but it soon became clear to me that I needed pills and alcohol to help me get through a whole day of even being at home with my wife. The drinking was my escape from reality and the reality was; I fucking hated myself and the cracks were starting to show. I tried searching my soul to find the answers to all my issues only to discover that I was struggling to care about anything at all.

The rest of the summer was quiet with shows taking place mainly at the weekends. One of the best of them was at the Hammersmith Apollo, London, when the band was asked to support INXS and The Beat or English Beat, as they were now known due to band member injunctions.

The English Beat was fantastic and backstage it was great to finally meet a band that could match us in the drinking stakes.

Watching INXS was a bit weird, for one, there was no Michael Hutchings and second, some talented Canadian singer called J.D. Fortune, who won a US reality show called 'Rock Star' fronted them — it just didn't seem right.

Ollie must have had the same thought pattern as me as I overheard J.D. Fortune ask his opinion of his show to which Ollie replied, "You were brilliant mate, but you're no fucking Michael Hutchings, that man was sick."

J.D. turned and walked away in disgust.

The band played a few outdoor gigs at the weekends and these gigs were always the best for pissing around and having a laugh, as it was not confined and there were more random people walking about. Joe was in his element at these gigs as sound check was his domain, he would check the microphones and would pick out someone poor stander-by, get their attention and shout,

"Hey...you in the blue shirt...check, check...ARE YOU GETTING IT IN THE REAR? Check, check, 1-2, 1-2, ARE YOU GETTING IT IN THE REAR? WAVE YOUR HANDS IF YOU'RE GETTING IT IN THE REAR."

The poor person in the distance would start waving his hands like an idiot and one time he even had a little old lady start talking back to him thinking she was helping out by shouting as loud as she could, "YES DEAR, I'M GETTING IT IN THE REAR."

At one show Joe let rip a massive fart on stage and it was so foul smelling that I could almost taste it from the side of the stage. Stu was gagging at the back and finding it hard to concentrate on playing the drums – he told us later that his eyes were burning it was so bad.

You could tell that the crowd could smell it and some were running off to the back of the venue and it had made me wonder if Joe had actually shit himself.

Joe quick as flash shouted to the crowd, "Who has fucking farted?" and after catching the eye of an attractive blonde in the front row, he tells the entire crowd that it was her — she left immediately.

For the first time Ollie starts dating. It was a girl he had met on the 'Stand Up 4 England' video shoot and this now meant that she was backstage at gigs and this obviously was pissing the other two off, especially when she started telling him how to dress and God knows what else behind the scenes.

He bought her to almost every show and she didn't lift a finger to help out, she just sat in the van drinking with everyone else stroking Ollie's forehead and massive ego. It annoyed me because she hadn't been there the first time round and it had fuck all to do with her.

It's nothing personal against her, and I'm sure she did it at the request of Ollie himself, but it irked me that she was there just because she was giving blowjobs to the lead singer.

Then there was the time she made herself look like a twat when she encountered a brilliantly sarcastic hotel receptionist.

We were staying in a very shabby run-down looking hotel in the middle of nowhere and, now, also bloody paying for an extra room for her and Ollie to shag in, which Joe and Stu weren't best pleased with and Joe seemed to be drinking more and smoking more as a direct result.

I had checked us in and they had all dispersed to their relevant rooms, while Joe and I went to the bar, when all of a sudden she came storming down with a face like thunder and in a rather rude tone asked the person behind the desk "Does the water always come through the ceilings here?"

"No Madam," answered the woman very politely, "Not always, only when it rains."

I looked at Joe and we fell about laughing, she turned around saw us laughing and stormed off. Ollie promptly came down to the bar and told us not to be rude to his girlfriend.

I think Joe replied with "Bollocks."

Ollie stood silent, his face showing his brain-wheel turning as he desperately tried to format a suitable quick-witted clever reply in his head beneath his stupid bobble hat, "Fuck you!" he shouted before stomping off upstairs.

While we were sitting at the bar another man came and sat with us and after a while we started chatting.

"So, what do you do for a living?" I asked.

"I work in the city," he replied.

"Cool," Joe said, "are you a stocks and shares man?"

"No, I work on the bins," he replied.

We laughed out loud and then spent the night drinking and taking the piss out of Ollie's girlfriend.

The band had seemed to have stalled once again, perhaps they we were never going to make it. Perhaps it was time to give up.

Life had become like one of those grabbing machines you see in the arcades; you know you will end up losing, but you will keep trying to grab that soft toy. Once in a while you may win, but the rest of the time that crane returns empty handed.

We only had a few coins left and a big decision to be made — do we go for the toy, or do we give up?

Chapter 25

Crashing into the Top 20

I had the band out on the road doing gigs as much as possible, sometimes just to all get away from being stuck at home bored, and on the odd occasion because we were actually getting paid.

The band had a gig up in the north somewhere – I think it was around the Sheffield area, but it might have just been a bit further up into bandit country. It appeared to be some kind of country and western club, as the walls were adorned with posters of all things wild-west.

The promoter welcomed us in and showed us to the dressing where he had kindly laid out some sandwiches, beers, bottles of water and a very large bottle of Jack Daniels and before I'd even had time to thank him, Joe had already poured himself a very large neat glass.

I asked the promoter about the wild-west theme and jokingly asked if the room would be full of cowboys. He explained that the club was used for line dancing, but the new owner wanted to turn the place into a rock club because all the line dancers did was dance, drink tap water and complain.

He advised that tonight's show would be a rock

crowd and that they had sold over 250 tickets – yeah right!

The band was to be the main act and, following two mediocre supports, went on to rapturous applause to a crowd who did indeed look like a rock crowd and were well over 250 plus strong.

As the set progressed, Joe, who was much the worse for wear having drank almost the entire bottle of JD, noticed a few older people at the back dressed in cowboy and girl outfits and as they finished their final guitar riffs of 'The Crash' — Joe stood and stared at the bemused cowboys and girls.

Then asked, "Have you got your nights mixed up?"

"Yes," an elderly lady replied, "we thought it was line-dancing tonight."

"Well, if you want line dancing my love, then line dancing you shall have!"

Joe turned and whispered to the other two. Then just as the band began to play the line dancers looked at one another and smiled; they knew exactly what was coming.

"Tumble outta bed and I stumble to the kitchen,
Pour myself a cup of ambition,
And yawnin', stretchin', try to come to life,
Jump in the shower and the blood starts pumpin',
Out on the streets, the traffic starts jumpin,'
With folks like me on the job from 9 to 5,
Workin' 9 to 5, what a way to make a livin','"

Yes, you guessed it, the band had launched into a cover of the Dolly Parton hit '9 to 5'.

The crowd laughed before they too started to jump around and sing along with the cowboys and girls and by the time Joe got to the last chorus, they were having a great time heel digging, double heel digging, weaving and grape-vining all over the dance floor. The band followed up with one final song by the Proclaimers '500 Miles' cover, and everyone there had a great time.

It was a good night, but it was one of those – *'I guess you had to be there nights'*, but it certainly was one of the lighter moments of life on the road with the band.

On the way home and now drunk I tried to explain to the guys that I was worried that things had not worked out and that we needed a fucking big break. I suggested we made one more single and that if nothing came of it then we would call it a day – we all knew that time was running out for all of us.

The three of them agreed. Ollie announced that he had a great song that he hadn't given a title yet, but would send it to me the following day.

Finally, after about fifteen phones he sent the damn track at 9pm — it was indeed a cracker.

The band was heading to the studio on the Saturday morning to record it, as I rang to remind them about their interview with The James Whale Show at Talksport in London later that night, they thanked me for the reminder as they had indeed forgotten all about it — as usual.

I spent the day out with my daughters before settling in front of the television with a four-pack of lager. The weather had taken a turn for the worse and it had started to rain, the clouds were really grey and dark. The skies opened up and the rain poured, thunder and as lightning filled the sky, I thought of the guys having to drive through the storm. The rain at one point was so heavy it was hitting my Sky TV dish with such force it was breaking the signal and was ruining my nights viewing.

I tried to have a conversation with Paula, but she was in one of her ever increasing moods and eventually I gave up and watched 'Enter the Dragon' on DVD instead.

My timings were perfect and just as the movie finished it was time to tune into The James Whale Show on the radio and listen to the boys, who were to be this week's special guests. James had always been a great supporter of the band as he admired their punk-rock attitude to the establishment; I think he must have been a secret punk-rocker himself once.

James was known for his plain-speaking, often confrontational broadcasting style and tonight was to be no different. During the phone-in session, he hung up on callers he disagreed with, and those who were not making their point quickly enough.

But he let the boys talk and I could sense they were relaxed and even Ollie had something to say for a change.

When the interview had finished, I turned the radio off and I headed for bed, and just as I fell asleep my phone rang.

"Hello," I said.

"Hi Gary, alright, it's Ollie," came the reply.

"I'm ok mate, what's up?"

"Well, we gotta bit of a problem," he said before continuing "we're on the motorway in the dark and the car's upside down."

342

"What, … hang on… for fuck's sake… what did you just say?"

"Well, it's a bloody storm out here, we hit some water and the car kinda just flipped over mate."

I started to panic and asked, "Are you all ok?"

I then heard Ollie shout, "Are we all ok chaps?"

"Yes," from voice one, "Yes," voice two, "Yes," voice three.

"Who else is in the car?"

"Joe's mate Chris," Ollie answered, "he's actually shit himself and it stinks in here."

"Do I need to call for help?"

"No, it's on the way already."

I could hear the cars whizzing by and the splashing of the rain hitting their vehicle.

"Sounds bloody dangerous, can you get out?" I asked.

"We are all trapped in, we can't get our seatbelts undone," Ollie said.

Then the battery went dead. I tried calling back, but nothing.

For the next hour I paced up and down having the odd shot of vodka. I was scared and worried about their safety. Then at around 1.00am I got a call from Joe's dad saying that the emergency services had got to them and everyone was fine. Feeling an instant hit of relieve I went back to bed and fell into a deep sleep, when I finally woke up it was 2.00pm.

I spoke to the guys as soon as I woke to confirm they were all ok. Stu told me that for the first ten seconds as the car took off from the road and flipped, he thought they were are all going to die.

"We should have gone in the van and not mum's car," he said — I think he must have been in shock!

It turned out that the first policeman on the scene happened to be a big fan of theirs and had actually been to some of their gigs and, in a surreal moment for the lads, the first thing the policeman said was "Hey aren't you that band Koopa?"

Thank God, the band had all survived. they were all shaken, but unharmed; except for Joe, who was milking it a bit complaining he had a sore neck. While hanging upside down in the car that night they had used the time wisely and had unanimously decided that the title of their new song would be 'The Crash' in honour of the event.

Knowing the band members were all ok and no real damage had been done, I started to set up the next single. It was obvious that the major labels were not interested and the small labels couldn't really offer us anything we couldn't do for ourselves — we needed some serious investment.

But where was this going to come from?

I was starting to get the feeling that our ship had sailed and that we were all fucked!

This time round we decided it was time to push that boat right out and press some CD's, but in order to get the CD single into actual record stores, it had to be seen as a legitimate record label release, as well as having a proper distribution company behind it. Both of these would actually be the easy bit as Boring-Paul, the publisher, could deal with this on our behalf. But we needed a name for our fake label.

I chatted to the boys and for a laugh, we told Boring-

Paul to call the fake label 'Juxtaposition' in honour of the band Foregone Conclusion who had been fronted by the fictional character David Brent from 'The Office'. We all laughed, but I'm not sure anyone else got the joke – but Ricky Gervais would get it.

The band loved watching his mockumentary sitcom and played it endlessly on their little portable DVD player while drinking and doing copious amounts of weed before and after shows.

Funny enough one of the reasons I now demanded my own hotel room was down to Ricky Gervais.

It boiled down to one specific night that completely topped me over the edge. After yet another heavy drinking session, everyone had collapsed into a drunken stupor and was now sound asleep when someone's mobile phone started constantly ringing eventually causing me to wake. It would ring for a few minutes, then stop before starting again.

"Will one of you turn that fucking phone off!" I screamed, but no one stirred.

On and on it went until I could take no more, I jumped out of bed and stormed over to the table where the boys' phones were charging, the three of them still blissfully snoring as I searched for the culprit. 'I bet its Ollie's fucking girlfriend checking up on his movements' I thought, as her late night calls were something that had become more and more common place as she was not always with him; girlie trust issues I guess.

Most girlfriends of musicians suffer from trust issues and with some justification, as I haven't encountered many musicians who would miss the opportunity of a blowjob or hand-job from an admirer given half the chance.

Remember the saying 'what goes on tour stays on tour!' that's more than just a saying, it's a sacred musicians bond and one that should never be broken. Well, at least not by the musicians! – managers can say what the fuck they like!

Despite checking their phones the bloody ringing started again and as I fell about the place half-drunk tripping over the mass of clothes, bags and beer cans, I accidently kicked over the bong causing all the dirty rancid water to spill over Stu's jacket and it really smelt bad.

I was trying to move around the room as the ringing was getting louder, when I discovered the source of my anger and frustration; the bands little portable DVD player on the floor in the corner of the room and, as I picked the bloody thing up the ringing started again, it was the bloody DVD menu jingle to 'The Office' — a ringing phone. "Bollocks!" I said under my breath, as I switched it off and returned to bed.

As I lay there I pondered on everything that annoyed me about the three of them; their attitudes, their drinking, their drug taking and worst of all that fucking Office DVD - sorry Ricky Gervais, but had you been there at that moment I would have tried to make you eat the fucking thing.

***

In an attempt to better the chart position of the single we put five different versions of 'The Crash' on pre-order. which was a mental idea, or so I thought, these days everyone is doing it. Of course I made sure that people could text to purchase, as the band had benefited considerably from the previous ones.

As well as the standard radio version, Joe had mixed extended and fake live versions, the band had recorded an acoustic version and to cap it all off, I had the brilliant and almost ingenious idea of creating an audio commentary version. What I had in mind was something like the audio commentary that you could get on movies where the cast and director discuss the movie as you watch along.

I'm still not sure why these exist, as all they do is ruin the film and who cares if Russell Crow had to eat ten pounds of raw meat a day while making 'Gladiator'. The Koopa audio commentary was meant to be insightful and was there to help the listener to understand the whole process of making a record, but it ended up being more like a comedy sketch as the band just fooled around for over six minutes.

As the band politely said at the end of the commentary "This was our manager's idea, so if it's rubbish, blame him!" which wasn't at all helpful.

No band before then had ever done an audio commentary and, in hindsight I now understand why.

Once again we needed another new music video to accompany our new song and that's when I was introduced to the band's friend Dangerous-Dave. He had told Joe he could help and that he had an idea, a location and also all the props needed, so we drove down to his house just outside Brighton the night before and prepared in our usual way; consumed a vast amount of mix of lager, spirits and fancy cocktails.

I had cocaine for the very first time that night. I had bought it a few days earlier from some geezer in the pub when I had been absolutely plastered and was feeling tired and a bit under the weather, but I had forgotten I had it on me.

Good job no one at home went through my coat pockets.

When you initially snort cocaine it burns a little, and it has a weird chemical taste that I would akin to 'Play-doh'. But within a few minutes, it makes you feel like a more sociable, cooler version of yourself.

On the day of the shoot we had another problem, Ollie was being a complete dick and was refusing to come out of the van because he felt too nervous. The problem was solved with four cans of Kronenbourg, laced with a little cocaine and ten puffs on the bong.

Dangerous-Dave had done a good job on the video and with it in place I sent the band on an all-out charm offensive to promote the new single, and with five different text codes we were going for it big time. At a show in Southend we managed to get most of the audience to text for at least three versions of the single and this was a trend we continued.

The pre-sales were racking up and we already had release we had over 4000 in the locker.

Such an amazing feat considering that we had no radio play unless you counted our old chum Steve Lamacq, who was pushing the song on his late night show. As for the rest of the music industry — well they had nothing, but utter disdain and contempt for us all by this time, and anyway we didn't fucking want their help.

Some of the reviews had been just offensive, especially from the 'Drowned in Sound' editor, who for some reason seemed to have a personal vendetta against us.

We considered visiting his office once with some mates as back-up, to set the record straight, but decided in the end that he wasn't worth it, although he was, and still is in our opinion, a total fucking wanker!

One reviewer said *'As people like Joseph Stalin have proved, the term "history maker" isn't always a good thing.'*

We were about to shake the industry once again and this time not only would the band finally get a bite from a label, but the industry would fight back; by forcing The Official Chart Company to revise its rules on downloads. These day downloads have to be redeemed to actually count as a sale, but as we set our sights on the charts once more — all we needed was the purchase.

Soon after the band released the single the rules were amended, and these new rules meant that the track had to be downloaded before it counted as a sale. This change was something that in certain circles in the music industry became known as 'The Koopa Clause.'

By the time the release day of the single came around, we had plenty of sales in the locker and I was confident we had secured at least another top 30. The midweeks came out the following day and there it was sitting pretty at number 15. This was going to be a tough one to hang onto, so the next few days were spent getting everyone we knew who had a phone and a computer to text and download, including: parents, sisters, aunts, uncles, the chap at the One-Stop shop, that geezer who ran the petrol station and his next door neighbours granny and of course ourselves.

The four of us worked together like a dream-machine, four terminators and this time there was going to be no stopping any of us. Even if it was our last hurrah.

We wanted to shove it right down the doubter's throats. But could we do enough?

I kept thinking that we needed more, much more if the band was going to get in the top 20 that week, and I think at that point I actually do believe that I wanted it more than them, the addictive side of my nature took over and that's when I found myself sat on my own in the dark having a very weird imaginary conversation with the band.

"How about we shake the tree once and for all?"

"How?" Imaginary Stu replied.

"Let's get some more SIM-cards and get the single in the top 20!"

Then imaginary Ollie said, "Fuck it, let's do it."

"You have nothing to lose," I said, before adding, "this will piss them all off!"

If the men with white coats had been passing at that particular moment they would have put me in a straitjacket and carted me off to the funny farm. To any neutral person observing the situation, it would've been quite clear that I was cracking-up and needed some sort of help. I was totally off my fucking nut!

So after my imaginary conversation and without consulting them, I was back on the phone to Dodgy-Dave to get in touch with Crusty-Chris and after a short while Crusty called back and said he only had about 150 left, but these ones all had £10 credit on and he only wanted £250 for them.

Which was a result really, as we could now put all five versions of 'The Crash' on.

"I'll have them mate," I said, "can you meet me in Chelmsford this afternoon?"

We agreed to meet in the ASDA car park in Chelmsford, which was far better than some dodgy dogging car park elsewhere, and after I checked a few, I returned home and started the boring task of filling every card with the five different versions.

I never told the band about this incident and let them carry on believing it was due to the growth of their fan-base and their increasing popularity. I also used all the negative online articles to spur everyone on, especially those suggested that everything was little more than an elaborate music industry hoax or a PR stunt.

The best rants came from other bitter managers who were just fucking jealous that we got in there first.

One band even put out a statement slagging of Koopa saying;

"We were absolutely disgusted with them, I mean what a cheap dirty trick, KOOPA have always been greatly respected by us for being a quality act, but this goes way below the belt."

It's clear to us that they were looking for angles to build their publicity on... bullshitting is one thing, but TOTAL BULLSHITTING at the expense of a rival band is cold man, fucking cold.

When asked by a journalist about the statement they had posted I paused and said, "I'm sorry that you feel this way, but please shut the fuck up and concentrate on your own music instead of trying to jump on our bandwagon, nobody gives a shit who you are – oh and who exactly *are* you by the way?"

I was sick to death of all the other bands bitching about it and this is something that my future acts Twenty Twenty, Loveable Rogues and Room 94 — would have to endure after they all had their own successes.

My advice to any other bands reading this is to concentrate on your own fucking music and never worry about what everyone else is doing. If an angle or an opportunity comes your way always consider it and if it's going to create hype for the band, then take it, otherwise go and listen to the theme tune to 'Rhubarb & Custard' and fucking calm yourself down.

***

It was the end of the week and once again we had done everything we could and I had even gone that extra little secret mile, so as before, all that was left to do was wait for those all-important results. When those all-important results came… we were fucking gob smacked.

I took the dreaded call around midday to find it was not good news — it was amazing news! The single had crashed into the charts at number 16 – FUCKING HUGE RESULT!

I rang the band immediately happy to announce that they were now officially a top 20 chart band and after an afternoon of drinking and listening to the chart show, I settled down to relax and to get very drunk.

We had all done a great job, but a phone call I would receive later that night would put the icing on the cake and a rather large cherry on top.

Chapter 26

An Offer We Could Not Refuse

It was a cold Sunday night and there was bugger all on television. Outside the rain was battering against the window and this was of course affecting the signal on my satellite box, so I was sitting in silence, pondering on a job well done when my mobile, which had been left on silent mode, started to vibrate along the glass coffee table top it was sitting on and was just about to vibrate itself off the edge when I picked it and looked at the number. I didn't recognise it and it was a Sunday — so intrigued I answered.

"Hi, is that Gary?" a man asked. His accent was strange and I couldn't quite grasp its origins.

"Yes."

"I represent Pied Piper Records based in Nashville," he informed before adding, "we really like your Koopa band and would like to discuss the possibility of signing them."

I sat there silent for a few seconds and I dropped my mobile on the floor.

"Hello?" came the shout from my phone, "are you still there?"

I picked the phone back up and replied, "Yes, yes, sorry I dropped my phone."

For the next ten minutes the guy explained that he was interested in signing the band and taking them to the US to record an album. He asked, that if he took care of all the costs and arrangements would I be interested in going over to discuss matters further and that he was happy to cover the extra cost to bring one member of the band with me.

Of course I said yes — who wouldn't like a free weekend in Nashville of all places!

I had just one more question, "Sorry, what was your name?" I asked.

"Craig," he replied.

I asked him to email all the details about the label he represented and then I picked up the phone and rang around the guys. Everyone was delighted to hear such fantastic news and Stu and Ollie nominated Joe to come with me to Nashville to help check things out – to be honest I think Joe nominated himself.

So in less than a couple of weeks Joe and I were drunk, pilled-up and asleep on our way to Nashville. We were met at the airport by Craig and his assistant Justin and taken to a private apartment belonging to the label, that would be home for a few days. I spent the weekend chatting, and drinking. Joe, however spent the weekend getting absolutely hammered and totally off his head on all manner of drugs I had never even heard of.

All went swimmingly apart from one sticky question about the bands fan-base and their following. I'll admit that I may have over-baked my answer just a tiny little bit, well a fucking huge bit, but after all — that is the manager's job isn't it?

We returned home from our whirlwind trip where over a weekend of booze and drugs, a deal seemed to have been verbally agreed. But where I should have felt as though I was flying high and happy, all I actually was was really tired. The rock 'n' roll lifestyle was definitely catching up with me and I was slowly dying from the inside out and seemed unable to deal with any of my issues.

I felt like I could sleep for three months. I never do sleep well when I'm not in my own bed and I wish I could bottle this particular trait so I could take it with me everywhere for regular use. It was a most welcome relief to be home.

Over the next few weeks and, without ever seeing the band perform live, the record deal was finalised and the label emailed me asking if I would discuss the topic of producers that they band would like to use on their album.

This was perfect for us because the labels in the UK were now onto our 'blags' and they wouldn't touch us with an extremely large barge pole – but then Pied Piper came along and man did we go for the jugular.

I asked them if there were any budgets for the producer and they replied saying that at this stage they just wanted the band to compile a list of their top choices. In the case of Koopa this statement was like unlocking the pub doors and declaring that 'The drinks are free for life and theirs an everlasting supply of weed out the back!'

We were all sitting high spirited backstage at a venue

called The Music Tek on an industrial estate, in the not so illustrious, Dagenham in Essex and the free lager and toffee flavoured vodka shots were going down all too easy, when I explained that the label wanted them to compile a list of prospective producers and that the sky was the limit — so they grabbed a fag packet and scribbled their list on it.

The final wish list on that packet of Marlboro lights read as follows:

1. Mark Hoppus – Blink 182
2. Dave Grohl – The Foo Fighters
3. Frank Black – The Pixies
4. Billie Joe Armstrong – Green Day
5. Steve Albini (Produced Nirvana)
6. Butch Vigg (Produced Smashing Pumpkins)
7. Rob Cavallo (Produced Green Day)

The band had just compiled pop-punk royalty! I advised them, I thought the label would take one look and simply reply with something like 'We approached them all, but they were not available so please consider these' – which would be a list of producers we had never heard of.

The band insisted that their list was to be sent and rather embarrassingly, I clicked 'send' on the computer and it was done. I awaited some kind of sarcastic reply questioning the bands mental state and their sense of reality —but it never came.

A few days later it did come and the reply was in my inbox. I had written in the subject line 'Producers?' so I knew this was a direct reply. I started to read it and to my utmost dismay, it stated that the label had opened negotiations with all the parties concerned and that they had received positive replies, and that over the next few weeks they would be in touch to confirm, which producer had been finalised.

I rang Joe and after saying hello, I declared. "Bloody hell, this guy is serious."

"That's fucking great mate!" Joe replied.

"Yeah, but then again this could just be the corporate bullshit game, so let's wait and see shall we."

I looked at the clock and it was 10.30 am. "Is it too early for a beer?" I asked myself out loud.

Worryingly I had been talking out loud to myself for some time now and worryingly still I found it to be quite therapeutic.

"Of course it's ok to have a beer, I'm celebrating! And while you're at it a couple of pain killers wouldn't hurt."

I was popping painkillers daily and drinking at every given opportunity and, on occasions, if nobody was in the house I would have a bottle of lager on my cornflakes – well, I did once and that was only because we were out of semi skimmed milk (I was not a full-on alcoholic just yet – I was very close though). I was completely unaware that I was now a borderline alcoholic and had a prescription pill problem. I was teetering on the edge, but oblivious to the edge of what.

It was all systems go and while the label made final arrangements to get the producer locked-in they started to arrange all the schedules, booking the flights and arranging the bands work visas.

The schedule arrived and the labels, master plan involved flying the band out to their Nashville studio to finish writing and producing demo tracks, by which time the producer would be sorted and the band could then stay in the States to record the album.

I informed my wife that sometime in March I would be heading off to America, which strangely was met with no resistance; she had no objections at all, the reason I would eventually find out in due course.

Everything was getting serious and I had to engage a lawyer to act on the band's behalf to complete the deal with the label picking up our legal fees. The band was also in urgent need of becoming a bona fide business so a meeting was arranged with an accountant to look after their financial affairs. He was obviously good at his job judging by the size of his mansion and his offices with a built-in swimming pool.

The deal was finally done and the band received a small advance, which pleased me as it was an opportunity to be paid some commission and reclaim some money back for all those receipts that were now stuffed in a brown paper bag under my bed for things I had paid for from my family's savings.

This was to be the time that I would quickly learn that we were not the band-of-brothers I had come to believe we were. I sat quietly going through all the receipts to ensure that all was present and correct and, by the time I had finished, the grand total due was around £2,000.00

On top of that I was also due my management commission for the record deal advance. So things were looking up for me, there was just one great big fucking problem, as the accountant explained — the band was refusing to pay the money owed.

I just couldn't believe it, so when I saw the them the

next day we had a blazing row and I told them how disappointed I was with their attitude especially after all my years of hard work.

Ollie said, "Don't be a money grabbing bastard."

"You bunch of bastards. After everything I've done for you," I yelled straight into their faces.

"We need that money to pay back our parents," Stu added.

I stood there contemplating punching all three of the little pricks in their respective faces.

"You are all off your fucking nuts... you fucking bunch of wankers!" I shouted as I stormed out before things got out of hand and ended in violence.

That night, sitting in the local pub I brewed over the band's attitude towards me, when I received a phone call from the accountant explaining that all the money owed to me had been paid into my bank account and that he would like to apologise on behalf of the band for all the grief they had caused me that afternoon.

I sat and wondered if he was just making it up and why hadn't the three of them just apologised to me in person. It was obvious from that moment, that we would now have trust issues and I was completely unaware at the time that behind the scenes, it was the label that were sowing the seeds of doubt against me in their minds – the good old fashioned backstabbing had begun.

Before the excitement of jetting off to the big apple the band still had a few commitments to fulfil and the first of these was in Doncaster at a shitty venue called The Leopard. The promoter, John was a nice chap and he would book the band to headline while also booking his son's band Area 15 as the main support – they sounded a bit like Koopa only on helium.

Doncaster has to be the worst town we'd ever visited with only Margate; with its run-down seafront full of closed amusement arcades a close second.

The town centre was a shit-hole full of abandoned, boarded-up shops with old signs in the windows declaring cheap rates, litter strewn everywhere and threatening chav looking boys and girls hanging around on every street corner, swearing and spitting. We had a special game for this town; a game called spot-the-fat-person-on-a-mobility-scooter and you got an extra point if they were smoking — It was an easy game with high scores.

John was great and always promoted the shows well and even though the venue was small and hot and the people were squeezed in like sardines, it was always packed to the rafters with teenagers.

The boys were on stage rocking and the sweaty crowd was leaping around the wooden floor, which at one point seemed like it would cave in under all the foot stamping and jumping.

I retreated to the exit doors, which had been opened to help bring in some much needed fresh air and stood on the top of the metal fire escape just in case the floor finally gave in and everybody plummeted to their demise, which of course never happened.

For a few seconds I wondered if the band had enough material for an album already so that they could have a number one album posthumously should the worst happen.

Fortunately, there were no disasters and while we

were loading the equipment back into the van I received a phone call from the label informing me that non-other than Mark Hoppus of pop punk legends Blink 182 had agreed to produce the album. The boys were beside themselves with joy and after hugging one another decided to celebrate by doing some bongs.

John had arranged our hotel for that night and, after checking in and spending a few hours in the bar drinking, the band decided to celebrate by being rock 'n' roll and subsequently trashed their room.

First Joe wrote their names with a thick black marker pen under every mirror and picture and, Ollie rather disgustingly, pissed in the kettle. Stu seemed perplexed as he looked around for something to do in order to join in on the trashing.

Suddenly he picked up the flat screen HD television and threw it out of the window, but he hadn't accounted on the fact that it was still plugged in, so it just bounced straight back and smacked him full in the face before just dangling there swinging back and forth from the window, still airing the evening weather report; so while we all fell about laughing, Stu embarrassingly pulled it back into the room just as the evening news started.

Things were busy prior to leaving for the States, and a week later the band had been booked to do a live radio session for The BBC, that had been organised by two BBC Radio Essex presenters called Mike and Ollie.

Basically, these are live sessions from established stars and the latest emerging talent at the BBC's historic Maida Vale studios.

The building on Delaware Road is one of the BBC's

362

earliest premises, pre-dating Broadcasting House, and was the centre of the BBC radio news service during World War II. The building houses a total of seven music and radio drama studios, and was most famously home to the legend that was John Peel and was where all of those classic John Peel BBC Radio 1 'Peel Sessions' were recorded.

While the band set about recording, I explored the building to take in all the history that you could just sense all around. I passed one of the largest studios and looked inside to see The BBC Symphony Orchestra rehearsing. Standing there listening was simply stunning and it really brought a chill to my bones. The band finished their session and Mike and Ollie advised it would be aired on their show the following week and would also be broadcast on The Steve Lamacq Show on Radio 1 just a few days later – things were actually on the up.

Joe and I had another engagement to attend that night; as guests on some late-night discussion show for BBC Radio 4, so we headed off in a taxi to BBC Centre.

On the way Joe asked, "Are you thinking what I'm thinking?"

"I fucking hope not!" I replied.

"Don't be a dick. I was thinking things are going really well, aren't they!"

"Yeah, but this is Koopa mate, who knows what's around the corner."

We arrived at the BBC and were ushered into a room where people were milling about chatting and helping themselves to the abundance of soft drinks, sandwiches and hot beverages available.

"What a shit rider!" Joe joked, "no brandy?" he added.

"That's the last thing you need!"

I surveyed the room and studied the people and noticed that everyone else was wearing brown corduroy trousers and casual jackets and looked like they were about to go on 'Mastermind' or 'Question Time.'

We were shown into the studio where for the first three quarters of an hour, we hardly spoke — what the hell did we know about an ongoing war in the Middle East in some country you couldn't even pronounce, let alone discuss the state of the NHS.

We were like fish out water, but when the conversation switched to the state of the music industry, we held our own against the toffee-nosed intellectuals, who continued to look down their noses at the two of us.

What a bunch of over analysing corduroy wearing intellectual wankers!

Chapter 27

The Band vs. Bob the Builder

The band had one more show in December before I could look forward to spending Christmas with my family.

The venue was somewhere near Braintree in Essex being held in a hall at a social club, that was also hosting a wedding anniversary in the hall next door. The promoter was a blonde long haired, bespectacled chap by the name of Jim and his son's band called Nothing Can Prove It were the headliners. Jim's son, Sonny was the drummer in the band and a damn good one at that. I remember that the lead singer had a SpongeBob-SquarePants tattoo.

Jim and I would go on to become very good friends for a while and would forge an excellent working relationship when his son joined a band, I would manage called Twenty Twenty, and through sheer hard graft and commitment from everyone involved, they would eventually be signed to a major record label before it inevitably went 'tits up' and everybody would fall-out and almost come to blows.

It was the usual tale of finger-pointing with many fingers pointed at Jim, but I couldn't blame him for the band's failure and it's a real shame that we now no longer speak.

The music industry does seem to have a habit of creating internal feuds turning friends into enemies.

It was cold, dark and foggy the night of the gig and I drove the short distance to the venue with my daughter Holly, who was going to help out on the merchandise table.

When we arrived, I discovered the boys looking glum and as usual, being ultra-unfriendly and choosing not to mix with the other bands backstage, but instead opting to sit in the back of the van drinking and smoking to entertain themselves.

I stuck my head in the van and noticed Stu looked peculiar; his face was very pale in fact he looked like a fucking ghost.

"You ok mate?" I asked.

"Yeah."

"But you look weird, you ill?"

"I just feel a bit hyper as I've just downed four cans of Red Bull and my heart's in overdrive!"

"For fuck's sake, you'll have a heart attack if you don't lay off that shit!"

I looked over and saw that Joe had already polished off at least half a bottle of cheap white label supermarket brandy, which would explain the far-away look in his eyes. His dependence on alcohol seemed to be increasing and he was slowly drinking himself to death.

He had also started drinking on his own more frequently, which to many experts is the final sign that you have become a full blown alcoholic and in need of help. The problem was I was usually too drunk to even notice his demise, or indeed even care, which is a most shameful thing to say – but I was battling my own demons at that point.

"Have you sound checked?" I asked.

"No."

"Why not?"

"Because Bob-The-Builder said there was no time for them tonight," Stu reply.

"Who's Bob-The-Builder?"

"The promoter, that bloke Jim, the one who thinks he's in charge," Ollie replied.

"Yeah, he's just a builder not a music promoter, I think he did our garden wall last year," Joe added.

"Either come in and have a drink or fuck off inside, either way shut the van door it's freezing," Ollie said.

I was driving and I had Holly my youngest with me and there's one thing I would never do and that was drink and drive — so I declined the bands kind offer and we went inside.

Holly and I found a suitable merchandising table, so while she laid out our cheaply made T-shirts, I had a chat with Bob-The-Builder – sorry Jim.

Whatever promotion Jim had done had certainly worked as the hall was packed with teenage fans, as well as friends and family of the bands and I had persuaded him to let Area 15 open the show, as it was nice to see that John had ventured this far down south with them.

Area 15 took to the stage and after a minute you could hear that there was a problem with the sound, as it kept cutting out. I told Jim what was going on and he whispered something in John's ear who then immediately scuttled off to the side of the stage.

Jim explained that because the venue was only a local social club and governed by the local council rules, being in a built up area meant that it had to be fitted with a noise limiter, which was causing the sound issues. Jim actually threw a few f-words into the explanation, as obviously he wasn't too happy with the situation either.

Now a noise limiter to a musician is the equivalent of a cross to a vampire or a silver bullet to a werewolf.

It was the work of the devil, otherwise known as the local council. Noise limiters are inserted between the main breaker box and the plug sockets supplying the stage area and in effect a noise-limiter acts as a mains cutoff, if sound levels exceed a preset threshold for a preset period, which in the case of tonight's show was about thirty fucking seconds.

I watched as John ushered one of the band members over and after a quick word in their shell-like they adjusted some switches on their kit and hey presto all was back to normal and they finished their rather toned-down set.

I went to the van and as usual was immediately smothered in fumes as I opened the side door. I informed them they were next on and that they had to tone things down a little due to the noise limiter. In hindsight, I should've just kept my mouth shut as I might as well have just waved a massive red flag to a pissed off bull.

I could see that beyond their red-sunken bong-filled eyes, they were planning a nasty surprise.

As I turned to leave I said, "Please behave tonight."

Ollie grumbled something along the lines of "Rashin'

Fashin' Fuckin' Bollocks, Gary," in his Mutley voice and as I walked away I could hear them whispering.

Just prior to performance time, I went back stage and could see that the band was really pumped up and hyper, or maybe perhaps just completely off their tits.

Joe looked at me and shouted, "We're going to blow the lid off this motherfucker!"

I instantly realised what they had in mind and shouted "Oh no for fuck's sake. Please don'...t," it was too late, they took to the stage and Joe with his legs astride in front of the microphone shouted to the crowd below "Good evening! Are you ready to rock this fucking joint!"

The crowd erupted, and with that Joe hit one of the loudest bass chords I had ever heard, which of course as planned, was instantly followed by total silence. The chord had instantly tripped the noise limiter. Joe turned to Ollie and smiled and muttered something like one nil to me. I put my head in my hands and sighed.

Ollie stood patiently waiting for the sound to return and then strummed his guitar as hard and as loud as he could, to create again total silence. He turned to Joe and gestured that it was now one all. The crowd stood silent for a few seconds and then started screaming....

"KOOPA! KOOPA! KOOPA!"

The boys were now high on adrenaline and sensing the crowd wanted to actually hear their music they started to play their set, but even though they adjusted their kit the limiter kept cutting out and I could see the band getting wound-up and angry. The limiter was absolutely ruined the gig for everyone in the hall and half-way through 'Lost in Madrid' the band stopped and stood silent as the crowd wondered what was happening.

Ollie was staring out from the stage looking stoned and angry, he started to shake and shouted, "This is fucking annoying me!" before adding, "I'm not fucking having this, I want to entertain these people!"

He stormed off the stage and marched toward the back of the hall, leaving everyone wondering what the hell was going on, he then grabbed a six-foot stepladder which leant against the rear wall, positioning it under the sound limiter located above the main entrance.

I was with Holly at the merchandise table and we just looked at each other in total disbelief before it suddenly dawned on me what was going to happen.

"What the fucking hell is he doing?" Jim asked me.

"I have no idea," I replied, but I did, I knew exactly what he was doing.

Then to everyone amazement they stood and watched Ollie climbed the ladder grab the white limiter box and start to violently pull it as if trying to wrench it away from the wall.

Joe started to clap his hand above his head and started a chant followed by everyone else in the hall. "Pull it off! Pull it off! Pull it off!"

Jim rushed to the bottom of the stepladder and started shaking it and shouting at the top of his voice, "Fucking get down you stupid little bastard," and within seconds the manager of the venue had joined Jim urging Ollie to stop or he would call the police.

Joe continued to urge Ollie on from the stage and

the crowd was baying for blood as the initial chanting turned to tension as everyone watched the events unfold.

Ollie fumbled around for ages looking for an 'off' switch while Jim and the venue manager tried to shake him off the stepladder. Ollie soon gave up trying and started to grab at the box with both hands and forcibly pull the thing clean off the wall, causing it to emit an electric shock sending him flying off the stepladder and onto the floor and causing the room to fall into total darkness.

Ollie had apparently fused the entire bloody building and had possibly electrocuted himself in the process. As chaos started to ensue I rushed over and looked at Ollie on the floor — he was unhurt and laughing out loud.

"You fucking stupid twat!" I shouted as I grabbed him by the arm and dragged him to his feet.

"Get the fuck out of here!" I screamed.

Ollie legged it outside and jumped in the back of the van and I could see Jim was stalking the hall drooling and snarling looking to find him and probably kill him. I instructed Joe and Stu to pack up their equipment as quickly as possible and asked Stu for the keys to the van.

"I'll meet you at the back doors in two minutes," I told them.

I told Holly to stay put and not to move, then I ran outside and jumped in the driver's seat of the van and started the engine. I think that the gravity of the situation had finally dawned upon Ollie and he sat silent in the back mumbling to himself.

"If you get arrested you can kiss goodbye to The United States you fucking idiot!" I shouted.

I crunched into reverse gear and using my side mirrors headed back towards the exit doors to where Joe and Stu were waiting as fast as I could. Then out of bloody nowhere stepped one of the band members of Area 15 and as I felt the bump I realised that I had run over the poor sod's foot.

"Bollocks!" I screamed.

I slammed the brakes on as I reached Joe and Stu and shouted at them to load the van as quickly as they could. In the meantime, I ran to check if the guy I had just ran over was alright as I could see him sitting on the ground rubbing his foot and crying.

"Oh God mate… you alright?" I asked.

"Yeah I'm fine," he said through the tears.

"Shall I call you an ambulance?"

"No, it's ok I've had my foot run over loads of times."

"Funny that, because this is the second time I've run over someone's foot."

I was told a few days later, that the band's own driver had run over this poor chap's foot about ten times since they had started touring and he still hasn't learnt to keep out of the way. Which led me to ponder if the guy's feet were made from steel.

I threw the keys to Stu and shouted "Get the fuck out of here now," and the three of them made a swift exit as I stood and watched as the van vanished into the fog and the dark before going back into the hall to see what was happening. I walked into pandemonium.

The room was still in total darkness and everyone seemed to be arguing. I spotted Jim and walked over to apologise for everything, he was very aggressive at first, but realising it couldn't possibly be my fault, he soon calmed down. However, he did say that it was a good job the band had made a quick escape because he was about to kick Ollie's arse up and down the fucking hall until he was screaming in pain and begging for mercy.

I looked him straight in his eyes and said, "Fair enough, I feel like doing that sometimes."

The lighting did come back soon after, but there was still no power on stage and the manager was more than ready to call the police and report the incident. If Ollie got arrested and charged with something like criminal damage, then that would be that — the band would be finished and the label would want their advances back; meaning I too would have to dig back into my life savings to pay back everything and I was not prepared to let that happen.

The crowd was getting restless and started to demand refunds, when the good guys steps in and saved the night. Jim's sons band Nothing Can Prove It, to their immense credit sat on the side of the stage, called everyone over and then proceeded to perform an hour long acoustic set, which Holly and I hung around for to enjoy.

We chatted with the fans and gave away some free T-shirts before the manager eventually came over and asked me to step inside his office.

As I walked in I feared the worst, as I had found out only a few minutes before, he had apparently told Jim that he was definitely going to have that nasty little fucker Ollie arrested. I stood looking forlorn and pathetic as he sat at his desk looking up at me; it felt like being back at high school.

I explained what it would mean to the band if he called the police and had Ollie arrested. I also explained that Ollie suffered from some kind of mental disorder that would explain his erratic behaviour and, while he lorded it over me, I also considered punching the pretentious fucker in the face.

He pondered for a while and then agreed that if all the repair costs to refit the noise limiter were paid in full, and Ollie would go in and personally apologise to him and all his staff, that he would not press charges. I shook his hand and left the office letting out a huge sigh of relief.

The following afternoon I had a prolonged argument with Ollie on the phone about the previous night's events and to my disbelief, he just couldn't seem to get it through his thick skull that he must apologise, not only to the promoter, but the manager and everyone else at the venue, for his outrageous behaviour and that he had to pay for all the damage he had caused otherwise he was going to be arrested for criminal damage.

"This is all fucking bullshit!" he shouted down the line, "they can all go fuck themselves!"

"Are you insane? Don't you want to go and record in America?" I asked.

"Yes of course I bloody do," Ollie paused for a second and then added, "I just don't want to apologise to that fucking Bob-The-Builder bloke."

"You mean Jim."

"Yes that fucker!"

"Is your mum there?" I asked.

Ollie handed over the phone to his mum Sheila and we discussed what needed to be done and she agreed to drag him along to the venue later that afternoon to see the manager and pay the damages.

Ollie came back on the phone and said, "Happy now?" all aggressively.

"It's nothing to do with being happy Ollie it's all about making sure you are able to travel to America."

"I will apologise to the manager at the venue, but that promoter bloke can fuck right off."

"OK, don't worry, I will deal with Jim." I said.

Later that day Sheila called to inform me she had driven Ollie to the venue, that he had been in and apologised in person to the manager and his staff and that she had paid the bill for the repair of the sound limiter and the peripheral damages, which had come to a grand total of £200.

I sent Jim a long email apologising for all the hassle we had caused and again thanked him for being patient and understanding and of course for not going round to their perspective houses and battering the fuck out of each one of them.

Chapter 28

From Russia with Not So Much Love

The last commitment to fulfil before we headed off to America was a show in Moscow, the Russian capital and as we eventually discovered, turned out to be at the invitation from a member of the Russian mafia whose son was a huge Koopa fan.

The whole process of getting the legal permission for a band to play in Russia is very tough, but luckily for us, the promoter had arranged all our necessary visas, etc. to be issued without any complications, but even then I still had to endure some cold-war espionage style adventure before we finally received them.

My mission from my Russian agent, should I be willing to take it, was to travel by train to London's Waterloo Station and stand under the main clock where, at precisely 3.00pm I was to be met by a woman wearing a long black coat and carrying a briefcase, who went under the name of Anna. I was to hand over all the passports and then arrange a further meet with her a few hours later to collect said passports once she had arranged the necessary visas. It was all very cloak and dagger, but in truth there was nothing sinister or shady going on and she simply collected the passports from me and returned them at the same spot two hours later whilst I had spent the two hours catching up with some old friends in the pub.

We flew a few days later into the strictly controlled check-in desk of Domodedovo Airport in Moscow. There was a huge sign written in Russian and English that stated 'Security has priority over everything,' and I have to admit there was a tense, almost scary atmosphere around the place as I waited for my turn to go through the security barrier.

I was watching people go into what appeared to be some kind of futuristic space pod. These were the full body security scanners that everyone had been talking about before we left. I was the first of us to be ushered forward by the guard and as I approached the white line on the floor he ordered me to stop.

"Do not move," he instructed me in his deep pigeon English and I did not move an inch.

The security officer then asked me to raise my arms and then he abruptly ordered me to step into the plexiglass cabin. The doors closed and I heard a short buzzing sound as I was scanned. Through the glass I could see another security officer obviously checking the scan. The doors then opened and I was ushered through. It was a most bizarre experience, unlike any security check I had ever encountered. I then stood watching and waiting as one by one the boys were scanned, praying that they were not stupid enough to have tried to smuggle in any drugs – which luckily that hadn't.

After collecting the guitars and our baggage, we made our way to the exit to meet the driver who would be waiting for us to take us to our hotel — well, that's what we thought!

The driver was waiting in the airport lobby holding a card saying *'Koopa'* and as I walked up to introduce myself, it was obvious that the guy didn't speak English, and just beckoned us to follow him. We were led outside to an underground car park where his vehicle was located and as we placed our guitars and baggage in the back of his vehicle I was struck by how cold it was.

"It's fucking freezing cold," I said as we got in the people carrier.

As we exited the car park there was snow everywhere and in fact we were told later that the first snowfalls had just arrived.

There were taxis everywhere it actually seemed busier than New York. It also looked as though driving in Moscow was pretty stressful too, as at every given opportunity our driver would shout, what I presume was abuse, at the top of his voice at the latest vehicle in front to cut him up.

I could clearly see his eyes in his rearview mirror and he looked like a mean-mother. I definitely wouldn't want to be on the receiving end of his road rage. The sort of guy that would be ideal for anger management classes I thought as he deftly drove us to our final destination.

On the journey we passed some very drab and dreary looking apartments that obviously stemmed from an era past, as well as many modern and colourful high-rise apartments. Then suddenly there seemed to be a western commercial building at every turn like McDonalds, TGI Fridays, BMW and Mercedes.

Old and new blue and white buses travelled up and down with cables attached reminded me for some reason of the trams in Sheffield and Nottingham city centre. I guess in many ways, this large bustling city looked like any other major modern metropolis.

One amusing distraction was the street sweeping trucks that mingled with the regular traffic spraying blasts of water onto the roads, giving some motorists a free partial car wash. As we passed it sprayed the side of the vehicle and our driver let out a loud yell of discontent.

When we seemed to arrive at our final destination, I looked out to check out the standard of our hotel —but didn't even see one.

Just then a young man wearing a dark suit with white shirt unexpectedly appeared from an insignificant looking doorway, he walked over opened the door and with a big smile said in broken English said, "Welcome. Please follow me."

Joe, Ollie and Stu looked at one another and then stared directly at me. I shrugged my shoulders and just looked back at them just as bewildered. We collected our stuff from the back of the vehicle and followed the young chap into an overall dirty looking building, then followed him up a narrow dimly lit staircase.

I turned and whispered to Ollie, "Was nice knowing you mate."

"Shut up you wanker," he replied.

At the top of the stairs the young man stopped, reached in his jacket pocket for a key and opened the door to what looked like some sort of apartment, before ushering us all in.

He turned to us and said abruptly. "This is where you stay."

We learned over the next few days that the Russians are very blunt and won't beat around the bush; they don't want or tolerate small talk and prefer to get to the point as soon as possible.

I looked around the room; it was like a squat. There were two beds, one double and one single, and the sheets looked as though they hadn't even been washed. In the corner was a small scummy sink that appeared to be coming away from the wall and I dared not even look in the toilet and shower room.

Before I could say anything the young man said to us. "You stay here until Greg the promoter come collect you." Then he turned around and walked out leaving us standing in total silence.

That's when the debate over whether or not we were ever going to see England again began. I have to admit for the next hour while we waited for Greg-the-promoter I was genuinely scared for my life. Have you ever seen the Eli Roth movie 'Hostel?' I think the guys were thinking exactly the same and they also had the double whammy of suffering from a bout of cold turkey, as it had been some hours since their last fix.

I considered calling home to let everyone know I may never be coming back, but I had no fucking signal anyway and I remained without any signal the whole time I was in Moscow. This led to the standard massive argument once back at home; that I in fact obviously loved the band more than I loved my wife and family.

We were discussing the probability that we had met our doom and were destined to never see anyone again when suddenly there was a knock on the door.

"Come in," I said sheepishly.

A tall bearded man wearing jeans and a white jumper walked in and said, "Hello. I am Gregor, but everyone calls me Greg. I am pleased to meet you."

He walked over and after exchanging handshakes all round, he apologised for the accommodation, saying that as we were only there two nights, he thought it sensible to put us in an apartment he owned right next to the venue, so that way everyone could enjoy a few drinks and not worry about getting expensive taxis. He also apologised for the state of it and that the maid would be arriving in the next hour to clean and change the bedding he also pointed out that there was a pull out bed underneath the double one.

With the accommodation, tour out the way he told us that he had someone who wanted to meet the band and gestured to us to follow him. So we headed back down the dark staircase and out of the building, the sky had turned, not dark, but jet-black and it was starting to heavily snow. After a short walk we arrived outside a very busy and noisy bar.

Greg said something to the two burly looking doormen and then instructed us to follow him inside where he seated us at a table at the back of the room. Soon after Greg introduced us to a man and a teenage boy, whose names evade me. The man was dressed smartly in a dark shirt with a dark tie, wore a massive gold chain around his neck and had huge gold rings on his fingers. The teenager was wearing a smart black Adidas tracksuit and also had a large gold chain around his neck.

Neither spoke much English, but after the initial introductions, we sat silently while Greg chatted to them in Russian. Greg explained that the elder gentleman was the bar owner and sitting with him was his son who was *the* biggest fan of the band and the reason why we were actually there.

From the corner of my eye I could see a silver tray filled with two very large bottles of Russian Standard vodka, seven shot glasses and a large plate of smoked salmon heading our way, carrying the tray was an absolutely stunning waitress, dressed in a tight fitting short black dress, she had silky black long hair and seductive come-to-bed eyes.

Greg explained that it was a Russian tradition to drink shots and eat salmon and that our hosts would be offended if we didn't partake. Well, I fucking hate the taste of smoked salmon, but even I knew that this was one tradition I dare not break.

For the rest of the afternoon we all drank expensive vodka, ate smoked salmon and the band answered all the questions the young fan had, all kindly translated by Greg. His father sat quietly and on the odd occasion turned to his son to say something in Russian. Once in a while he looked at us and smiled and obviously we smiled back at him. I was starting to get a strange feeling about these people.

Even though our gut feelings were screaming at us to stay alert we still all managed to get hammered that night, and just as we were leaving I saw a man at the end of the bar tap our waitress on the backside, causing her to turn and smack him in the face with her tray just before two tough looking men grabbed him and dragged him off. I was expecting to hear a single gunshot outside at that point, but it never came —I've watched far too gangster many movies.

Greg suggested everyone go on to a nightclub, but after a long day travelling we all decided to head back to the apartment and Greg kindly walked us back. The snow was falling even heavier by then and Joe, who was drunk as a skunk and unable to even string a sentence together, decided to make some snow-angels on the way back.

We watched and laughed as Joe floundered on the ground like a beached whale.

Greg asked, "Is he always like this?"

"Yes, Greg," I replied, "I'm sorry to say that he *is* always like this."

The following night Greg would witness first-hand just how Joe could be after a heavy drinking session.

That night I slept in the single bed, Joe on the pull-out and the two brothers shared the double and, apart from all the snoring and farting, everyone got a good night's sleep even though the band had been fretting about their next fix. We decided to head out the next morning to grab some breakfast and then do the whole tourist thing. It was extremely cold outside and the bite of the wind turned your face instantly red. The wind was blowing the snow around and opposite our apartment an old man was shoveling the snow from the path leading to his shop, we turned the first corner and there it was —the big M!

The best thing about McDonalds is that the food is

the same all over the world, you know what you want before you go in, you can easily just point to the pictures to get exactly what you want, and you know that it won't kill you – well, not immediately anyway.

Burgers and coffees consumed, we set off to see Red Square and The Kremlin with its imposing walls and towers that completely took my breath away.

Finally, after drinking in the pleasure and beauty of the area we took a little pit-stop at an outdoor restaurant to have a coffee with a whiskey-shot to warm us all up before meeting up with Greg to prepare for the show that evening.

The venue was already full of young people bustling around in anticipation and, after setting up and sound checking, the band set about preparing for the show by downing the free bottles of vodka that the owner had given them. I'm sure that they had also convinced the young Russian fan to help them acquire some weed as that sweet chocolate smell filled the air back stage.

The show went well, and although the band was half-cut they managed to put on an energetic and entertaining performance. After the show we were offered a table and free drinks and as the live music came to an end a DJ started pumping out some techno-house tunes and the crowd hit the dance floor. I also noticed that the club started to fill with beautiful half naked ladies, some of whom were sitting chatting to punters.

Greg came over excited and kept repeating "Everyone's happy, it was a great show guys! If there's anything you want, just ask."

Then he ushered over some of those very attractive ladies who sat at our table and started drinking vodka shots with us for a couple of hours. This was going to be a great night I thought – Oh, no sorry… no it wasn't.

We had barely left the table and we must have drunk a river full of vodka when Joe stood up and announced to all of us that he needed a piss. He stood up, knocking over his chair, stumbling back, he fell onto the table behind him full of people, sending all their drinks, bottles and glasses flying, causing them to hit the floor and smash into tiny pieces. One of the men at the table looked down at Joe who was now lying on the floor, grabbed him up and then pushed him through another table, causing that to then upturn and send its contents also spilling to the floor.

It quickly became like one of those wild-west style brawls.

Ollie and Stu was up ready to jump in, but I quickly shouted. "Don't be stupid. Sit back down."

Greg stepped in and grabbed the guy while I ran over and picked up Joe, who pushed me away and stumbled forward instantly falling through yet another table, this time spilling drinks all over two lovely looking young ladies who instantly started screaming at him in Russian.

We needed to get out of this situation and fast, and as two stone-faced doormen approached, I could see they were spoiling for the opportunity to rearrange Joe's face and perhaps even remove some of his body parts. I told Stu and Ollie to go outside and while I tried to get this sorted. I was in a state of fear, fully aware of the company we were in and worried that we would not get out of this one alive.

One of the doormen grabbed hold of Joe and put

him in some kind of choke hold, but then suddenly there was a loud shout in Russian from across the other side of the room. The doormen stopped, and immediately let go of Joe. I looked over and there stood the bar owner flanked by two menacing looking men in dark suits. It was more than obvious that this man was the governor and our fate lay in his next few words. Greg approached him and after a brief conversation the man nodded and shook Greg's hand. Greg walked over to Joe and me and said, "It is ok. He will let you go."

I didn't have the courage to ask Greg the burning question that was racing through my mind – what would have happened if he had decided not to let us go? Suffice to say that I grabbed Joe and, along with Greg, we left the bar and met the other two who were standing shivering outside (I wasn't sure whether they shivered from fear or the freezing cold night that had descended on Moscow, or both).

We were walking back to the apartment and Stu and Ollie were all but carrying Joe, who by this time had virtually passed out and as things calmed down I decided to ask Greg what the man back at the bar had said.

Greg then explained as best he could in his broken English that the owner was a local businessman who had fingers in many pies and that if we had not been going home tomorrow, he would have had his men teach us all a lesson in manners.

"Fucking hell!" I said out loud.

The following morning, we were all packed for the airport and I double checked everyone had their passports, but when I went to get mine from the side pocket of my travel bag it was missing.

I asked Ollie and Stu if they had seen it.

"No," they both replied.

"Joe, what have you done with my passport?"

"I haven't seen it."

"Please stop messing around. This is fucking serious."

"If I've lost my passport I'm in deep shit," I added.

My breathing started to become erratic and I started to wonder if Greg, the maid or that driver had stolen it in order to sell on the black market. I imagined being beaten and dragged to a prison cell in Siberia or shot and left somewhere, I was getting myself worked up and after another half an hour of frantically searching I was almost in tears, shaking and sweating profusely. I was on the verge of breaking down.

"I just wanna go home," I said tearfully, "I need to go to the British Embassy. Is there a British Embassy in Moscow?"

"How the hell do we know," came the reply from Stu.

"We have to leave to get to the airport. Do you need dropping off anywhere?" Ollie asked.

"Are you fucking kidding me, you wankers? Are you seriously going to fucking leave me here?"

"We will get you some help when we get back to England," Stu replied.

"No, please don't leave without me," I pleaded with them.

"Helppp me, please," I shouted before finally a tear fell from my eye. I could feel total panic setting in and my whole body started to shake uncontrollably with fear. I was hoping for the best and finding my passport, but all the time fearing the absolute worst.

Then Ollie shouted "Da-dah!"

The sudden feeling of overwhelming relief made me go light headed then, after the moment of clarity of realising that I would be going home after all, I turned to the three of them and yelled "You bunch of complete fucking cunts!" Before sitting on the edge of the bed and putting my burning head in my sweaty hands knowing that eventually these three would be the fucking death of me.

Chapter 29

Never Underestimate
the Other Guys Greed

With the trip to the United States looming, I had some much needed time to myself and took the opportunity to spend some quality time with my daughters. I also made sure I fueled my habit by visiting the pub every night and taking some pills to help me get through the day and then make me sleep at night.

Paula was not talking to me much to be honest; we had nothing to say to each other anyway.

When the time came to leave for the States I felt sad to be leaving my girls for so long, but I needed to go to make sure everything went according to plan. I was also though very excited, as the next chapter in the band's career was about to begin and this time we had backing with a label being on board helping make it all happen. Little did I know that this would be the trip that would change everything between the four of us, as well as be the tipping point for me and my addictions.

It would also be the trip that would almost cost me my life.

**

The flight to Nashville was pretty uneventful as I did my usual routine; got very drunk and swallowed some sleeping pills. This system worked well for me, it was like I had my very own 'Star Trek' style transporter, all I had to do was climbed aboard, strap myself in, fall asleep to be awoken as we landed, 'our teleportation system.' Joe and I called it.

I woke up and noticed I had been resting my head on the stranger sitting next to me, and just as we stopped on the runway, he also woke and started to wipe the drool off his shirt that he assumed was his own, as I watched I thought it might be a good idea to own up, but then as I looked over at the boys, who were all laughing so I decided not to.

Craig and Justin from the record label met us at the airport. This was the first time Stu and Ollie had met the pair and instantly Ollie thought that Craig, or Crag (in American) was the doppelganger for the character 'Hurley' from the TV show 'Lost'. Obviously from that moment onwards we would adopt that alias.

We left the airport and headed for their headquarters. The journey lasted about an hour and we ended up in the middle of bloody nowhere.

I turned and asked Justin, "How far is the nearest town?"

"Well, there's a grocery store about twenty minutes' drive. Town is about three quarters of an hour away."

I looked around and for a moment closed my eyes to enjoy the sunshine that was warming my face. We were encircled by woods and all I could hear was the sound of birds and insects. The large cabin structure that would be our home for the next month was beautiful and was painted in a dark green colour that blended effortlessly into its surroundings. It had a lovely stained wooden balcony that extended the whole way round; it looked like one of those ranch houses straight out of the old wild-west movies.

It had a large living room complete with 80" wide screen television and cable set top box, as well as; a PlayStation and X-Box games consoles with a selection of games including a copy of FIFA Soccer 2008 as the Americans called it.

There was a large kitchen with a massive double fridge full of bottled beer and water.

Craig, Crag or Hurley as he was now known, had an office at the back and upstairs were three bedrooms for Justin and two other employees; Janice the cook-stroke-cleaner and a guy called Odd-Bob who ran the studio. There was also a large bathroom.

Odd-Bob would also double-up as the boy's private drug dealer as he knew a guy…who knew a guy…

Out back was a massive purpose built brick BBQ and also a brick-built fire pit that was situated next to what was once the swimming pool, but now seemed to have become storage for general junk like old desks, chairs and cardboard boxes.

I asked Justin where the band would be sleeping and he told us to follow him and we were led into a long hallway, through a doorway down a long wooden staircase that sloped to an area below that was pitch black.

I turned to Joe and whispered to him "Here we go, Texas Chainsaw Massacre time."

Justin reached out and turned on the light switch at the top of the stairs.

"You and the band have your own apartment downstairs," he said.

It was great, there were two bedrooms, one for me and one for the boys, a large living room again with wide-screen television and cable box. A large shower and toilet room and finally a small kitchen area complete with another fridge full of beer. It was more than suitable and we were all happy.

Justin then handed the boys an envelope each and said "Craig said this is to keep you going while you're staying here."

Immediately after he left the boys opened the envelopes and were delighted to find $500 in each one. That's fucking nice I thought. I will just add at this point that, at no time, did any of the band members offer to buy me any food, or even stump up and get me a beer. The whole time we were there! I paid for my own – comrades in arms?

The band's seduction by the label had begun and they were in a position where they had their cake and they were not only going to eat it, but they were going to consume every last piece of it and things would only get worse as the weeks progressed. So, as the three of them sat there counting out the $10 bills and supping on their cold cans of beer, I sat contemplating getting the very next flight back home.

The first few weeks passed and, to be honest, life was slow and boring. The band was in the studio preparing demo tracks for Mark Hoppus and I spent the time chatting to whoever I could to keep my sanity; which included many conversations with the cleaner. The label people seemed to simply ignore me and I could sense that they didn't want me around.

You have to bear in mind that the band would be in bed until about two in the afternoon, get up, shower, shit, eat, drink and smoke bongs before heading to the studio until the early hours of the following morning.

The evenings were so boring; I had even stopped sitting out on the porch at night after Justin told me, for a laugh, that once a grizzly bear had attacked the previous owners.

The band had a new friend in Odd-Bob and they would all head off in his truck twice a week to go and score some drugs somewhere. Once in a while I would come up from the apartment to find people literally sprawled all over the furniture drugged-up to their eyeballs and a huge cloud of sweet smelling smoke floating around the room. The boys were in heaven and I was in my own personal hell. I went and asked Odd-Bob if he could get me some prescription painkillers and he duly obliged and these, along with a lot of beer and vodka, helped keep me sane.

I should have gone home, but I had noticed that Hurley was always sniffing around the boys and he was joining them from time to time for a bong here and there. They were becoming much closer and I seemed to be getting further and further away. They barely talked to me unless it was to complain that the fridge was running low on beer again. I had just become their butler and worst of all, my self-esteem was so low at this point that I just accepted it.

Was this just my own personal paranoia setting in or was something more sinister going on? I came to realise that I should trust no one and to never ever underestimate other peoples greed.

It was also around this time that I started getting headaches that seemed to last all day every day.

I tried to call home at least once or twice a day, but never managed to get my head around the time difference so kept waking everyone up. I enjoyed using Skype, and seeing my daughters would put a smile on my face. I had the odd discussion with Paula, which always seemed to be rather frosty and ended in an argument, so I tended to not speak to her that often in the end.

On one happy phone call the girls were excited to tell me that they had just got two kittens and had called one Izzy, after someone in 'Greys Anatomy', and the other Moss after the character in the 'IT Crowd'.

***

One night everyone was heading into Nashville for a few drinks and, although I was suffering from a really bad headache, I decided to shower, get changed and tag along. I was also aware that I needed to keep one eye on the band and the other eye on Hurley, as they were spending a lot of time in his office – 'chatting!'

The night was going really well, and the downtown Nashville atmosphere is unlike any other. We strolled from one bar to another and at every stop the live music and entertainment was utterly amazing. The only problem for me was that my headache had started to get much worse, but as everyone was having such a great time I tried to ignore it. The throbbing in my head, though persisting and had started to make me feel confused and nauseous.

This was without doubt the worst headache of my life. I was sitting on the steps outside a bar looking in and could see everyone drinking, dancing, laughing and having a great time.

I just didn't know what to do — I had an extreme thirst and my mouth felt dry. I thought I'd get up and go for a walk thinking that will help to clear it up, but I was sorely mistaken and from the moment I stood I felt an excruciating pain in the top part of the back of my head, and then again as I took a step forward, and then again and again as I tried to walk. I was really struggling, I felt dizzy and faint and had cramp in my legs, which didn't bloody help — I was in serious trouble and as I tried to cry there were no tears.

The pain was so excruciating that I had to stop and I stood still just staring at the brick wall that was opposite me.

I started mumbling to myself, "If I run into that wall, perhaps this pain will stop."

I was quite literally about to take a run at it when Justin and Joe walked out and grabbed me as I stumbled forward.

"Gary, are you ok?" Joe shouted.

I tried to talk, but the pain was so overpowering that I just collapsed to the ground right there in the street.

They say that your life flashes before your very eyes when you are about to die, and let me tell you right here, right now, it's true. As I fell to the ground and lay there I felt panic and fear at first and then saw my whole life started to pass me by in an instant. I saw my long departed Nan, standing above me telling me everything was going to be ok and then I blacked out.

I woke up in hospital with my right arm attached to a drip and was informed by the doctor that I was very lucky to be alive. I had been suffering from dehydration and, if I hadn't got to the hospital when I did, then within a few hours I would most likely have been dead.

I remained in hospital until the doctors were fully satisfied that I was rehydrated and they were sure I had no further complications or damage to my internal organs.

Justin was the only person who came to see me and he was the one that collected me and drove me back to the cabin once I had been finally discharged. When we arrived back we found the cabin was empty, as the band had gone out to dinner with Hurley, so I went to bed and slept like a log for the next thirteen hours.

When I finally woke, I spent some time to gather my thoughts before showering and going up to see everyone. I realised that I'd had a very lucky escape and while staring at my terrible reflection in the mirro,r I vowed to change – but my reflection just stared back as if to say – bet you don't!

My hospital stay had cost the label $1500, which made me chuckle and say out loud to no one "Well, at least I got something out of the bastards!"

I called home to explain what had happened and I received no sympathy whatsoever from Paula, who simply blamed the band and my poor lifestyle choice and after I put down the receiver I thought that actually she was spot on.

After a few days of laying off the booze and drinking plenty of water I started to feel much better, but all around me the excess was abundant and no one showed any sympathy towards my close encounter with death, and I found myself constantly harassed by everyone for being boring when not accepting an alcoholic drink. So inevitably within a few days I slipped back into my old ways and my current addictions were once again exposed.

I had even added cocaine to my daily intake – much to my shame.

The time had arrived for the band to perform at The South By Southwest Festival this was to be their showcase event. We were called into the office and informed that, as Austin was not that far from where we were located in Nashville, we would be travelling by car. I wish I'd seen a fucking map before we left because here was another case of someone with very little knowledge of geography and even worse common sense.

FYI, it's 859 miles from Nashville, Tennessee to Austin, Texas and by road takes approximately thirteen hours!

We set off on our mammoth journey. There were two vehicles, Hurley and Justin in one with Ollie and Stu and Joe and myself in the other with a couple called Lindsay and Seamus.

Lindsay was in charge of the bands press and Seamus was a filmmaker who had also recently been a camera man on the latest 'Jackass' movie. Both of them were really nice and they bought their lovely little pug dog on the journey, who to be honest, was better company than Joe.

The journey was long and boring and as Hurley wanted to make it there in one day it meant breaking the speed limit. Both cars were bombing along some highway when suddenly out of the blue we found ourselves in hot pursuit by a police car with its sirens blaring out.

Seamus slowed down and, as the police car drew alongside, the officer gestured to pull over and of course he obeyed straight away. As we sat there waiting for the police officer to get out of his vehicle Joe jokingly suggested, "Just drive man! we are almost at the state line."

"Shut up please," Lindsay replied.

"What shall I do with all these drugs?" Joe asked.

"What the fuck, Joe, are you kidding me?" Seamus shouted.

"Yes I am."

"Don't be a fucking dick," came the reply from Lindsay.

Joe sat back and laughed, so I slapped him on the forehead and told him to shut up.

The officer walked up and did that classic policeman move by tapping on the window and asked Seamus to exit the vehicle before having a long discussion regarding speed limits. All the time I was staring at his holster thinking his bloody gun was huge.

Soon after we were on our way again with a speeding fine Seamus now had to pay and we still had eight hours to endure in this motorcar with Joe, who I don't think had washed that day and, most definitely, had eaten something nasty before we left. The rest of the journey was uncomfortable and unpleasant on the nostrils, as Joe burped and farted all the way to Texas.

The following day I felt like shit and with a creaking back that still had not recovered from the tiring car journey, I set about getting the band registered for their showcase. I had a wander around the main town, taking in the sights and sounds and I eventually found myself in a large marquee and watched Brit band Scouting for Girls do an outdoor showcase performance before meeting back up with the band at the gig's bar for some pre-show cocktails.

Not one of the band seemed to care that they were playing an important gig that night as in the drinking stakes they were going for it lock, stock and barrel, by first drinking Long Island Iced Teas, followed by some beers, then moving onto vodkas and red bulls before finishing off with some Jäger bombs.

It was time for the band to take to the stage, but Joe was missing and it was down to me to try and find him – he was nowhere to be seen. I could hear someone knocking on the backstage exit door, but they were being ignored by the burly security man on guard.

"Hi there, I'm looking for one of my band members, have you seen him?" I asked.

"No."

"That might be him trying to get in."

"No, that's just a dishevelled drunk, we found hanging about backstage."

"Could you possibly open the door, I think that might be him."

The security man opened the door and surprise surprise there was Joe.

"Yes, that's him," I declared, "can you let him in please he needs to be on stage."

By the time the three of them finally took to the stage they were all completely smashed and I could see that Hurley was not impressed.

He pulled me aside and accused me of not being able to control them. I explained that this was normal, and that he should wait until after the show before placing any blame on me. I didn't care what he thought to be honest as I was drunk and not really listening to a word he saying.

The band played on and apart from Stu accidentally flinging a stick out into the audience and Joe declaring "I am fuuuuuuuuuuuuuuuuuuuuuuuuuuuked up!" the show went well and the meager crowd that had bothered to walk to the venue just outside town, enjoyed the performance. However, you could sense that Hurley's alarm bells were ringing and he was less than impressed.

That night, Lindsay had arranged for everyone to go and see Bowling for Soup, a band who were headlining an event in the main town centre. She was good friends with their manager and was aware that they were about to do a big tour in the UK later in the year, so had arranged for us all to attend the after-show party in order to network.

The show was magnificent and afterwards we were ushered backstage to meet with the band members Jaret, Chris, Eric and Gary and share a few beers. The guys ended up getting on like a house on fire and by the end of the evening I was left feeling confident that there was a great chance the boys would get a slot on the tour.

Once again Joe was hammered and while everyone was fast asleep, he had gotten up to take a piss; he had, however missed the bathroom door and walked instead straight out of his hotel room and took a piss in the corridor, then as he staggered around, he found an open door, thinking that it was his room he then proceeded to lay down and go back to sleep.

In the morning the cleaning lady found him curled up naked in the linen room.

By the time I had showered, dressed and left my room, everyone else was already waiting in the reception and Hurley was busy pacifying the hotel manager to avoid further implications.

I now had the pleasure of another 859-mile drive back to Nashville, which in the end took much longer, due to all the unscheduled stops for pissing and vomiting.

Joe was in a right state and not only looked, but smelt like a tramp. He had really been hitting the bottle and as I looked at this young man next to me, I had the horrible feeling like I was sitting next to a dead man – he was in an almost zombie like trance and I was quite worried about him.

At this rate he was going to be dead by the time the bands album was recorded.

Chapter 30

That Bloke from Blink 182 & Heather Graham's Bush

After a few days spent recovering from all the travelling it was time for the band to record their debut album with Mark Hoppus. Just the boys, Hurley and myself flew to Los Angeles and, after arriving at LAX, we headed off to the band's next home for the month, which turned out to be a lovely rental apartment in the hills near Universal Studios that came complete with swimming pool.

There were two bedrooms and while Ollie and Stu took first dibs on one, I was landed sharing the other with Joe that would turn out to be a big challenge for my senses.

I hated sharing a bedroom with another man; the experiences I had encountered with Garry-the-dwarf at The Red Lion had scarred me for life. Joe would snore and fart his way through the night and, on some occasions would even sleep walk into my bed. He, also, just like the other two, liked to play pranks on me and the final straw came one night when his schoolboy game of sneaking up on me in the dark while I slept, groaning with a torch light at his face caused me to jump up and try to punch him, but luckily for him I'd missed.

We had a few days before the band started recording so we just chilled by the pool drinking. I also arranged for us to meet up with an old ex-pat friend of mine, Stuart, who I had previously met whist drinking in the famous Rainbow Bar.

I called him Roadie-Stu. He'd been a roadie for The Who in the sixties and after their big US tour decided he would not be returning home and took up residence in L.A.

I really liked him, but of course at that time it didn't even dawn on me that I would be introducing the boys to their new drug dealer.

Roadie-Stu would regale us with all the rock 'n' roll stories he had in his locker while we sipped potent Long Island Iced Teas at The Rainbow. He even introduced us to Joey Covington the drummer of Starship, who once pissed, would repeat the same old lines time and time again "The sixties and seventies are gone! Dope will never be the same or as cheap! Sex will never be free again and rock 'n' roll will never be as great!" Sadly, Joey died in a car crash in 2013 and perhaps that was the rock 'n' roll way out that he would have preferred.

Also at The Rainbow we got to share a few shots with Slash and watch Lemmy play the slots.

I learned a lot about the history of rock 'n' roll from Roadie-Stu and he was also instrumental in helping the band get a gig at The Whiskey A Go Go, as he knew the owner well.

Our first day of recording was here, and as the band

stood outside the studio unusually quiet I could feel their nerves as they just stood silently staring at one another.

"I'm about to meet my fucking idol!" Ollie said.

"This is fucking brilliant!" Joe added.

They were in total awe of Mark Hoppus as it was because of him and his band Blink 182, that the three of them were initially inspired to become a band in the first place, and here they were standing outside his Los Angeles studio about to record an album with him – they were absolutely dumbstruck and they were shitting themselves in excitement.

Ollie in particular was as nervous as a chav awaiting the paternity test results on the 'Jeremy Kyle' show.

When we knocked on the door it was Mark Hoppus, who opened it. Ollie just stood there with his mouth open, speechless.

Everyone else shook hands and eventually like some demented fan Ollie walked up and while shaking his hand said, "You're Mark Hoppus."

"I am indeed Mark Hoppus, it's a pleasure to meet you Ollie."

Ollie just looked him in the eyes and with a tremble in his voice repeated, "You're Mark Hoppus."

"You can let go of my hand now," Mark replied.

Mark laughed and we all followed him inside where we were introduced to Chris Holmes the recording engineer and given a full tour of the studio and all its facilities. Then, with all the niceties over it was down to business with Mark telling the boys that he was really looking forward to working with them.

Mark had a great personality and one of the first

things he did was to sit the band down before saying, "Let's start with AMA."

Ollie, Stu and Joe looked at one another in bemusement.

Mark said it again, "AMA chaps, AMA."

"Sorry Mark what do you mean," Joe said.

"Oh sorry I thought you were Blink 182 fans?" Mark replied.

"We are mate!" Ollie muttered.

"Just don't know what AMA means mate," Stu added.

"Have you not seen our DVD's?" Mark asked, "this is not a good start is it?"

"Many times," Ollie replied, "but just not heard that before."

"Well, AMA is the thing I say to reporters in the DVD'," Mark said, "It means ask me anything."

Just then the penny finally dropped and while the boys laughed nervously, Mark burst into laughter and said, "I'm just fucking with you!" Jumping up and high-fiving the three of them while shouting, "Let's make an album!"

After a great day in the studio and with spirits really high we decided to play something called the pop-punk drinking game that night. The rules are simple; you just put on any pop-punk compilation album or playlist and do the following:

1. 1 shot every time they say "Friends."
2. 1 shot every time they say "Girl."
3. Everyone downed a pint every time there is a gang vocal.
4. 1 shot every time they talk about drinking.

You'll be pissed after 3 songs – give it a go, but don't dare play if the only playlist you have to hand is Bowling for Soup or you might not make it out alive.

The next few weeks literally flew by and as song after song was completed. I could feel that the air was filled with excitement as the new tunes came together. Mark and Chris made the guys feel at home and I could sense that everything was going to plan with the atmosphere in the studio almost electric.

When it was now time to record the drums, Stu was told he could use Travis Barkers famous glow signature green acrylic drum kit and Travis even popped in to give Stu some tips. Mark ended up doing some backing vocals and playing some bass on one track, after he joked that Joe was not up to the job as he was a shit bass player, I even did some backing vocals on a few tracks (God forbid).

Mark constantly updated his fans with photos and videos of himself working in the studio with the band and there was a real online buzz about the project, all the fun and excitement of the situation made for a very happy camp.

In between recording the band had their show booked at The Whiskey A Go Go and although Mark said he would be there he didn't turn up that night. The gig itself was a bit of a shambles as the sound was awful, but Ollie did get his chance to remind the barman who had refused to serve him earlier that year that he was back *and* performing and we made damn sure he honoured his free drinks boast.

In between recording I chilled by the pool or sat drinking with Roadie-Stu. Joe was steadily drinking more and more and one night caused trouble in The Rainbow, when he tried to pick a fight with a member of Cypress Hill. Suffice to say we made another one of our swift-exits via a taxi and I teased Joe all the way back that the guy from Cypress Hill was in the car behind us and was waving a gun out of the window.

Once we had arrived back at the apartment and had locked all the doors, Joe had some bongs to calm himself down before crashing out in the bedroom and I went to bed after popping a few painkillers and tried to get to some much needed sleep.

Joes snoring was so loud that I didn't sleep at all and I even considered covering his face with a pillow to shut him up for good. The snoring was piercing my skull and driving me fucking crazy. Eventually I could take no more so dragged him out of his bed by his feet and, without even waking him up, threw him and his duvet into the large closet that contained an iron, ironing board and a vacuum cleaner and then placed a pillow over his face and closed the closet door. Peace at last!

I was surprised when he woke in the morning that he didn't say a single word about it. But after I watched him drink a large glass of brandy for breakfast, I told him what I had done and informed him that the cupboard from now on would be his sleeping place for the last few days we were there. He seemed ok with it, but didn't have a choice anyway.

The most disgusting thing about him sleeping in the cupboard, was the foul smell, which emanated from within. I also had the pleasure of dealing with the maid when she complained that she had to clean what appeared to be semen from the cupboard ceiling – she was not impressed.

The band's awesome experience recording their album with Mark Hoppus was coming to an end and Hurley was back in Los Angeles for the last few days. While the band was finishing off some recording bits and pieces he asked if he could have a chat so we walked off to find the nearest coffee shop.

He then proceeded to explain that he had been giving things a lot of thought and he wanted to manage the band, as well as be their label, and right there on the spot he offered me $25,000 and a first class flight home —if I handed over the management reigns to him. I was in no mood for his offer and instantly refused as I still believed that despite all the drink and the drugs, they were still going to make it big. How I wish I had accepted that offer — what a narrow-minded idiot I was.

The band's debut album was finished and they had enjoyed every single minute of it. There were hugs, handshakes and more hugs in the studio before I finally managed to get the guys out of the place. They were physically and mentally exhausted and in need of some sleep, but instead we were informed that everyone had been invited to a BBQ at the home of 'Jackass' movie director Jeff Tremaine, who just happened to be a good friend of Seamus and Lindsay.

The BBQ was fantastic and the food tasted great. Some of the 'Jackass' team including Dave England and Preston Lacy were there and everyone was enjoying a very pleasant L.A. evening.

Jeff lived next door to actress Heather Graham, who

had stared in Austin Powers 'The Spy Who Shagged Me', which just happened to be one of the movies the band watched in the back of the van. Joe had been drinking all night and was being loud and obnoxious and decided he would peek over the hedge that divided Heather and Jeff's properties, in hope of getting a view of the lovely Miss Graham, but with little success.

He then wandered off to the end of the garden before vanishing in the dark. We presumed that he was nipping to the end of the garden for a piss rather than use the actual toilet – after all he was a bit of an animal when it came to toilet habits.

Soon after though he returned looking very red faced and flustered. I was standing drinking a beer with Ollie and Stu as he approached.

"You ok Joe?" Stu asked him.

"I have just cum in Heather Grahams bush!"

I spat out my beer and asked, "Sorry.... What did you say?"

"I just wanked on Heather Grahams hedge!" he said as he burst into laughter.

"You dirty little fucker," I said in total disbelief, "we need to leave right now," I informed all three.

"You can fuck off I'm staying," Ollie declared.

"Ok, you fucking prick, you stay," Joe, shouted at Ollie.

Ollie was again in one of his moods, where in the red mist his brain would only think of himself and everyone else could go fuck themselves.

I quickly ordered a taxi as this was only going to go one way — thankfully the taxi arrived in less than 5 minutes, as Ollie and Joe had already started hurling insults at each other. Later that night when the pair of them returned, they also had a blazing row, which mainly centred around Joe's drinking and outrageous behaviour before turning into a 'fuck-you, no fuck-you session'. Joe eventually retired to his closet and fell asleep and I spent a few hours chatting to the others about the recording experience, as well as Joe's ever-increasing passion for over indulgence.

The following morning, we packed up all our stuff and headed back to the airport and flew back to Nashville for a final few days at the cabin in the woods before eventually heading back home. I was feeling tired, fat and sweaty. I was drinking too much, taking too many prescription pills, talking to myself again in the mirror, missing dear old Blighty and most of all home.

The final night before we were due to leave the label threw a party at the cabin, which in all honesty was the last thing I needed, but the band was as always up for a drink and a drug binge at someone else's expense. With the party in full swing and the alcohol flowing Hurley asked me if I would meet him in his office for another quick chat. He offered me a seat and before my bum had even reached its resting place he informed me that the band had now asked him to manage them, as they thought I was no longer able to take them any further in the music industry, and that he could get them the kind of things I could only dream about.

I stood up and looked him in the eyes and said "Fuck you, if they want to sack me then tell them to grow some bollocks and tell me to my fucking face," before storming out and slamming the door shut.

I stormed over to the three of them and was met with a barrage of lies as they spurted out that it was all Hurley's fault and that he shouldn't have said that to me. I was so fucking angry that I stormed out and stormed off into the dark woods that surrounded the cabin, before realising where I was and running back in again in case a wild grizzly bear attacked me.

All the stress was definitely taking a toll on my mental and physical health; I felt absolutely dreadful.

I took some deep breaths to calm down and sat on the porch and pondered what my Dad would do in this situation and I was reminded of a time he was landlord of The Red Lion.

***

The pub was heaving and one man who was obviously from the local gypsy community was being very loud and disturbing other customers sitting around him. Dad walked over and politely asked him to keep the noise down a little and, after mumbling something back in his thick Irish accent, he jumped up and started swearing at Dad who then grabbed hold of him and frog marched him out of the pub. As he left, he was shouting abuse at everyone and looked at Dad and said 'I'll be back' – and this was years before 'The Terminator'. Dad turned and walked back in the bar. Job done.

About 10 minutes later a battered old van pulled up outside and six gypsies jumped out and started baying for my Dad to come back outside, as my mum screamed for him to stay where he was while she called the police. He, however, calmly turned around and walked outside.

Some of the pub regulars started to follow, but he turned and said calmly, "Stay there."

He walked and approached the gypsy gang. One of them was a giant of a man and had the biggest hands, I've ever seen — even the goalkeeping legend Pat Jennings would have been impressed with the size of this geezer's hands.

Dad stood as the men circled him shouting abuse. Just then the giant man took hold of a concrete post that he had ripped straight from the ground. I looked on in amazement and for a moment thought they were going to kill him, but he just stood his ground and the whole scenario seemed to freeze before my eyes.

Suddenly a car appeared and screeched to a halt outside the pub and a scruffy little man jumped out.

Turns out he was the head of the gypsy community in the village and had just been told what was unfolding, so had raced up to the pub to put a stop to it. He shouted at the men and one by one they walked up to my Dad to shake his hand and apologise before getting back into their van. The giant gently put the concrete post back in the ground before he too shook Dads hand and apologised.

The little scruffy man said something to Dad and the pair of them walked in the bar and shared a few beers. Later that day I asked Dad who that little chap was and he explained that he was the head of the gypsy families and someone he played golf with every Saturday.

"That's lucky," I said.

"That's not luck son, that's business."

***

I sat and brewed over Hurley stabbing me in the back and then trying to twist the bloody thing as well; I had the horrible feeling that the backstabbing was far from over. It was going to be extremely challenging, moving forward and there was going to be major trust issues all round.

We flew back to England. I had nothing to say to any of them and I don't think I said a single word on the way to the airport or leaving the airport back home – of course in between would have been slightly difficult as I had had my usual drink and pill combo and had passed out.

The band was due to go straight out on tour when we got back with The Towers of London and even though I thought this would be a great tour just for the sex, drugs and rock 'n' roll, I told them I was ill and stayed at home to spend time with my daughters — so their new best buddy Dangerous-Dave drove them around.

When I did finally meet up with them again to clear the air, there was a lot of initial tension. They said that they still wanted me to be around, but wanted Craig to be their main manager and me to be their UK manager and that I would still retain my percentage.

I had no trust or respect for them at this point and my self-esteem, health and state of mind were shot to pieces, so I caved in and just let them get on with it all and let them do whatever they wanted, which as usual involved the excessive smoking of weed, binge drinking and not giving a fuck about anyone else.

I just clung on to the little strand of hope I had for

the album, that I hoped would eventually break the band and would make me some money back before it was all over.

The finished album had been delivered from Mark Hoppus and it certainly sounded very impressive, Mark had captured the angst and anger that was so obviously brewing inside the boys – especially Ollie. So ever the optimist, I totally thought this could be the bloody one!

I wondered if this might just be the album to break the band both in the UK, but more importantly in the USA. Surely with the support of Mark Hoppus— only the best bass player in one of the world's most famous bands Blink 182 — along with the label we would be able to work some great angles to the industry and the media, especially the specialist rock shows on the radio and the rock press like Kerrang Magazine, Big Cheese and Rock Sound.

I was so excited that I put all my pent-up anger aside and got ready for the band to break big.

I felt that everything was finally on the up — then I received a phone call from Joe and the shit hit the fan once again.

Chapter 31

Balls as Big as Town Hall Steps

The album sounded fantastic and as I sat listening to it for the third or fourth time I was rubbing my hands together at the prospect of the band finally getting some recognition when the phone rang.

It was Joe.

"I'm loving the album mate," I said all excited.

"We all hate the whole fucking album."

"What?"

Joe went on to inform me that having listened to the album numerous times, none of the them liked the way the album was produced or mixed and that, without consulting me, they had already spoken to the label who had sent them all the raw data files so that the band could re-record the parts they were unhappy with, as well as remix the entire bloody thing.

"Have you all gone fucking crazy?" I asked.

"Nothing to do with you," Joe replied, "you leave the creative side of things to us."

I stood silent and stunned by the whole conversation – I was numb. He further explained that they knew what sound they wanted from their album and that Mark Hoppus had not achieved it.

I could sense paranoia in every word he spoke and I knew if this was allowed to carry on that it would eventually pull the band apart and even worse was that those twats at the label seemed to be in agreement with the band being allowed to remix the album — it was total madness and I wondered what the fuck was going on.

"Have the label said they have no problem with you doing this?" I asked.

"No, they don't have any problem, they trust us, do you?" Joe replied his words slurring as he did.

I clocked the time, it was just after 11.30am. Just by his voice I could tell that he had been drinking and obviously thinking – a fatal combination for him! I was fully aware that his alcohol consumption had taken a turn for the worse and he was now drinking heavily at home as well as on the road. I knew all too well that once he succumbed to drinking at home alone, he would have a serious problem.

It was a real shame that the only thing Joe could do to a dedicated level was drink and smoke bongs. He was definitely drinking himself to death and seemed beyond anyone's help. He always had that strong alcohol odour around him on tour and even after showering and brushing his teeth it would return within 10 minutes.

I wanted to say to him "You're going to drive yourself to an early grave if you keep drinking as much as you do!"

But it would be like the pot calling the kettle black and we would just end up having a row – so I said nothing.

"Well, if the label said you can do what you like with it then I guess that's that," I said.

"They did and that is indeed that," Joe snapped back, before adding, "speak later," and hung up.

I let out a long sigh of disbelief and then decided to email the label to let them know how unhappy I was; that firstly, they hadn't bothered to consult me first before talking to the band the band, secondly allowing the band to remix the whole fucking album, which I thought was a huge mistake and thirdly that they shouldn't let the band have such control. It was a real heart-on-sleeve moment and, in hindsight, may have been a little over the top, but I was in a state of shock over their bizarre decision.

Within my email I also informed them that I had already sent one of the album tracks to a well-known DJ friend of mine who loved it and said that having Mark Hoppus on board was a real coup and that the rock press would be all over it like a rash.

The next morning, I got a call from a very angry sounding Hurley.

"Why did you send one of the tracks to a DJ?" he asked.

"To get some feedback."

"You have betrayed the trust of the label and the band!"

"What the fuck are you going on about?" I replied, I could feel myself getting angry.

"I arrive in the UK tomorrow and the band have asked me to discuss your position."

"What do you mean?"

"Well, they are worried that you have doubts about

their ability to correct all the problems they have found on the final mix of the album," he informed me.

I was getting really pissed off by this point and while he was talking to me, I envisaged strangling him to death, pulling his teeth out with pliers and chopping him into tiny pieces and feeding him to the pigs – whatever it was going on inside my head, it wasn't good and it was a total red mist, a black anger that just took over. I gathered my thoughts for a second and replied, "Ok, where do you want to meet?"

"I'm arriving tomorrow I suggested we meet at the accountant's office in the afternoon once I've had my meeting with the band in the morning."

I responded with a simple "OK," and pressed end call.

I was fuming and started pacing around the room thinking 'Who the fuck does this cunt think he is?' I felt like I was going to explode, my brain couldn't cope with all the emotions, I felt like I was slowly going mad and all my inner demons were starting to surface, and in the end, it would take a cocktail of vodka and painkillers to eventually calm myself down.

The following day it was cold and dreary, just like my mood. I arrived at the meeting at the accountant's office ready for an argument. I remember I was listening to some 'Avenged Sevenfold', which was pumping me up before the meeting so I was ready for a rumble.

Dave the accountant, mediated the meeting between the label and myself, which actually became pretty one-sided, as Hurley pointed out that I was losing the trust of the band and my attitude was affecting the mood in the camp. And the band had asked him to convey that, if things continued in this manner they would call it time on our working relationship. I could hear what he was saying, but the only thing going through my mind was that I wanted to reach across and slam his curly haired fucking head onto the table with all my might — but as I kept that locked inside (I could feel myself slowly turning all 'American Psycho') as he continued to talk.

The meeting came to a close with me still telling him that I felt he was wrong to let the band play about with the album and him not listening to anything I had to say, so after a half-hearted handshake we agreed to disagree.

Mark Hoppus, only became aware of the band remixing his work when one of them foolishly posted a photo on their MySpace page with the heading *Remixing the album in our home studio*. The post was deleted soon after along with any promotional support from Mark Hoppus.

I was fighting a losing battle with not only the band, but also the label. I felt that everything was crumbling around me and that everyone hated me – my own personal paranoia taking its own firm hold.

However, as hard as I tried I just couldn't quit the alcohol and the painkillers. I tried to quit, but my first attempt to go cold-turkey lasted just one day and the following morning the stress of getting out of bed led me straight to the pill bottle and the lager in the fridge.

My relationship with Paula was now in complete tatters and I trusted no one. I needed help, but I had none from anyone. The only constant was the band and that was starting to slip away from me; suddenly something snapped and at that very moment, I knew I could either swallow all the pills I could get my hands on and end everything right there, or grow some fucking balls and sort out my fucking self-inflicted problems.

I looked in the mirror and I could barely recognise the person staring right back at me – this was not me. I looked scruffy, fat and sweaty. I was dishevelled, my hair unwashed, and my teeth un-brushed and I was wearing the same underwear I had been wearing for the last three or four days – I could almost smell the fat on me as well as my foul body odour – fucking hell, what had I done to myself; I looked like a disgusting old dirty tramp that you would cross the road to avoid.

I had finally realised I had gone from being a loving family man to a cruel, selfish bastard and that this had to stop. I was tired, tired of concealing the true fact that I had issues with the booze and pills, tired of playing-down all my problems. Drinking had become the centre of my social and home life; It was *me* urging others to order more rounds, *me* cutting back on activities that I once enjoyed because they didn't involve drinking and it was *me* that was in very dangerous territory. Waking up three to four times a week with a hangover, not remembering things that had happened the night before or only having a foggy recollection — all of which was a not-so-subtle clue that my drinking and pill taking was out of control.

I looked in the mirror again and screamed out loud "SOMEONE PLEASE HELP ME!" and finally the penny dropped when I realised the only person who could help me was *me* – I had to recognise the problems in order to deal with them.

Scared and nervous I picked up the phone and made an appointment to see the doctor; the long road to recovery had begun along with the help I sorely needed from both a medical and mental health position.

I also made another major decision that day, that I had finally had enough with all these people I was working with. In layman's terms I decided to grow a fucking huge pair of balls and sort my poxy life out and trust me when I say these new balls were as big as 'town hall steps,' I was going to take no more shit from anyone — especially myself.

It was tough, but somehow I managed to stop the abuse of my body and get some clarity.

The band was due to start the tour with Bowling for Soup and although my natural instinct was to stay at home, I took a phone call from Stu begging me to go with them as Hurley had fucked off back to the states and wouldn't be back until the last date in Bristol — so I agreed to go.

However, just before we left, the label emailed me stating that Dangerous-Dave would be joining the team as the sound engineer and would also be sharing some of the driving with me. I hadn't agreed to do any driving so phoned the label for clarification and to see what the fuck was going on. Apparently the band had kindly offered my services as driver of the hire vehicle during the tour, which was bloody news to me, so I asked how much they were going to pay me and after a little bartering we agreed a suitable fee.

I was actually quite happy with this arrangement as it finally meant earning some money, however I had reservations and suspicions about Dangerous-Dave and within the first few days of the tour I had convinced myself that he was definitely sent to spy on us, and that he was fucking snitching back to the label every day – fucking grass.

On top of this, the lazy fucker hardly drove and left me to do all the long distances and when he was asked to take over, he would give the excuse he was too tired or he'd been drinking. I would encounter this again situation when managing Twenty Twenty with a co-driver that didn't like driving at night and who would drink four cans of lager before declaring that he had forgotten he was his turn.

One particular night, I had driven all day and was exhausted, so I asked him to take over the wheel for a while. He shouted from the back that he had been drinking so couldn't; I cracked and called him a fucking wanker and when we finally arrived at our destination we had to be pulled apart by the band.

"Fuck off grass," I yelled.

"What do you mean," he was red with anger and spat as he shouted.

"You fucking know what I mean you kiss-arse."

The band restrained us both until we calmed down and I realised that I must off been wearing a massive chip on my shoulder, so I backed down did the honourable thing and held out my hand and apologised. Dave reached out and shook my hand. From that moment instead of pulling apart, we pulled together and for the rest of the tour just got on with what needed doing – but that didn't mean we were suddenly the best of friends.

Being the designated driver actually worked out well, as it kept me from drinking now that I was cleaning up my act. It was also a way to stay out of any conversations with the band. Things were still a little frosty due to my views on the remixing and re-recording that I still believed was a massive error in judgment by them both.

The tour itself was going really well, and the band was performing as well as I had ever seen them and their onstage presence was electric. However, it was now Joe's turn to become increasingly more and more paranoid to the point that the other two couldn't leave the room without him knowing where they were going. On top of this he had taken his drinking to a whole new dimension. downing at least one bottle of cheap supermarket brandy during the day as well as topping up with beers and countless bongs.

Ollie and Stu kept on drinking and smoking bongs like they were going out of fashion, but it was Joe who was out of control and on a downward spiral of self-destruction. I truly believed that he would just drop dead one day or choke on his own vomit in his hotel room after a gig.

There was nothing I or anyone else could do or say to him that would get through to his thick skull, I guess I actually hadn't been the best role model, but I did resign to the fact that he was going to die any day.

On the other hand, I was now becoming really focused and completely off the booze, but have to admit I was still popping a few painkillers to help me get through some of the long drives from venue to venue. I genuinely was having a few problems with some back-pain and they did help.

I was avoiding everyone in between shows to keep away from temptation even if it meant sitting in my hotel room alone drinking cups of tea and watching late time television. I'm not sure what was worse, being drunk or having to endure hours of the same mundane shit television – shit sport shows about cars and rip-off gambling shows. And that's if the channel hasn't just shut down during the night.

When I first met the band they had been insepara-ble and they all drank to their future, but now it was like they consumed copious amounts of alcohol and got high just to be able to get through spending the whole day in each other's company.

It was the last night of the Bowling for Soup tour and the weather again like the mood in our camp, was mis-erable. It was cold and raining with that horrible fine rain that manages to soak you all the way through to your very bones. The wind was up making it feel even colder. But hey, this was Bristol and even though it was a summer night in July you wouldn't expect anything less from this windy rainy city.

So there we were everyone wet, cold, tired and all so fucking miserable.

To pass the time, the band told us the story of how they had embarrassed their mate Chris the previous night. Chris had come along on the tour as the mer-chandise manager and back at the hotel, after play-ing some weird drinking game he had stripped off and passed out naked in the band's hotel room. Seizing the opportunity to humiliate him, the boys had dragged him fully naked out of the room and positioned him in the hotel hallway and just left him there in all his glory. They had been surprised by the fact that he had not woken up and slept there all night long.

We all laughed out loud, but poor Chris was less than impressed with the turn of events and was bemoaning the amount of OAP's that had, as he put it, 'Had a good gander at his bollocks,' as well as the telling off he had received from the hotel manager who had also threatened to have him arrested for indecent exposure, but had decided not to after Chris had explained thoroughly and apologised.

"I hope you were dressed when you were with the manager or is that why he let you off?" Dave asked.

"Oh yeah, did you have to let him touch you?" I asked as we all burst out laughing.

"I had a towel around me and come to think of it, he did pat me on the thigh a few times," Chris replied before he walked off into the venue.

The tour itself, had gone really well for the band and the guys from both Bowling for Soup and the main support band Go Audio were always up for a chat and everyone involved seemed to be getting on with one another. Little did I know that that night's events would take a turn for the worse and the atmosphere in the camps would become a little strained to say the least.

The support band's dressing rooms at Bristol Academy are tiny with was just about enough space to swing a cat and realistically the room could only hold three or four grown men, so there was little chance that two bands and all their crews were going to fit.

So, as is the norm in these situations, the band would slope off to the tour van to amuse themselves in their usual way with drugs and drink and Joe's with his beloved £4.99 litre bottle of white label brandy.

Joe, by this stage, was a full-blown alcoholic paranoid drug addict, but wow could he still play the bass and belt out a tune. I would just stand and wonder how the hell he managed to stand up let alone play the bass guitar *and* sing.

The three guys did have a brief break from the back of the party van to do a quick sound check, which mainly involved them shouting "BUTTSCRATCHER" through their microphones as an homage to Peter from the cartoon 'Family Guy' which seemed to have been their chosen show to watch during the whole tour.

As soon as sound check was over, which took only 5 minutes in their case, they went back to the van for a proper session of more bong filled madness and alcohol before the gig. I went to check in on them about an hour before stage time to find them pissed and doped up to their eyeballs.

I shouted, "What the fuck guys, can you even stand up to play?"

"Never fear Gazza old son, we're on it," Ollie replied.

"You're all fucking wasted!"

I considered informing the promoter that they were unable to play tonight due to illness, but after a moment I said to them. "Fuck it, who cares, I fucking don't anymore!" and I slammed the van door shut as hard as I could.

By this time Hurley had arrived and was accompanied by some media types that were there to checkout the band. He said hello and asked how the boys were. "They're fine," I lied before I continued with, "to be honest they are very tired, but they are professionals so the show will be great as always."

Then I walked away – he was the last fucking person I wanted to have a conversation with right now.

I did rush over and give Dangerous-Dave the heads-up about the situation and he then promptly ran over to Hurley, but I actually had given up caring at this point and just didn't give a fuck anymore.

The band was totally out of control and there was nothing I, or anyone else could do about it, they were calling all the shots and they just didn't give a flying fuck about anyone, but themselves and not just themselves as a band, but also individually. Ollie and Joe were getting further apart as each gig passed, to the point where, if Ollie liked something, Joe hated it and if Joe liked something, Ollie hated it – their bickering was ripping the band to shreds.

As show time approached, I noticed Joe had another bottle of brandy in his hand and it was already half empty.

"More brandy mate?" I said.

"Yeah a fan just gave me this one as I walked to the venue."

"But it's half empty already."

"Yeah, I had a few sips."

"But you've already done a bottle in the van this afternoon, you'll fall off the bloody stage."

"Oh well, I'll just fucking move back from the edge a bit then," he bellowed back sarcastically and with an air of aggression.

Bollocks to him I thought it's only a twenty-minute set he will be fine.

Famous last words as it turns out.

Chapter 32

The Bristol Incident

The O2 Academy in Bristol is an awesome venue and tonight was packed to the rafters, mainly with hormonal teenage boys and girls who all emanated that waft of odour, that is a combination of teenage sweat and pre-band tension. If you have never experienced this smell, then you're in for a treat; it really is unlike anything else. It's different from my day, nowadays when the lights dim the crowd who were all looking down at the smartphones, instantly all look up at the same time like a mob of merkats, all of them rushing to record tonight's events through their screens.

I have never understood why they do that when they have paid for a ticket to see a live band., they might have just stayed at home and watched on their TV screens. What is wrong with just standing, watching and listening for God's sake? And it's so annoying when all those crap-sounding clips fill the Internet the following day.

These recordings really don't help any bands at all and they just make great bands sound ordinary, good bands sound shit and shit bands... well, just sound even shittier.

The band took to the stage and the crowd started to cheer. No, wait, let's rewind, two members of the band took to the stage, and one, namely Joe Murphy, stumbled on quite a few moments later, almost knocking over a microphone stand, and as I had earlier predicated very nearly fell off the edge of the stage into a bunch of frightened sixteen-year old girls.

He just managed to steady himself and stand still for a moment before delivering an opening line to the packed, hot, sweaty venue; that didn't just take me by surprise, but also stunned everyone in the crowd including

All the parents standing at the back of the room whom obviously didn't really want to be there in the first place, but had been persuaded by their children due to the venues strict policy that under 14's must be with accompanied by an adult.

Joe let rip a long BUUUURRRRPPPP in to the microphone and then shouted, "Hello CUNTS we're KOOPA," as loud as he could.

For a brief second, time stood still and I just looked at the three of them and said out loud "Oh shit!"

Then I looked at Dangerous-Dave, who had his hands in his head and then Hurley, who just stood there with his mouth agape in total shock. Just then the first chords were struck on their guitars and everybody started jumping around, forgetting the profanity that had just preceded, well, except for the parents who now seemed to be frantically discussing the use of the c-word with the security.

Halfway through their set the boys decided to do their impression of Peter Griffin again, and soon had the whole audience repeating "Butt scratcher!" This did seem to go on far too long and I could see out of the corner of my eye Hurley looking just a little perturbed, and could sense that the media people with him just didn't get what was happening.

As the band launched into their last song, their cover of The Proclaimers '500 Miles', they had all the crowd singing along, bopping up and down like those nodding dogs you used to see in the back of cars, and they even managed to unite the parents who had now calmed down and were also singing along.

With their set finished and their job done, the boys grabbed all their stuff from the dressing room and headed off to the back of the van, without a word to anyone else. I did overhear Ollie expressing his disgust at Joe's performance and they walked out of the building arguing and swearing at one another.

I was on my way to check they had taken everything from the dressing room, when I encountered what I can only describe as one of the most shocking and traumatic events in my lifetime.

The corridors back stage were very narrow and whilst I walked along taking up most of it singing "I would walk 500 Miles," from out of nowhere came Chris Burney of Bowling for Soup, a man of some considerable size. He had walked out from the shower room stark bollock naked and stopped directly in front of me.

"Sorry", he said, sheepishly realising that he may have scarred me for life.

"No problem Chris," I replied.

But for some reason instead of one of us backing up,

he just stood there looking at me, probably out of embarrassment, but in return I just stood there looking at him. It was a very awkward situation that we both found ourselves in.

Then it happened — He tried to squeeze past me and, in the process, I could feel his wet wedding tackle rub across my thigh – it seemed to take forever until he was finally passed.

Then Chris said, "See you later," and walked off up the hallway, his huge butt cheeks burning horrible images in my eyes. I was, and remain, scarred to this day, by the image of those wobbling buttocks.

While Dave finished packing the equipment and the boys were in the back arguing, I wandered over and chatted with Hurley, who expressed his disappointment in Joe and advised that he would definitely be having words with him later. Good luck with that mate, I thought.

Soon after Ollie and Stu came over and he suggested that they go to the pub for a drink.

"Where's Joe?" I asked them.

"Who fucking cares," replied Ollie.

Oh no here we go again, I thought. I decided to stay and watch Bowling for Soup perform their set. (if you have never seen them, I would recommend that you try as you have missed out on a great live show full of fun banter).

I was enjoying the show, when half way through something very bizarre happened and, for no apparently reason, Joe suddenly stumbled out onto the stage.

The Bowling for Soup guys looked slightly bemused as their security man ran on and grabbed Joe, who was now waving to the booing crowd — well, I think he was waving. I stood and watched as he was then escorted by the venue's security towards an emergency exit and then quite literally thrown out onto the street before they slammed the door shut behind him.

Joe had managed to stun me for the second time that night. "Fuck-in' hell!" I said out loud before rushing outside to find him slumped on the floor leaning against a wall talking to himself.

"What the fuck were you thinking?" I shouted as I helped him up from the cold wet pavement.

"Fuck off you cunt," he snorted back at me.

"You need help mate,"

"I said fuck off you cunt."

Joe had an amazing ability to be a complete prick, as he had requested, I fucked off back inside the venue to watch the rest of the show leaving him leaning against the wall.

When the show was over the house lights came up and everyone started to leave, and to clear my conscience, I thought I'd better go and check on Joe to make sure he was ok, and as I walked out I saw him outside signing autographs and having his picture taken with fans. Not sure if they really wanted a photo with him, but he seemed pretty insistent that they did. He seemed to be getting quite familiar with one young girl, nothing creepy or out of line, but just a little too clingy so I decided to go and drag him away from her just in case.

I ushered him away and took him to the pub where everyone else was enjoying a few drinks. I settled down with a diet coke and tried my luck on the quiz machine and I would have won a tenner had I known that 'The most money ever paid for a cow in an auction was $1.3 million.'

You could feel that the atmosphere in our camp was a little jaded to say the least. Word had gotten round about Joe's exploits and Ollie, Stu and especially the label, were all far from impressed.

Stu then took me aside and said "Joe's had far too much to drink and we need to get him out of here."

He was right Joe was stumbling around the bar, bumping into people and trying to have slurred conversations with complete strangers, just then Hurley came over to ask, if I wouldn't mind driving Joe back to the hotel before he got too out of hand.

"I'll get a taxi for the others," he explained.

"No problem," I replied, "I'm tired anyway."

I asked their mate Chris, who had finished packing away the merchandise, if he would give me a hand. And he was more than happy, as I think he wanted to get a head start on the boys and not suffer another naked-night in a Travelodge hallway.

As we ushered Joe outside, the evening started to get a little bit nasty and, as we grabbed his arms and started walking towards the van, Joe started babbling on how the other two were making plans behind his back. It was clear that he was completely paranoid about everything and I'm pretty sure he was developing some kind of dual personality.

He was rambling on about Ollie and Stu, and how they were plotting against him. He insisted that they were having a discussion right at that minute with the label, about starting a new band and leaving him out in the cold. We assured him that that was not the case and that the others would be back at the hotel soon and he finally agreed to get in the back of the van.

The hotel we were staying in was only a few miles away and was located by the Severn Bridge, and as we set off the rain started to pour down and by the time we reached the motorway it was raining so hard, it felt as if it was trying to break through the windscreen.

As we got further, the van started to get very shaky and I turned to Chris and said "This bloody wind is awful."

"It's not the wind shaking the van mate, it's Joe going mental in the back."

Chris pulled back the curtain that separated the front from the back of the van, and there was Joe thrashing around like some kind of deadly twister.

"Joe, calm down!" I shouted.

He rebuffed my request with a volley of verbal abuse, which mainly involved questioning my parentage.

The van was now shaking so bad that I was struggling to remain in control of it and on a dark, wet and a windy patch of motorway I started to swerve from side to side.

"Joe we're going to crash and die if you don't fucking stop!" screamed Chris at the top of his voice.

"Fuck you all… I hope we all die," Joe shouted back.

Chris turned to me and begged. "Please pull over."

"I'm on the motorway, I can't just bloody stop!" I shouted before adding, "we are nearly there now."

Joe started throwing stuff around, he was like a madman picking up stuff and hurling it towards us.

"He's throwing all Dangerous-Dave's photo equipment at me!" Chris yelled.

Dave won't be happy, I thought as I put my foot down I could see the toll booths in the distance and knew I just had to get there as fast as I could.

I was finding it very hard to concentrate, as Joe had now given up thrashing around like a spinning top and instead decided to start kicking the back of my seat repeatedly which really fucking hurt.

We were just approaching the toll, so I decided to pull over onto the hard shoulder and slammed the brakes, causing Joe to fall back on the van floor.

I turned around and yelled angrily. "Joe, for fuck's sake, you're gonna kill us!"

He looked bedraggled and his eyes were sunken. He looked up slowly and menacingly like something out of a horror film and, for a split second, I could swear that his head spun around 360 degrees like the scene from 'The Exorcist'.

"I'm... going... to... kill... everyone!" he said in a demonic tone.

We didn't have to say a word as I took control and decided to just go for it and get to the hotel as quickly as possible, as it was just a few minutes away. I pulled up to the automatic toll booth threw in the coins, and as the barrier lifted up I put my foot down and sped away so fast that the van tyres screeched.

I could see the hotel in the distance as Joe started to kick the back of my seat again, but this time with such immense force, that it nearly gave me bloody whiplash.

"Chris, grab his feet!" I yelled.

"You grab his feet!"

"I'm driving you grab them, you twat!"

Chris went quiet for a moment and then recoiled. "You wanker!" he yelled.

"You ok?" I asked.

"No, he just kicked me in the face and it fucking hurt."

The rain was still belting down and Joe was screaming like a man possessed. My mind was racing. I'd seen so many horror movies like 'The Hitcher' and 'The Texas Chainsaw Massacre' where a madman was in a vehicle, and they never ended well, and in our version Joe was the bloodthirsty maniac that had just escaped from the insane asylum – we were in big trouble.

Suddenly and more importantly for the two of us, it all went quiet in the back and for the last remaining minutes of the journey, except for the odd mumbling, we heard nothing. Perhaps he had calmed down or passed out.

Chris was still whining over the boot he had taken to his face as we pulled up outside the hotel. We got out of the van, put on our coats and looked at each other before looking at the locked side door that contained Joe and then looked back at each other again.

I did the thing any brave man would do in this particular situation and told Chris to unlock the side door.

"Fuck off!" he said.

"Don't be a pussy mate, he's your friend," I said, "listen, it's fine… it's all quiet,"

Chris responded with a look of pure fear on his face. "That's what's worrying me."

After a little bit of a macho stare-off I declared Chris

a big girls blouse and decided to approach the van my-self.

"Joeeeeeeee, are you ok?" I whispered nervously.

Silence. Nothing. No reply at all. "Joeeeeeee?" I said with in a weird squeaky mouse like voice.

Suddenly, BANG!!!

We jumped back. Well, that's a lie, we shit ourselves and jumped back about twenty-five foot. It was just like one of those sci-fi films where everyone is standing in front of a door and suddenly the creature on the other side slams into it. The door was being kicked so hard it was denting to the point you could see footprints embedded on it as it started to buckle. The hire company was not going to be impressed I thought.

Then it all went quiet again so I had another go and approached the van and said, "Joeeeeeee are you ok?"

There was no answer. By now the night porter had heard the commotion and stuck his head out of the reception door and said, "What's with all the noise gentlemen?"

I looked at him and replied, "Nothing mate, we are just about to book in."

I told Chris to stay put and I walked to the hotel lobby to indeed check us in. The night porter was back sat at his desk reading 'Loaded magazine' and I could see he was admiring Jordan's breasts, as she was this month's centrefold.

Once back outside, I asked Chris if there had been any developments.

"No."

It wasn't raining anymore, it was bloody chucking it down and we were standing there like a couple of idiots getting soaked until Chris decided to chance his luck. He somehow managed to get the door open and looked inside.

Joe was crouched in the corner. This situation was all turning a bit like the movie 'Blair Witch.'

"You alright mate?" Chris said sheepishly.

"Not really," was the calm reply.

So I walked over and looked in myself, bad timing on my part as at that specific moment, Joe decided to lunge at us both with a screwdriver. I believe it was one of those yellow and black 'Stanley' screwdrivers, but I didn't hang around to make sure I was correct.

Joe was screaming at us, "I'll fucking kill both of you for making me leave Ollie and Stu."

Correction this was not 'Blair Witch,' this situation had gone full on Hitchcock's 'Psycho.'

I swear he just missed stabbing Chris in the head and, as I stood there, I felt my throat take a large gulp of adrenaline filled saliva as I thought – fuck me that was close!

Feeling the impending danger to our lives, we ran as fast as we could into the hotel lobby causing the night porter to jump up and shout, "What the hell's going on?"

I was surprised at how quickly I was joined by Chris, who shouted, "He's gone fucking crazy."

"Who has gone crazy?" the night porter asked, "I'll call the police," he continued.

"No mate please don't its ok its just our mate and he's had just a little bit too much to drink," I said.

"Ok," he replied, "But if there's any more disturbances I will."

As we watched from the relative safety of the now locked reception doors Joe finally emerged from the van, his face looking like that of a snarling beast. He walked up to the glass and looked us up and down and then before our eyes, he seemed to change back to being Joe. It was like watching Jekyll turn into Hyde and then Hyde turn back into Jekyll – it was totally random and scary.

Thank God I thought, he has finally realised that he had been acting like a nutcase when suddenly his expression turned again, but to one of desperation. Joe turned away and lent back against the closed doors and seemed to fixate on a big oak tree about twenty-five feet from the van.

I turned to Chris, "Is he going to run into that tree?"

"It wouldn't be the first time."

Just then, right on cue as if a starter gun had gone off in his head, Joe raced towards the tree, like a Glaswegian meeting an Englishman who had called him a 'kilt-wearing pussy', he head-butted it full pelt. Looking out from the hotel lobby Chris, the porter and myself just cringed and all shouted "Aw! Ouch!" at the same time.

It looked like it must have been really painful. Joe fell to the ground and, after the initial shock of watching a fight between tree versus man, and realising the tree had obviously come out on top, Chris and I unlocked the reception door and rushed over to where Joe lay slumped on the wet grass with his forehead oozing blood.

As we were about to bend down and pull him up thinking it was all over much like Michael Myers in the very first 'Halloween' movie— when no matter how many times you shoot him, he just keeps getting up — Joe flung himself up, mumbled some kind of gibberish to himself and slowly turned his head towards us then just stood and stared at us both.

Assuming Joe might be hurt and have some kind of concussion, we moved closer.

"You ok mate?" I asked. No reply.

"Joe, are you ok, shall I call an ambulance?" once again no reply.

"Joe I'm calling an ambulance."

"No!" was the reply, "You bastards, you're all against me. Ollie, Stu, the label, you, Chris, and that bloke standing behind you!" he ranted as he pointed to the night porter.

"Don't be stupid," I replied, but really thinking, for fuck's sake please let this night end.

Joe stood up, brushed himself off and said, "I'm fucking fine you wankers," and he walked off to the hotel.

Thank fuck for that now we can all go to bed I thought.

How wrong can one man be — this night was far from over.

Chapter 33

So I Guess This is the End of the Road

So there I am, staring at Joe thinking that with almost two litres of brandy, beers and weed in his system, he obviously never felt a thing after he head butted that tree, but boy would he feel it in the morning.

I was contemplating that the evening had been quite eventful and had just started to follow Joe back into the hotel, when he turned to us and with the rain bouncing off his face and blood dripping from his head just stood there staring at me with blank, empty eyes – he had a weird absence of expression.

Then in a very calm and soft voice he said, "Well, that's enough of this for me in this world, goodbye."

Then Joe ran away in the direction of the Severn Bridge.

"What the fucking hell are we supposed to do now?" I asked as I turned to find the answer on Chris's face.

"Just fucking leave him. He'll be back soon enough!" Chris replied.

I was thinking that this was just a stupid drunken cry for help, but then again, you do have to worry about the mentality of a man who is so drunk that head butting a tree does not make him see sense.

I stood and looked out into the darkness beyond the poor tree that Joe had just tried to dent with his head, and my first instinct was to go to bed and leave him to dwell on his bad behaviour, sleep it off, then realising the error of his way, apologise to us all in the morning, and all the usual crap that follows these drunken incidents, but I was just not sure enough and my gut instinct was to call Hurley and tell him what had happened.

"He's done what?" he said.

"He head-butted a tree and then ran off shouting goodbye to the world."

"I guess he will be back soon."

"I'm not so sure, I think he might have gone completely fucking mental," I exclaimed.

"Why?"

"Why? Because he fucking tried to kill us first!"

Then after a few minutes explaining the trauma trying to get Joe back to the hotel, he sighed what seemed to be the longest sigh I can recall.

Then he said. "I'll leave this matter with you, he's already done enough damage to the band tonight."

"What about Ollie and Stu?"

"The other two are staying with me tonight as they don't want to be in the same room with him."

Then he hung up.

"Thanks a fucking bundle," I shouted at my mobile.

I had a brief chat with Chris and, after a few minutes of wandering around in the dark and the rain shouting, "Are you there Joe?" I decided the best option I had was to call the police. I pressed 9 then 9 again on my mobile and my finger hovered over the final 9... should I call them or not?

Yes, I thought and pressed that final digit. I got through to emergency services and said police please and was patched through. "What's your emergency sir?" I was asked.

My gut instinct to say 'Oh nothing, just that some fucking idiot in a band, who head-butted a tree, has now run off into the woods to kill himself,' but I stayed calm and collected and replied "Our friend who has been drinking and has run off shouting he was going to kill himself, and we are worried he is going to jump off the bridge."

They responded calmly, stating, "Don't worry sir, we will send a car out to look for your friend."

They took the call very seriously, as apparently, someone else had just phoned and reported seeing a man whose clothing looked dishevelled and who had blood on his forehead, running through the woods near the bridge screaming obscenities.

The sighting led to the following events that turned the night into one of those scenes not too dissimilar to the movie 'The Fugitive' starring Harrison Ford and Tommy Lee Jones.

If you have seen the movie, then you will know what's coming —for those who haven't this is how the situation unfolded. While we stood in the hotel lobby waiting for what would be the first of five police vehicles, dispatched to investigate the sightings of the running man, pull up outside the hotel, the residents were starting to stir to see what all the commotion was about.

One of the policeman asked us both some questions about what had happened and then relayed the information down his radio. I might add at this point that Chris and I neglected to mention the screwdriver incident, as we felt it might lead to us having to press charges.

The other policeman, a giant of a man, approached and informed us that they were searching for our missing friend (I use the word friend lightly indeed as by now I wanted to kill him myself) and that he had just requested aerial and canine support – at this point, I took a moment to lighten the situation and turned and joked with Chris, that if Joe got bitten by the police dog it would be pissed in seconds and probably need some jab to ward off infection.

The policeman wandered off into the dark to investigate, with the light of their torches bouncing around off the trees. Then suddenly we could hear 'chaka chaka chaka' as the whirling blades of the police helicopter approached the area with its spotlight gyrating, as it started to circle in search of our alcoholic, drug riddled, shambolic and probably concussed bass player.

Chris turned and said to me. "Can you hear that?"

"Yes mate reminds of a song."

"What song?"

"Chaka, Chaka, Chaka Chaka Khan let me rock you.. Chaka Khan…"

We laughed as the helicopter soared past us high in the dark sky above. Soon after, the canine unit arrived and out jumped a policeman who had a great big bushy beard with four German shepherds (And, yes, I mean dogs… this is not a Monty Python sketch).

The policeman unleashed his beasts and they all proceeded to head off in the direction of the woods, and soon vanished into the darkness until all you could hear was the dogs barking.

There was very little I could do now, so I went and sat down in the hotel reception with a dazed look upon my face and my head buzzing from a combination of worry, despair and tiredness.

I looked over to see that Chris was busy chatting away to some random woman that had appeared from nowhere, wearing an almost see-through dressing gown, and could tell that he was trying to manoeuvre her into a position where he could get the full view of what was beneath.

The hotel porter was talking to some residents, who had been awoken from their slumber, demanding to know what was going on and making disgruntled noises to express their anger. One woman looked on the edge of hysteria and was raising her voice, which caused the hotel porter to look at me and give me a terse nod as a show of his annoyance.

Chris came over and put his hand on my shoulder and muttered, "Not your usual night at a gig, is it?"

I let out an elongated sigh and laughed before replying, "You're not wrong there mate."

What seemed like an eternity passed, but was actually, in fact, only about an hour before finally, out of the darkness, another police car approached the front of the hotel and out got two tired looking policemen and one sorry looking soaking wet Joe.

Joe had not 'dived off the fucking bridge' as I was fully expecting, and if I was totally honest, with the way I was feeling, sitting there at that moment in time, I was almost a little disappointed, as finally if he had of jumped, at least one of us would have been put out of their fucking misery.

Turns out, that Joe had not even got as far as the bridge before apparently feeling faint, throwing up and sitting down by the roadside feeling sorry for himself. He looked like a wrung out dishcloth, soaked to the bone and dishevelled. He also had a swollen forehead that looked like it was pulsing.

The two policemen took hold of him and walked him towards us. "He's all yours, sir," one of them said in a polite commanding voice, followed by. "Get this fucking dickhead to bed," from the other.

We took possession of Joe, nodded to the police officers and without a single word, walked past all the onlookers to the hotel, past the reception desk and along the narrow corridor towards his room.

We sat him on his bed and Chris soaked a towel in cold water, and placed it on his forehead.

"Hold that on there mate," he instructed Joe.

"Get some fucking sleep Joe," I said and turned to leave the room along with Chris.

"Goodnight," Joe replied.

As we walked down the corridor, I turned to Chris and said, "Goodnight! – good fucking night! That's all he has to say, good fucking night! —I'll give him good fucking night!"

"Is that all he has to say, after all the mayhem and madness he had just caused us?" I continued.

"He's just not on this fucking planet these days mate," Chris replied.

Just then Hurley rang. "What the fuck does he want?"

"What's happening?" Hurley asked, in a rather demanding tone.

And as I proceeded to fill him in on the full details about the evening's events, he cut me off by saying.

"I'll call you back in 5 minutes."

I sat waiting for him to call, while all the time trying to stop myself from nodding off to sleep – I was so tired, that my mind was on the blink and I even became jealous looking at my computer, as it went peacefully into sleep mode.

Just as my eyelids could take no more, he rang back to inform me about the discussion he had been having all night with Ollie and Stu.

"The other two are in the hotel room. I've just filled them in and will discuss this more in the morning, but, they want Joe out of the band," he said before hanging up.

Yes, I thought to myself, I bet you have filled them in – but that's another story.

I sat down on my bed and switched my phone off. I was shattered and the night had taken its toll on my body, mind and soul. I reached for the pot of painkillers next to me, popped the lid, and stared at the contents.

I knew a few pills and the bottle of lager, I had sneaked out of the dressing room earlier, would help take away the strain I was feeling as I sat there alone, but for some reason, I just couldn't bring myself to take any or even open the bottle of lager.

I just wanted all of this to just go away and that left me with just one option.

I'd had truly had enough and right there, right then, I made a decision that would change my life. I opened that lager and then poured it directly down the sink and then I took the painkillers and flushed them down the toilet and then I switched off the light and for the next few hours slept like a baby.

Bright and breezy the next day I woke, shaved and then showered – I felt totally empowered. I got dressed and prepared for the meeting. I knew that this was the beginning of the end for the band, as well as everyone else involved. Joe had sunk to a whole new level of desperation, and he now had a lot to answer for, as well as needing some serious help with his alcohol and drug addictions, and help with his depression and volatile paranoia.

Then there was Dangerous-Dave, who had now discovered his camera was broken and he was not going to be easy to deal with.

Hurley, Stu and Ollie arrived and Joe was ushered into the car and after Hurley gave Chris and I some money for food, he said. "We will speak later," they all drove away and as they did the hotel manager came running up, all hot and bothered shouting, "I would like a word with you please sir," at me.

I walked into the hotel reception before asking, "What's the problem mate?"

"We have an issue to resolve."

I really wasn't in the right mood for some pompous prick in a blue suit, to start laying down the law to me, but I controlled myself and asked politely what that issue was.

"The issue is quiet big sir; I need to bill you for all the refunds I have had to give to customers for the disturbance that your chap caused last night."

"How many people complained?"

"About twelve rooms in total."

"Fucking hell," I said before apologising for swearing and continuing, "How do we sort this out?"

"We need to bill your credit card for the rooms we refunded," he said, before continuing, "We have this card on file that we can bill all the charges too if you like?"

I leaned over and looked at his computer screen, the card on file was under the record label's name, so I looked up and said to him with a smile, "No problem mate, use that card," and I walked out.

It was a long drive home in the rain from Bristol, and it seemed to take forever, but the sound of the rain on the window seemed somewhat relaxing, so I turned off the radio and listening to its pitter patter. I pondered as I drove — was this really the end of everything?

It was a quiet journey home as Chris slept all the way until I dropped him outside his house, but that suited me.

It had been an emotional, exciting and, at times, downright nasty journey (that's the time spent with the band not the drive home from Bristol), but it was ultimately time to close the book on all things 'Koopa'. I could take no more, and the strain of just being a part of it all had taken its toll on my body, mind and soul and, to top it all off, I had a damaged eardrum from all the loud noise.

Ollie, Stu and Joe only seemed to have one thing in common these days and that was that they were all fucking impossible to deal with.

I was starting to win my personal battle with the

booze and drugs, and I decided that all things must come to an end at some point, and that point was now. I didn't even want to talk to them, so I chose to email everyone and informed them officially that I could take no more of the shit they put me through, and that I wanted nothing to do with any of them ever again.

Hurley was the only one who made any effort to reply, and he thanked me for everything on behalf of the band and the label, before signing off as 'the band's manager' – what a fucking total wanker.

At first. I struggled to get back to being normal — as much as I hated it, I missed the band at first. and it made me feel sick to the stomach not being a part of it any longer. But I fucking needed to step away in order to save my life.

I sat in the dark alone, for what seemed hour upon hour. considering what I was going to do. Surely no booze, no pills and no band would equal no fun, but in actual fact, it was the complete opposite and with a little help from family and friends along the way, I eventually managed to get myself together.

After some long, bitter arguments with my wife Paula we did, for a short while, seem to have some kind of new understanding, but the long-term damage had been done and was irreparable.

Whilst I settled into life away from the band and the label, I was told that Joe. had somehow managed to persuade the others that he could clean up his act. and with Hurley now managing them. they did manage to finally release their version of the album, even if it was only in Japan.

They even flew over to play some shows with Metro

Station, to help promote the album, which did make me think to myself for one brief moment — 'Damn I could have gone to Japan."

I kept an eye on what they were up to out of interest and when they returned with the album still unreleased in the UK, I noticed that they had a headline gig at The Twist in Colchester and I thought long and hard about going before deciding 'Fuck it! I'm going to go along and give everyone a piece of my mind.'

The inferno of interest, chart hits and publicity had all but gone, mainly due to a complete lack of cohesive planning by the 'label' and yes, I do use that word very advisedly. The band also had little in the way of a genuine fan-base by now, which was sad to see as they were still fucking great live.

As Koopa came on stage that night to release their new single, in their home town of Colchester, they played to about thirty people. And as I sat at the bar drinking iced water, with the band, as well as the record label representatives, all fucking ignoring me, I decided there was no point making a fuss — It was over and this just confirmed that I was right to get out when I did. To see the looks on those record label faces said it all, not another cent ever came from the label, and the band was therefore commercially dead.

I sat catching up with some old friends and I text my wife (well, she still was for the time being) to tell her that it's all definitely over for me with the band and she replied that she was pleased and that perhaps I could start being a father again to my daughters, she also threw in a couple of swear words as usual. Of course she was right on the money and her swear words were due – it was time to change my life radically and start all over again, but this time with lessons learned. It was like a massive weight had been lifted from my shoulders.

I knew I was right to walk away and when you know you're right, its worth so much more than the money.

I was about to leave The Twist club, when I saw Hurley. I stood and looked at him for a few seconds and as I stared directly into his eyes, I could see that he knew it was coming to a cataclysmic conclusion and the sad look on his face said it all — he had finally realised that he had been taken for a ride and that he had been just another sad victim of the mantra that put me and the band on the map...... Blag, Steal and Borrow.

As I left behind the band, the label, and all the hurt I couldn't help but think that the great and late Malcolm McLaren, former manager of The Sex Pistols and how he had said that he had been proud of me and perhaps had he still been with us today, would may have allowed me to call this book … **The Great Rock and Roll Swindle Part 2**

There are some people that have labelled me a blagger, a charlatan, a hustler and even a pirate, but they are just jealous bands and artists who wish they had come up with the idea first. I prefer to describe myself as an opportunist.

I guess what I'm trying to say is that I'm unapologetic for what I helped Koopa achieve and that whether you agree with our mantra of blag, steal and borrow or not – I just don't care anymore.

We failed miserably trying to do things by playing-the-game, so I decided fuck that! Let's think outside of the box and come at this from another angle and in doing so, we blagged the entire world's media and the music industry and created music history while doing so.

Are we con men? – no we fucking ain't! We simply had a great plan and we had it first, and best of all we caught all those so-called experts in the music industry with their pants down.

But of course for every action there must be a reaction – that's just how karma works isn't it?

I've come to understand that everything changes, every hour, every minute and every second. Think about it for a while and you realise that it's true. And nowhere is that statement truer than in the snarling beast that is the music industry.

So did I enjoy being a manager in the music industry, I ask myself?

The answer is simple, no — because it has no time for the little man, the unsigned and the skint.

It's a fucking shit business I always told myself through gritted teeth as my misguided optimism would see me frustrated time after time. And what did I do after being rejected, well, I just dusted myself off and carried on believing that eventually I could conquer the industry.

I also take full responsibility for replacing my old friends and family with the pills, lager and vodka that I totally embraced — as they didn't pass judgment on me. But pills and booze are not really your best friends, deep down, they just want to screw you up. I went too far into the abyss and eventually my new lifestyle turned into something of a horror story, almost costing me my life, my sanity and would most definitely be the catalyst for yet another failed attempt at marriage, massive weight gain, loss of hearing and probably the being diagnosed with kidney cancer.

So as I walked away for the final time I pondered that I would never see Joe, Ollie or Stu again, never work in the music industry again, never drink alcohol again and never ever take drugs again...

Well, never say never...

One out of four ain't that fucking bad – Is it?

The End

If You Could See My Face You Would See the Great Big Smile You Have Put On It.
A Big Thanks to the Following:

To my wonderful sister Jill for being my official photographer

Tottenham Hotspur Football Club, the best team in the world #COYS

Bruce Lee, Raquel Welch & Farrah Fawcett-Majors for being on my bedroom wall

Pie & Mash, Rossi Ice Cream, Wimpy & Pot Noodle – the best food ever

The Koopa boys who made my life hell as well as unbelievable: Joe Murphy (I am glad you turned your life around), Stu (keep drumming) & Ollie (keep being Ollie)

Those Lovebale Rougues, Eddie Brett, Sonny Jay, Te Qhairo

The TT lads, Sam Halliday, Jack Halliday, Sonny Watson Lang

Room 94, Kieran Lemon, Dean Lemon, Sean Lemon & my surrogate son Kit Tanton

The Promise, Mike Bird, Colin Jones, Chris Nash, Michael Bazzoni

The lads: Terry Wiliams, Little Willy, Ali the Turk, Ginger Keith, Dennis W, Gary Rush

Lewis the coppers son, Ali Keys, John Blane, Lance Grant, Simon Smith, Roy Ashby, & Cousin Ray

All my team mates at Boreham F.C, Quay Sports, Directa Hotspurs and Broomfield F.C, especially Dave Lawrie for setting up all those goals

The following for helping make this book happen:

Jon Sheller, Ruth Killeen, Clifford Marker, Percy the dog, Neil Jones & Nigel Heath

Friends in the industry who I hope will still be friends after they read the book:

Albert Samuel, James Fern, Andrew Pountain, Mark Adams, Andrew Dutton, Roy Bickley

Mark Abery, Matt Parsons, Richard Smith, Paul Maynard and Rick & George – Red Triangle

Some great bands and artists I have met along the way: Go Audio, Bowling for Soup, Space

Diamond Days, Scouting for Girls, Dave Giles, Robbie Coles, Angus Powell & James Plimmer

Some people that were there in the good and bad times:

Jonathan Doyle, Jim Lang, Bob Watson-Lang, Charlie Arme, Richard Barnes

Ditto Music, Graham Middleton, Paul Buller, Lord Zion, George M, Stuart Collins & George M

Those wonderful film makers Gavin & Zoe

Some new friends I made:

Tracy Lemon, Mark Lemon, Sarah Dombrick, Sally Johnson

Katy Anne, Sheila Rowe & Nick Gibbs-McNeil

To all the fans of all the bands I have worked with especially the Room 94 fans – you are the best in the world

Our pets, Moss the cat & Lily the Jack Russell

To anyone else I have missed out - Spank you I mean thank you!

And finally…. to that traffic warden who once gave me a ticket while I was buying a homeless man, a cup of coffee … well you're still a wanker

This Is Blag, Steal & Borrow the Album

1. Some say that life is just like a song and my life has been just like a compilation album. So I have compiled a Spotify playlist that contains the tracks of my years, tears, failures and successes. Just copy the link into your browser and sit back and enjoy.

2. There's rumours there might be a CD released sometime – and as Eddie Cochrane once sang that would be 'Something Else'.

https://play.spotify.com/user/garyray610/playlist/5bSsrAaUN Zs11Fe9vZ7acX

Track Listing

1. White Cliffs of Dover – Vera Lynn
2. Maybe It's Because I'm a Londoner – Flanagan & Allen
3. Seaside Shuffle - Terry Dactyl and the Dinosaurs
4. All The Young Dudes – Mott the Hoople
5. Mama Weer All Crazee Now – Slade
6. You Ain't Seen Nothing Yet – Bachman Turner Overdrive
7. In The Summertime – Mungo Jerry
8. Girls, Girls, Girls – Sailor
9. The Beautiful Game – Jackdaw4
10. Centerfold – J. Geils Band
11. Highway to Hell – AC/DC
12. You Won't Find Another Fool Like Me – The New Seekers
13. Red Light Spells Danger – Billy Ocean
14. Kung Fu Fughting – Carl Douglas
15. I Eat Cannibals – Toto Coelo
16. Dance with the Devil – Cozy Powell
17. Don't Believe a Word – Thin Lizzy
18. What a Fool Believes – The Doobie Brothers
19. Just What I Needed – The Cars
20. Rebel Yell – Billy Idol
21. This Flight Tonight – Nazareth
22. From New York to L.A. – Patsy Gallant
23. This Town Ain't Big Enough for the Both of Us – Sparks
24. Just One More Night – YellowDog

25. The Things We Do for Love – 10cc
26. Magic – Pilot
27. Hell Raiser – The Sweet
28. From Russia with Love – Matt Monro
29. Back Stabbers – The O'Jays
30. Stuck in the Middle with You – Stealers Wheel
31. Gotta Pull Myself Together – The Nolans
32. Bad Moon Rising – Creedence Clearwater Revival
33. The End of the World – Skeeter Davis

Here's some albums from the artists I have worked with. Go have a listen.

You can find them on iTunes, Sptify and Apple Music.

Koopa

Twenty Twenty

Loveable Rogues

Eddie Brett

Room 94

More True Life Stories
from Percy Publishing

**Ray Quinn
This Time Round**

**Kevin Paul
Inside Gossip
of a Celebrity
Tattoo Artist**

Stories as Life
as a Private Contractor

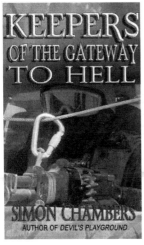

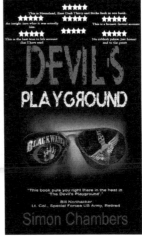

Some Fiction Titles Available

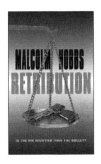

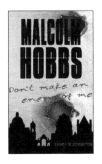

PERCY
PUBLISHING

Visit www.percy-publishing.com for more information.

Facebook: www.facebook.com/percypublishing

Twitter: @percypublishing